Man from the Valley

Memoirs of a 20th-Century Virginian

Sketch by John Perts, 1969
Courtesy of the Artist

Man from the Valley

Memoirs of a 20th-Century Virginian

by Francis Pickens Miller

The University of North Carolina Press
Chapel Hill

Manufactured in the United States of America
Printed by Heritage Printers, Inc.
ISBN 0–8078–1161–0
Library of Congress Catalog Card Number 71–132255

To H. H. M.,
the good companion

✐ Contents

𝒯 Illustrations

✐ Preface

I was born a liberal. I couldn't very well help it. For four hundred years my ancestors had been French Huguenots, Scotch Reformers and Covenanters, and then American Revolutionaries. They never belonged to the establishment and were seldom friendly with it. We seem destined to oppose those who hold too much power—especially when they hold it for too long.

By a liberal I mean one who believes—

That improvement in human society is both possible and desirable.

That life itself connotes change—where there is no change there is death.

That change in society can best be achieved through representative institutions which serve the general welfare and compromise differences through an appeal to reason.

That freedom for the individual depends upon his rights being guaranteed by the Constitution.

That the criterion of public policy is its relation to the nature of man—not to an abstract theory, ideology, or principle.

There are many kinds of liberals: I consider myself a humanistic liberal.

My people, as far back as the record runs, all came from one small area—from the lands that lie around the channel through which the North Atlantic flows into the Irish Sea separating Scotland from

North Ireland. The Millers came from Ayrshire, the Harveys from Kintyre, the McElwees from Argyll by way of Londonderry, while the Pickens came from Ulster on their way out from La Rochelle after the revocation of the Edict of Nantes. They were an independent breed. In the Old World they were anti-Stuart and anti-Papist. In the New World, ever since Jefferson's time, they have usually been identified with the more liberal wing of the Democratic party.

They were, above all, people of the Book. The Bible, for them, was the source of all wisdom, the word that spoke with final authority. And by that word they believed that both men and institutions would finally be judged. For seven generations before me all Miller men in the direct line except one have been Presbyterian ministers. My father, the Reverend Henry Miller, born at Pontotoc, Mississippi, was educated at the University of Mississippi and then studied theology at Princeton and Hampden-Sydney. My mother, Flora Boyce McElwee, was born in Lexington, Virginia, where her father, Dr. William Meek McElwee, was also a Presbyterian minister. My older brother was a missionary and my younger son is a minister.

What a child inherits is a decisive influence in shaping him, if he is proud of it, as I was.

✒ Acknowledgments

In writing my memoirs I had in mind primarily my two sons and my grandchildren. Consequently some of the tales told were too personal or too domestic to be of interest to a wider audience, and the original draft was too long for publication. However, I did not trust my own judgment to do the required cutting.

I needed some one who knew me well enough to distinguish between the relevant and the irrelevant and who would not hesitate to prune where pruning was necessary. Murat Williams consented to do this for me. We had so much in common (Virginia, Oxford, wide knowledge of the world, political philosophy, and the same religious faith) that a minimum of consultation was necessary and I found myself in general agreement with his suggestions for revision. Our collaboration deepened a friendship that was already firm enough, and my debt to him is simply incalculable. I like to think of him as a person who will carry forward in Virginia the tradition that I tried to represent in my time, and this is the measure of my gratitude.

I was particularly happy that Florence Lang was willing to type the final draft. During my 1949 and 1952 campaigns she was my secretary and I could not have had a person who more fully possessed that rare sixth sense of knowing where any paper was at any time—a priceless asset in a political headquarters.

✐ Introduction

Fifty years ago, when a poor student rejected his rich uncle's offer of a chance to inherit millions and got cut off without a cent, one had to assume that the youngster had something else very important on his mind.

Thirty years ago, when a rising politician spurned an all-powerful politician's offer of welcome to his governing machine, one had to believe that he really had bigger plans of his own.

Francis Pickens Miller turned down both offers.

A modern career counselor would say that he was out of his mind. But early in life Francis Miller had resolved that certain things had to be done and he would do them. It might have been comfortable and it certainly would have been prestigious to command millions in the Chicago banking world, but he did not pause long to say "No" to that. He could have had quite a share of power as a stalwart of the Byrd Machine in Virginia, but when the elder Harry Byrd invited him into the select organization, Francis Miller replied with a firmly polite negative that startled the omnipotent senator.

The rejected rich uncle cut him out of his will. The rejected party chief waited for another means of reacting.

What Francis Pickens Miller had in mind to do on his own was a staggering budget of nonpersonal ambitions. The incredible thing is that he achieved most of them, even though the list grew longer as the years passed.

He never held high public office. That was not essential, though even under the poll-tax regime one hundred and thirty thousand Virginia votes were cast for him. He did see his purposes achieved and without long delay, because his opponents were converted more quickly than even he might have hoped. Machine men in 1949 purported to be horrified when Miller, campaigning for governor, espoused the claims of black Virginians to equal rights. They derided and attacked him in newspaper advertisements because he said he would make appointments to public office on the basis of qualifications not of race. Yet within less than a dozen years after such vituperation, one chief opponent, Governor Lindsay Almond, put his arm around Miller's shoulder and said, "Pickens, you have been right all along." Within less than twenty years another Byrd-selected governor, Mills Godwin, was justly proud of having put into effect what was no more than the essence of Francis Pickens Miller's program. In 1969, a headline in Virginia's great newspaper, the *Norfolk Virginian-Pilot,* declared on its editorial page: Miller was "The Political Winner, After All."

Francis Miller was always ahead of his time.

In 1930, Miller and his wife, Helen, published a book titled: *The Giant of the Western World: America and Europe in a North Atlantic Civilization,* almost twenty years before the North Atlantic Treaty was signed.

In the 1920s and early 1930s, Francis Pickens Miller's central occupation was working for the Church Universal, as chairman of the World's Student Christian Federation—thirty years before the ecumenic movement really caught on. Karl Barth told him in those early years that he would have nothing to do with Miller's "international orchestra," but Miller was ahead of Barth.

Francis Miller did not limit his interests.

It was Miller as much as anyone who organized the leaders of public opinion in the United States in 1940 to make it possible for Franklin Roosevelt to offer fifty destroyers for the Royal Navy when Britain was close to destruction. How he did this, even how he arranged General John J. Pershing's crucial speech in support of the plan, is a rare story of how the popular will can be awakened by a man whose main assets are his own convictions and his determination.

He taught international relations at Yale Divinity School. He fought overseas in two world wars. He initiated a public affairs publishing venture which ultimately sold more than 50 million pamphlets. He introduced *son et lumière* into the United States. He led in desegregating an important Virginia city, Charlottesville. Whatever he has done he has done with an eye always on the future, with a focus on the young and an appeal to those willing to face an inevitably changing world.

Some who have known him in one or two of his roles are surprised to learn that he has been a man of many lives.

How one man could undertake to do such a variety of good things would leave a biographer incredulous and a novelist baffled. To some his theme might seem to change too often, but, fortunately, he has written his own story. In its variety and changing fields of action there is a single-mindedness, all summed up by a hard-boiled newspaper editor, who introduced Francis Pickens Miller to an audience at the University of Iowa as "a man who has always seen what had to be done where he was, and has done it."

Murat W. Williams

Man from the Valley

Memoirs of a 20th-Century Virginian

I ✒ The Valley

same years Buchanan

When I arrived on June 5, 1895, my father was pastor of the Presbyterian Church in Middlesboro, Kentucky, and during the next five
years we lived for brief periods at Versailles, Kentucky, and Mount
Sterling, Kentucky. By that time mother's father had become pastor
of Bethesda Presbyterian Church at Rockbridge Baths, Rockbridge
County, Virginia. Dr. McElwee was a gentle spirit. He belonged to
the generation that knew by heart entire plays of Shakespeare,
whole books of the Bible, and endless poems of Tennyson and
Browning. I thought he was wonderful.

Every summer mother took my older brother William and me to
the Baths and because of the increasing ill health of her parents,
after February, 1898, she spent about half of her time there. Finally,
upon the death of both Dr. and Mrs. McElwee in 1901, the congregation of Bethesda asked father to become their pastor. He accepted
and so the Valley of Virginia became our home.

My first clear and vivid recollection is of our move from Kentucky
to Virginia in February, 1901. Father was bringing William and me
to join mother. We got off the Chesapeake and Ohio train at Goshen
and father hired a one-horse buggy to drive us the eleven miles
through Goshen Pass to Rockbridge Baths. It was snowing and it
was cold. The going was difficult and the buggy was old. Shortly
after entering the Pass, just before we reached a spot called the
Devil's Kitchen, the front axletree broke away from the body of the

buggy and the horse galloped off in the snow taking the shafts and the front wheels with him. Our isolation was complete. There was not a house for miles and there was no other traffic on the road that day. Father tucked the heavy lap robes around us and started walking for help. Several hours later he returned with other transportation and eventually we reached the manse at the Baths. It had been a frigid reception to Virginia.

For the next fourteen years my home was in Rockbridge County and I consider myself a Valley man. To Virginians there is but one Valley. It is the long strip of farming land from twelve to twenty miles wide that lies between the Blue Ridge and the Allegheny Mountains running from Roanoke to Harper's Ferry. In its lower reaches it is called the Shenandoah. But Rockbridge County lies further up than the source of the Shenandoah and there it is just called *The* Valley.

The north fork of the James River (now called the Maury River instead of the North River) cuts through the Allegheny Mountains at Goshen Pass and flows in a generally southern direction across the county. It was upon a bluff on the left bank of this river two miles below its exit from Goshen Pass that our manse and our church stood. From the porch we looked north to the Pass, flanked on the west by Hog Back Mountain and on the east by Jump Mountain—so-called because of a legend that an Indian girl threw herself from the sheer cliff at its eastern extremity when she saw her lover killed in a fight between Indian tribes at its foot. True or not, there had at any rate been a fight there, because as a child I watched men from Richmond digging up the skeletons of warriors slain in battle.

Looking across the river on a clear day we could see on the western horizon the tips of the summits of House Mountain, ten or twelve miles away. Behind the manse was a modest hill called Buncombe with woods on top and cultivated fields on its lower slopes between the woods and our yard. In the winter these fields were ideal for coasting and the woods supplied rabbits, persimmons, and sassafras.

Rockbridge Baths lay one-half mile farther up the river on the road to Goshen. It consisted of the post office, Tom Anderson's general store, the blacksmith shop, a flour mill, six or eight residences and most important of all a summer hotel with springs and baths from which the place took its name. The owner of the baths and the general medical practitioner for our part of the county was Dr. Samuel Brown Morrison—the grand old man of the place.

It was he who, with Hunter McGuire, tended Stonewall Jackson after the latter had been mortally wounded at Chancellorsville. I have always liked to recall that the same doctor who was with Stonewall as he crossed over the river cared for me when I was a child. The life of a country doctor around the turn of the century had its rewarding aspects but the practice of medicine itself was onerous and frustrating. Medical science was still rather primitive. Typhoid fever, pneumonia, and tuberculosis were common and smallpox reappeared sporadically. The life span was much shorter than it is now and death was more common, particularly among the young.

The main road going south from the Baths passed directly in front of the manse and between it and the church. After following this road for two or three miles a side road branched off toward the east to Timber Ridge, our nearest railway station, which was five miles or one hour's driving time distant. The main road continued on to Lexington, eleven miles or two hours' driving time away. Lexington was our courthouse and metropolis. Twenty-five hundred people lived there and it was the site of Washington and Lee University and Virginia Military Institute. But more important than the living people or institutions was the fact that Robert E. Lee and Stonewall Jackson were buried there—the men who embodied the best we knew in life.

The community of which Bethesda was the church stretched out from the Baths three or four miles in every direction. Around 1900, the Presbyterian Church was the only church for whites and since the total population did not number much more than six or seven hundred people, almost every family was in one way or another related to it.

Except for the minister, the doctor, the postmaster, the storekeeper, the blacksmith, the sawmill operator, and the miller, the entire community was composed of farmers. The principal crops were corn and wheat. It was not a money economy. Money was scarce, and barter was common. Each farm was pretty well self-contained and self-supported. Food was produced on the place. Cattle were raised for milk and meat, hogs for killing time, and chickens and eggs for eating and barter; there were apple orchards and occasional peach, pear, and plum trees. Blackberries were picked in the fields and huckleberries in the mountains. And a large vegetable garden was taken for granted.

All the men in our community who were fifty-five or older had fought in the Civil War. It is one of the ironies of history that these free farmers of Rockbridge who never owned slaves and had no economic interest whatever in maintaining the system of slavery should have supplied the Confederacy with some of its best shock troops—the men of the Stonewall Brigade. They gave the lie to the economic theory of history. There was Mr. Firebaugh who was blown up in the crater at Petersburg. But he was eating when the mine went off and dug himself out with his spoon. There was Mr. Hart who said he had served in Stonewall's "foot cavalry" and probably did not exaggerate too much when he recalled the incredible distances the brigade had marched in two or three days' time. The best storytellers in the county were our cousins, the Moore brothers in Lexington. There had been five of these brothers originally. They had all joined the Rockbridge artillery at the beginning of the war, had served through it until Appomattox and had all survived. As a little boy I was particularly fascinated by cousin Ed Moore's recollections because they nearly always had to do with foraging for food.

Life in the Rockbridge Baths community was typical of scores of other Valley communities at that time. The only community-wide institution was the church. But there was a great deal of co-operative activity. When Mr. Shewey's barn burned and he decided to build a new one, he announced a date for a barn-raising bee at his place. In advance of the date he hauled from Mr. Snyder's sawmill enough lumber for framing the barn, and Mrs. Shewey prepared vast quantities of food. When the day for the "bee" arrived, all the neighboring families assembled—men, women, and children. The men immediately set to work and by evening had completed the frame, interrupted only by the communal meal which the womenfolk had got ready while the building went forward. For the children it was a grand picnic. After the frame was up Mr. Shewey, in the days that followed, put on the roof and siding himself. No one was paid any money to help in the barn-raising. Participation was considered a natural neighborly act.

Work on the roads was also a co-operative enterprise. All the roads were dirt with occasional side ditches for drainage and "thank-you-ma'ams" running across the road where the grades were steep to carry the water off and prevent gullying. The soil was red clay. In dry weather this made an excellent road surface. But in wet weather it became first slick and then sticky. In winter the roads got so bad that even the wheels of a light buckboard would sink six or eight inches into the mud, and the rims would collect the red earth until they looked like inflated rubber tires. When spring came there were deep mudholes and ruts to be filled in and smoothed out.

In those days the county board of supervisors was responsible for road maintenance. Each county was divided into districts and one supervisor was elected to the county board from each district. It was the duty of the supervisor to have necessary road work done in his own district. I have no doubt that some men received pay from the very limited funds available for working on the roads, but I am equally sure that others gave their time free of charge. I know this was true of my father who was a tremendous enthusiast for road improvement. Though he was a minister and the only university educated man in the community, I have seen him working on the road with the group of men whom the supervisor had collected.

The public school at the Baths did not play the part in communal life that schools now play. There was no such thing as a P.T.A. This was before the day of automobiles and there was no public transportation so the children walked to school—it might be only a few hundred yards or it might be up to five or six miles round trip. Nor were there any organized extracurricular activities or sports at the school, though during the winter months Mr. Frank Snyder, a farmer who sang tenor in the church choir, conducted a singing class for the young. This was quite a social event. I attended, but never learned to sing.

With due allowance for the weaknesses of human nature at Rockbridge Baths, as everywhere, I have the impression that our community there came as near as any community could to fulfilling Jefferson's ideal for the citizens of a republic. Agriculture was still dominant. The artisans whom Jefferson feared were nonexistent. It was a time when and a place where one felt secure in his person. We did keep a rifle in the house, but everyone did the same, and it was more for killing hogs and hunting than anything else. Doors were left unlocked as a matter of course. During the ten years I lived at the Baths the worst crime I can recall was occasional chicken stealing. During those years I never heard of a murder or any other major crime, nor do I recall ever seeing a policeman or officer of the law in our community.

In view of the fact that everyone had to drive to church in a buggy, or ride on horseback, there were few services and almost no organized activities. Sunday morning church service was the big event of the week and the sanctuary was usually fairly full except in foul weather. I vividly recall what Presbyterians term the long prayer. At times it was indeed very long. Occasionally my father would ask one of his elders, Mr. Alfred McCurdy, to make this prayer and I was fascinated by the performance—not by the language but by the sing-song tone in which the prayer was uttered. No one else prayed like that and I had no idea why he did. Many years later I found the explanation. On a Sunday morning in Oban, Scotland, I attended a Gaelic church. I could not understand a word of the service, but when the prayers were said it was as if I were back in Rockbridge Baths, Virginia. The lilting was exactly the same as Mr. McCurdy's. His people had carried that way of praying from Scotland to America and two hundred years later were still saying prayers in the same way.

In addition to the Sunday morning service there was, of course, a Sunday School where Miss Ella Firebaugh taught me, and a little Missionary Society (The Kemper Band) in which I learned about Africa and China and gave pennies to pay for a steamer on the Congo and to aid the Chinese when they were starving because of Yellow River floods.

My father also preached once or twice a week at outlying chapels. During the week he spent part of his time preparing sermons for these services and the rest in visiting members of his congregation. In addition he did the work that had to be done at the manse— gardening, taking care of the horses, cutting wood, and all the other chores that were a part of life in those days. As William and I grew older we gradually took over these duties from him.

When I was fifteen my father died from pneumonia contracted while riding horseback in a cold winter rain to visit a sick person. I never got to know him well, but I knew him to be a sad man. It seems in retrospect that his sadness may have been due in part to some deep unspoken disappointment in life. It was also due to the fact that the shadow of the Civil War, in which his father and brother, Confederate officers, had been killed, darkened all of his days.

My father was ten years old when the war ended. As a child he had said that one day he was going to ride his donkey to Edinburgh, Scotland, to study at the University there—but that day never came. The war had blasted all his dreams. However, in spite of the war his attitude toward the Union was positive. This was made clear by what he did at a student convention in Louisville, Kentucky (June 6–10, 1877), which he attended while a graduate student at the University of Mississippi. He, as a young Mississippian, seconded the proposal made by a representative from Princeton University for the organization of a national student Y.M.C.A., and this was only twelve years after Appomattox.

In his political views my father leaned strongly to the liberal and progressive side. Though living in the Valley of Virginia he sometimes subscribed to Henry Grady's paper, the *Atlanta Constitution*, and sometimes to the *Baltimore Sun*, even though they arrived several days late. His preference for these papers was a measure of his distrust of the editorial opinion of papers in Richmond. He was a supporter of William Jennings Bryan when the best people in Virginia were anti-Bryan. And he was so much an admirer of Theodore Roosevelt that I was given and expected to read all six volumes of TR's *Winning of the West*. I was also presented with a life of Napoleon who ranked high in father's scale of the makers of hsitory because of his liberation of Europe from decadent monarchies. Among ancient secular authors he regarded familiarity with Plutarch's *Lives* as essential in the training of the young and read these aloud to us.

The art of public speaking was, in father's opinion, the finest art a man could cultivate, and, thinking that I had a good voice, he set about training me to use it. When I was only eight or nine years old he would make me memorize lines; then he would have me stand on the carpet in front of him and address the lines to him as if he were an audience. After each effort he would comment upon pronunciation, inflection, cadence, and volume. The purpose of the exercise was to teach me how to use the tone of the voice to enhance the meaning of words and the thought of sentences, and also how to throw my voice. In later years, I have been told that a speech of mine could be scored almost as if it were music.

Discipline was a part of father's nature, but I do not think of him as a harsh disciplinarian, since I do not recall his having thrashed me more than two or three times. For the most severe of these thrashings I have, in retrospect, been grateful. It was given because I had told a barefaced lie. Another thrashing, which was only effective to some extent, was administered because I, young snob that I was, refused to ride in the buckboard with a poor and rather dirty old woman to whom father was offering a lift.

My mother, Flora Boyce McElwee, was her two sons' constant companion, confidante, teacher, and friend. She had had three other children, and lost them all. My character was largely formed by my mother. Her roots were deep in the Valley through the Harveys and the Moores who had been there since it was first settled. She spent her early years in Lexington and it was from the McElwee home that servants carried to General and Mrs. Lee their first meal when the General arrived to assume the presidency of Washington College. He took a fancy to little Flora and gave her rides on his horse, Traveller, seating her up before him on the saddle. On each Christmas until his death he also sent her presents.

At fifteen my mother entered the Augusta Female Seminary at Staunton, Virginia (now Mary Baldwin College), and graduated three years later. Her teachers and their subjects profoundly influenced the rest of her life. She had that ancient Scotch thirst for knowledge; her interests widened with the years; and in her relations with people she was a complete egalitarian. An aristocrat, a millionaire, and a pauper were all alike to her. She agreed with Bobby Burns that "A man's a man for a' that." Further she had an innate quality of sympathy and compassion which were the fruits of her Christian faith.

For ten years after leaving the Augusta Female Seminary, mother spent much of her time nursing two older sisters, both of whom eventually died of tuberculosis. She was twenty-eight when she married my father and thirty-nine when we settled at Rockbridge Baths.

Our home, as I remember it, was orderly and quiet. We had a telephone on a party line which sometimes worked but one had to be careful in talking on the phone because Mrs. Sterrett often listened in and gossiped about what she heard. There was no running water in the house. Each bedroom had its washstand with pitcher and bowl. All water had to be carried in buckets from an outdoor cistern which collected rain water from the roof. There was a privy at the lower end of the yard, and on the coldest days of winter it was an agony to have to make that trip.

Breaking ice in the pitcher in order to wash one's face was not uncommon on a winter morning because the fires were not lit until we got up, and mother believed in fresh air. Father's study on the south side of the house was the most comfortable room at this time of year, but William and I were not supposed to enter unless invited. That made it all the more fun, when father was away, to slip in, snuggle up on the couch, and lose oneself in a Walter Scott novel or shiver with fright at Gustave Doré's drawings of the Old Testament prophets.

Mother did the housework and cooking, assisted from time to time by one of Ed Keyer's daughters from across the way. Ed was the

Negro janitor of the church. But William and I were expected from the first to take care of our own rooms and help with housekeeping generally. Mother made our clothes until we were twelve or thirteen, in addition to making all of her own. The only exception I can remember was a dress that her brother, Will McElwee, brought her from Paris around 1902. This event caused immense excitement. There was also a sealskin coat with leg-of-mutton sleeves which she had had since she was a girl and in which she seemed to me to be the most beautiful person conceivable. The homemade clothes William and I wore were very neat and practical, but that fact did not lessen the smart when children who had store-bought clothes sneered at us.

Father's income as a minister amounted to only twelve hundred dollars a year, supplemented by an annual "pounding." On the day for the "pounding" those members of the congregation who were well-disposed and able to do so brought all kinds of food for the manse larder and storeroom—it might be a ham or apples, sausages or canned fruits or pickles, and jellies, apple butter or preserves. But good as these things were they did not last long and we needed much more food than that during the course of a year. What we could not afford to buy, we had to grow on the place. The manse had a large vegetable garden, for which William and I were mainly responsible after we were ten or twelve years old. Milk and butter came from our own cows and I can still feel the sense of outrage when a cow on a cold winter morning would occasionally kick the bucket over just when I had about finished milking her.

We had chickens, partly for food, and partly to produce the eggs which could be traded (along with butter) at Tom Anderson's store for things that we could not produce ourselves—like flour, sugar, salt, pepper, and tea. In the spring we set quite a few hens because the casualty rate among the chicks was appalling in spite of the use of lime and disinfectants.

We had no cattle so we had to purchase whatever beef we ate, which was not much. But we did buy hogs for slaughter and pork in its various forms was our mainstay during the winter months. I thought no food could be better than a hot corn pone well-buttered and spiced with lots of cracklings. From time to time our menu was also varied by a rabbit caught in one of our box traps on Buncombe.

For transportation of all kinds and for plowing the garden we had horses. Our pride was in them. Father had always wanted a team, and he finally got one—Frank and Charlie. Several years later I

drove them much too fast one day over the eleven miles returning
from Lexington and shortly afterwards Charlie died. But Frank became my boon companion and remained so in spite of the fact that
he knocked the living daylights out of me once when I was currying
him by kicking me full in the chest. He lived on until after I returned
from World War I, and it was a thrilling moment then when he responded to my whistle.

We helped cut wood in the forest for our fuel, and, in addition,
William and I were general handymen. When there was painting or
whitewashing to be done or when doors or furniture needed to be
repaired, we did it. If a roof was to be put on the porch, we put it on,
and when a new chapel was being built, we helped built it. We also
cut the grass and weeded the flower beds, and I spent hours on
my knees in the front yard uprooting plantain and dandelions with
a kitchen knife.

The manse was a center for manual work. It was also a center for
study. Mother had a theory of education; that the training of the
mind should be made interesting. As a graduate of the Augusta Female Seminary, she felt she was better equipped than the local
school to prepare her boys for college. Further she had already had
some experience in teaching the children of one of her sisters who
had died. Consequently neither William nor I ever entered a classroom until we entered the University at fifteen.

Our education at home began after breakfast with family prayers.
Father made a practice of going through the Bible at the rate of a
chapter a day skipping sections like genealogies and other passages
less suitable for reading aloud to the family. Following prayers we
completed our daily household duties and then began our studies.
Mother usually had us recite between ten and twelve in the morning.
We prepared our lessons during what was left of the morning and
during part of the afternoon and evening. The total number of hours
spent in study varied from day to day and increased as we grew
older. William's diary shows that during the year before he enrolled
at Washington and Lee he averaged as much as nine to twelve hours
a day, and I rather think that this must have been also true of me as
I tried to do whatever he did.

Our curriculum was mother's own idea. She thought studying
English grammar was a waste of time. It was not necessary to know
English grammar if a child knew Latin grammar and so after intro-
ductory courses in that I began at seven to read Caesar's Gallic
Wars. The initial effect was catastrophic. It was the first time I had

ever confronted something which seemed insoluble, insurmountable, and overwhelming. My sense of defeat and frustration was complete and going out into the upstairs back hall I wept uncontrollably. But in the end I began to read Caesar. Father also taught us a little Greek.

Then there was history. Mother was not interested in political and economic history as such. She was primarily interested in the actors on the stage and she felt that before studying American history we should know something about the people from whom we came across the Atlantic. Our introduction to Scotland was Walter Scott's *Tales of a Grandfather* and for France and England we read the history textbooks mother had used at Augusta Female Seminary. When we got around to American history we were introduced to our own country through Bill Nye's humorous *History of the United States*. Nye found it difficult to take anything too seriously and he enjoyed deflating pomposity in public servants. His book was illustrated with cartoons and one that made a vivid impression on me was a drawing of General Braddock after his defeat by the Indians. It simply showed a stretcher on which was being borne a human form with a very fat belly covered by a sheet. On the apex of the sheet rested a cockade—that was all.

Following history came our European heritage of art. In those days a little monthly magazine was published in Boston called *Perry's Pictures*. It was devoted chiefly to brief articles about famous European artists from Giotto to the present time, with black and white photographs of some of their better known paintings. Mother subscribed to *Perry's Pictures* and we were required to write short essays on various artists, giving the facts of their lives with brief descriptions of their work.

We learned as a matter of course the basic facts of geography, both about the United States and the rest of the world. Our reading included a book by Rockbridge County's own Matthew Fontaine Maury, the geographer who taught at the Virginia Military Institute and who had requested that after his death his body be carried through Goshen Pass when the laurel was in bloom. And we learned about Asia and Africa from the lives of missionaries.

But I think the stars interested mother more than anything else. They fascinated and preoccupied her. So we studied a very primitive and rudimentary kind of astronomy. She had inherited from her mother maps of the heavens which showed the constellations with the mythical figures for whom they were named drawn in. With this basic document and good opera glasses we were well-equipped for our course which consisted in going outside on clear nights to become familiar with the heavens—and also remaining in silence to wonder. After William went to college I continued by reading Garrett P. Serviss's *Astronomy with the Naked Eye* and *Round the Year with the Stars*. In this way I established such a friendly rapport with some of the constellations that they were a great consolation to me in later years, particularly so, I remember, on one bitterly cold Christmas eve in France in 1917. I knew that the folks at home were seeing them too.

Finally, there was mathematics, to which mother attached the greatest importance as a discipline for the mind and as an encouragement to logical thinking. We finished simple arithmetic and algebra and began geometry. It was odd about mathematics. I always got higher marks in it at the university than in anything else, but I never understood it.

Our school in our home was for several years an "integrated" school. Ed Keyer's daughter, who worked for mother, sat with us for some of our studies and learned as much as she could, since there was no other school for her to attend. This seemed to all of us a perfectly natural thing to do, and it helped prepare my mind and spirit for the changes that were to come fifty years later.

Such was our course of secular studies.

Then there were our sacred studies. On Sundays, in addition to going to church, we memorized lengthy passages from the Bible—mainly psalms and the sayings of Jesus. I learned by heart the Westminster Shorter Catechism and was told that if a boy did that he would never run in battle when he grew up! Mother also read to us the lives of people whom she considered great Christians. My memory of Sunday is that it was, on the whole, the nicest day of the week—utterly unlike the stereotyped picture of the Puritan Sunday that is now generally accepted. My people would not, of course, have accepted the appellation "Puritans." That meant Englishmen and they were Scotch Presbyterians with a love for Bobby Burns.

Our home was the center of a prodigious amount of play as well as a center for manual work and for study. In those days entertainment was self-entertainment. There were no commercial games, no commercial sports, no movies, no theater, no paid lectures—in short no organized entertainment of any kind. The only store-bought playthings we had were the few miraculous mechanical toys which Cousin Nannine Patterson sent at Christmas time from Chicago.

Otherwise our play was self-invented, contrived, organized, and executed by William and myself with or without the help of our parents.

From the first we were very warlike. As a result of *Tales of a Grandfather* we preferred to emulate Scotch warrior clansmen of the thirteenth and fourteenth centuries. William Wallace and Robert the Bruce were our heroes. We made excellent bows and arrows and whittled out fairly formidable broadswords, formidable enough for me to kill a copperhead snake with mine at a Sunday School picnic. So engrossed were we in the Scotch drama that our Aunt Fannie Symington (she subsequently married my Uncle Will) bought cloth that resembled the Campbell plaid and made complete outfits for the two of us including kilts, tartans, bonnets, socks, and all. We even had a bagpipe which Uncle Will brought from Scotland. And we wore our Scotch regalia on special occasions almost up to the time when we went off to college.

It would be a mistake to suppose that we were exclusively war hawks in our sports. As I recall them now they were extremely varied. We built a mill by a stream on Edward Shewey's farm with a race and a water wheel that turned. In the well-equipped carpenter's shop located in an outhouse in the back yard of the manse we were constantly making and repairing things for the fun of it. Our supreme effort came in the summer of 1907 when in a little more than two weeks we built, painted, and launched in the river below our bluff a small rowboat. We even made a paddle for it, but condescended to use store-bought oars.

In mild weather we went swimming at the Baths pool or played baseball and I paid the usual price for these pleasures. My head was cut open from diving on a rock and my nose broken from catching behind the bat without a mask. During an average winter there was good skating above the dam on North River and splendid coasting on the slopes of Buncombe.

We also engaged in civic action. In order to let the farmers who passed by know what weather to expect we made a complete set of weather signal flags and flew them from a pole in our yard. The Farmers' Almanac was probably the source of our weather intelligence.

Occasionally our playmates were the children of townspeople who were spending the summer at the Baths. Between them and me there was always a measure of mistrust. I remember that on one occasion I spied three small boys in nice store clothes walking down the road by the church in the direction of Lexington. One of them was a distant cousin. But I was seized with a sudden impulse to chase these foreigners away. So hiding Indian fashion behind trees in the church-yard I pelted them with stones until they were out of sight.

This dislike for city folk was enhanced one day by the visit of a New York businessman to the manse. He came courteously to pay his respects to the minister. But when he left he tried to give me five dollars, thinking that I would be overjoyed, since in those days that was equivalent to a week's wages. Instead of being pleased I was incensed. He had humiliated me by trying to tip me, and I would have none of it.

In 1904, mother was determined that William and I should see the St. Louis Exposition. Because we had so little money, the three of us traveled in a day coach on the C & O from Goshen and stayed with a rich friend of mother's while in St. Louis. This was our first expedition from the Valley into the great outside world since taking grandfather to Chicago in 1901 to visit his son and my uncle, Robert Harvey McElwee. It was terrific. Mother had hoped that we would see things that would increase our cultural interests. I only remember three things—the unbelievably long fingernails of the Empress of China in a portrait of her which was displayed at an art gallery (for China was still ruled by an Empress in those days), a bamboo village inhabited by primitive Filipinos who wore as few clothes as modern Americans do on summer beaches; and a sham battle between Boers and British. The Boers galloped out onto the field led by General Kruger himself (the program said) but were met by determined British redcoats well-hidden behind rocks and trees. I have forgotten who won but the noise and smoke were glorious.

Then in October, 1907, the whole family went to the Jamestown Exposition organized to commemorate the 300th anniversary of the first permanent English settlement. Father had missed the St. Louis Exposition and he wanted to make sure that he saw Jamestown. I suppose that Exposition was the greatest flop of any ever held. The only memories I have of it are thoroughly unpleasant—the horrid barracks in which visitors lived, the swarms of flies everywhere, and the smell of dead fish washed up on the shore of Buckroe Beach in Chesapeake Bay.

In 1908, William left for college and for the next two years I continued my studies and did the work on the place as best I could. In September, 1910, I too entered Washington and Lee.

II ✐ Student Days and
a Decision in Chicago

Getting into a college or university during the early years of this century was a very different matter from what it is now. Far from being swamped with applications, the majority of colleges were finding it difficult to attract enough students to function properly. The aspiring student, unless mentally retarded, could in general go where he wanted and would be received with open arms by the institution to which he applied.

My family could not afford to send me far away to college and the proximity of Washington and Lee, together with the fact that William was already there, made it the obvious choice. There were no College Board Entrance Examinations in those days; if there had been I am sure I could not have passed them. George H. Denny was the president of Washington and Lee. Just after my fifteenth birthday my mother wrote Dr. Denny explaining that she had done for me about all that she could and that in her opinion I was ready for college. He thought that was fine and sent some entrance examination papers prepared by the college itself. It would have been difficult to fail these, so in due course I was admitted.

Washington and Lee was then a small institution with only about four hundred students, excluding the law school. But it was a proud university having received its first considerable endowment from General Washington himself, and then having had as its president Robert E. Lee, whom we thought of as the greatest gentleman the

South had produced. Further, it had been founded as a Liberty Hall more than half a century before Jefferson had succeeded in getting his university established east of the Blue Ridge. But in spite of the college's unique history, by 1910 it had not yet acquired a student body drawn from all parts of the country. Apart from its football players it was still a southern and to a considerable extent even a Valley institution.

The campus was a lovely spot. It lay on a small ridge which ran from the town to the river, its southeastern slopes covered with grass and trees. Riding the crest of the ridge was the main building, crowned by a wooden statue of Washington. It had been designed and built around 1824 by a local craftsman named Jordan, and the Doric columns along its front symbolized the austere spirit of its Scotch Presbyterian founders. To understand the Valley in relation to the rest of Virginia one only has to look at this main building and contrast it with the ornateness of Jefferson's designs for his university at Charlottesville. Lower down on the slope and facing the main building was the chapel where the body of Lee rested. Valentine's recumbent statue of the General had already become a southern shrine.

Shortly after getting settled in the home of my cousin, the widow of Professor Nelson, I went down to Ed Deaver's store on Main Street and bought my first store suit and town shoes. Thus adorned I walked over to the college, registered, and enrolled in my courses. Next came a visit to the college book shop to purchase supplies. I did not need many books because William had saved his. But it was wonderful to know that I could buy a book if it were needed, because for the first time in my life I had a little money in my pocket and I could spend it as I wished.

To secure an A.B. degree (at W & L it was not B.A. but A.B.) the student was required to collect a certain number of credits from different fields. The result was that upon graduation most students knew a little about a lot and not very much about anything. This was true of me. To make matters worse most classrooms were places where information was imparted and not where minds were stimulated to think.

Extracurricular activities were not as highly organized or as numerous as they are now, but there were enough to occupy the two or three hours a day that we could spare from our studies. It was the student Y.M.C.A. that interested me most. There were weekly meetings and organized study groups. It was in one of these groups that

I first began to take a serious interest in our race problem. I collected a number of students who were willing to discuss together a little book entitled *The Negro in the South* that had just been written by W. D. Weatherford, the student Y.M.C.A. secretary for the southern region. What he said set in motion trains of thought and action which profoundly influenced my attitudes.

Washington and Lee's honor system is the most precious legacy she has bestowed upon her sons. The system covered cheating in classroom work and breaking training rules in athletics. Its operation was entirely in the hands of the students themselves. The university administration had nothing to do with it. When any member of the student body became aware of an infringement by another student, he was expected to report it to the appropriate officers of the student body. If the evidence was sufficient to warrant investigation, the student charged was brought before a council of his peers and due process analogous to court proceedings was followed with the arraigned boy choosing his own defense attorney, usually from the law school. All proceedings were secret in order not to injure the reputation of the accused should he be proved innocent. If he were found guilty, he was told to leave the university immediately. Experience of the honor system profoundly influenced my attitude toward men and institutions. Anyone committed to the principles of such a system was bound to find himself embroiled from time to time in later years as I have been with people who were not so committed—and my impression is that in the United States at the present time the uncommitted vastly outnumber the committed.

Between 1910 and 1914, the influences that began to give direction to my life came not so much from college as from the summer conferences organized by the Student Christian Movement. In the South these conferences were under the auspices of the Y.M.C.A. and in New England of an independent committee. At the end of my freshman year, in June, 1911, I went to the southern conference which was being held at Montreat, North Carolina. There I heard John R. Mott and Robert E. Speer speak.

Mott had been born in 1865 in Iowa and was educated at Cornell University. He was a Methodist layman and somewhere along the way he had caught the vision of Wesley's "The World Is My Parish."

Long before men were talking about a League of Nations, Dr. Mott had dreamed of a world federation of Christian students such as that which he and his collaborators organized at Vadstena Castle,

Sweden, in 1895. A number of wealthy Americans became interested in Mott and with the money they provided he traveled all over the world speaking in the universities and organizing national student Christian movements. He had a series of prepared addresses which he gave to students, some about his travels and some on religious themes. One that I heard many times began: "Religion is primarily a matter of the will." Mott was not a theologian and his faith found very practical expression in life. The first time I heard him I was enormously impressed. Here was a giant of a man, I thought. He talked about Moscow, Calcutta, Tokyo, and Rio de Janeiro as if they were nearby towns, and he spoke of people belonging to different nations and races as if they were members of the same society. This man extended my horizons to the whole habitable world and provided me with a universal frame of reference. For the next fourteen or fifteen years he was my hero.

As far as the basic Christian virtues are concerned, Robert Speer was a finer person than John Mott. He too was a world statesman, administrator of a vast missionary enterprise, but he was more than that. The legend was that when he was a student at Princeton only one other student, namely Aaron Burr, had ever equaled his scholastic record. But though he possessed a first-class mind, religion for him was not primarily a matter of the will, it was primarily a matter of the heart. When he spoke my heart was moved.

In June, 1912, my brother and I went to the Student Christian Movement Conference at Northfield, Massachusetts, which was attended by students from the eastern and middle Atlantic states colleges. The evangelist, Dwight Moody, had spent his last years at Northfield and was buried on a little hill called Round Top looking north up the valley of the Connecticut River. On a fair summer evening at twilight it is one of the most idyllic spots in the world and Moody's spirit seemed very present. He had said, "What you are speaks so loud that I cannot hear what you say," and on his tombstone was written, "The world passeth away and the lust thereof, but he that doeth the will of God abideth forever." No moments in my life have ever seemed more precious than when we sat on Round Top as darkness fell, singing "Fairest Lord Jesus, ruler of all nature." It was a time for thinking deep thoughts and dreaming great dreams. I began to do both, and was again stirred by addresses from Mott and Speer.

From Northfield we proceeded to Cambridge, Massachusetts. During the rest of the summer we became acquainted with much of historic New England, but for William and me the high point was learning the form used by Harvard oarsmen. There were two boat clubs at Washington and Lee. William was stroke of the Harry Lee crew and I was aspiring to a seat in the boat. As our club had been losing the annual race with the Albert Sidneys for several years we were eager to learn a better stroke. After inquiry we had been told that Jim Wray of Harvard was one of the best crew coaches in the country, so as soon as we could get settled in we went down to the boathouse and asked Mr. Wray if he would teach us the stroke he used. He said he would be glad to do so, and by the end of the summer we had mastered the form favored at Harvard which we carried back to Lexington. Using that stroke in 1913 the Harry Lee crew won and continued to do so for several seasons thereafter. Years later it suddenly occurred to me one day that we had never asked Mr. Wray what he would charge for teaching us, nor had we given him a cent. The idea of pay never crossed our minds because we engaged in sport for the fun of it and we assumed that Mr. Wray was also a gentleman who would be offended by the offer of money over and above his salary.

When the summer of 1913 arrived, it proved to be a time of adventure and more conferences. Dr. Weatherford had asked William and me to go to the National Summer School for Y.M.C.A. secretaries at Estes Park, Colorado, and mother was included in his invitation. So after attending the Southern Student Conference (which had moved from Montreat to the new Y.M.C.A. grounds at Blue Ridge on the other side of the valley) the three of us boarded at Black Mountain the special car in which all the southern secretaries were traveling and headed west. We had never seen the Great Plains or the Rockies, and we were as excited as if we had been pioneers venturing into the unknown. The throngs in the station at Kansas City gave us our first glimpse of real Indians and real cowboys, but every daylight hour on the train brought the thrill of new discovery. Finally the Rockies themselves came into view and after changing trains in Denver we arrived at a station from which old White Steamer buses took us up the canyons to Estes Park.

At that time Estes Park was still pretty much in its natural state, unspoiled by tourists and vacationers. There was a small village some distance from the Y.M.C.A. camp and a few outsiders were spending the summer in their own cabins, but we were unaware of their presence. The only private home of any pretensions near our camp belonged to Mr. A. A. Hyde who had acquired wealth through making Mentholatum and who was one of the principal benefactors of the Y.M.C.A.

The classes and lectures of the summer school occupied mornings and evenings, but there was plenty of time for recreation. Patty, Mr. Hyde's daughter, was a good horsewoman, knew the area by heart and loved the mountains. It was great fun riding with her on the trails that led to the Continental Divide.

The people who attended the summer school fascinated me. They came from all over the country and some of them had backgrounds and held views with which I was entirely unfamiliar. There was Frank Graham of North Carolina, one of the finest characters the South ever produced, who became a lifelong friend. At the opposite pole was F. N. D. Buchman, Lutheran minister and Y.M.C.A. secretary at Pennsylvania State College who wanted me to be his friend and who during the next two years used his considerable influence on my behalf, but whose friendship I repudiated in 1916. There were also assorted Europeans at the school including several Germans, but the man from abroad who interested me most was Dr. David Cairns of Aberdeen, Scotland. His profession was theology, but his passion was the battlefields of the Civil War, and the fact that my mother had known General Lee endeared us to him.

At the end of the summer mother and I took the train to Chicago to visit Uncle Harvey in Lake Forest on our way back to Virginia. His home faced Lake Michigan at the foot of Deer Path Avenue and by our standards he had quite an establishment, with a coachman turned chauffeur, two gardeners, a housekeeper, and several maids. There was a large lawn with a roadway winding among the trees.

During the visit Uncle Harvey asked me one day to go into town with him and have lunch at the Chicago Club. He was a lonely man. His only child had died and he and his wife were not at all congenial. He had made his money in the eighties and nineties out of lumber and by the time he was forty he was a millionaire. From then on golf was his principal interest and he became one of the best amateur players of his day. He also continued to have an active interest in financial affairs through his membership on the board of a Chicago bank which through successive mergers became the present Continental Illinois National Bank and Trust Company. I was told that he owned more shares than anyone else in the bank at that time.

The only thing I didn't quite like about Uncle Harvey was his hostility to Woodrow Wilson, whom I admired. He hated Wilson in the same way that comparable individuals hated Franklin Roosevelt a generation later. This hatred seemed to be due to the fact that Wilson favored measures that would benefit working men. I was puzzled by his attitude since it was obvious that working men had by their labor in the north woods created much of the wealth that Uncle Harvey then enjoyed.

I went with him to lunch at the Chicago Club, little realizing that one of the decisive moments of my life would occur during that hour. In the course of our conversation he said that when I finished college he wanted me to come out and join him. He explained that I would be given a job in the bank and that if I made good someday I might rise to be one of its senior officers. I received the impression that he wanted me in a sense to become his son and heir. To reinforce his proposal he added, "Francis, I don't want you to throw away your life the way my father did."

Was it possible that my uncle could think that his own father—that saintly poetry-quoting dear old man whom I had known and loved as a child at Rockbridge Baths—had thrown away his life by being a country minister? It seemed incredible. But that is what he had said, and my heart froze within me. At the end of our luncheon I explained that I would have to think it over and would write him when I got back to Virginia. But my mind was already made up. I knew that I could not work for anyone who talked about such a father in that way.

Shortly after returning to Lexington I went across the street to Uncle Will McElwee's house where mother was staying. I went upstairs to her sitting room which was empty, closed the door, got down on my knees by her sofa, and prayed that I might do the right thing. Then I sat down at her writing desk and penned a note to Uncle Harvey, thanking him for his offer, but explaining that I had other plans for my life. The decision was right, but I have often reflected since upon the callous cruelty of the young. I had to do what I did, but I wish I could have done it with more sensitivity and with more sympathy for that lonely man. My reply naturally cut him to the quick. He eliminated me from his will and I did not see him again for twelve years.

Sometimes one is tempted to ruminate on what life might have been like if he had decided differently at a critical moment in his youth. Would I as a multimillionaire banker in Chicago have been for Adlai Stevenson? I wonder.

There were three big events that made the coming year for me. First there was a National Student Volunteer Convention of five thousand students at Kansas City during the Christmas vacation. The motto of the convention was "the evangelization of the world in this generation." We were told that the whole world was rapidly turning toward the Christian faith and all that was needed was for a few more thousand American students to go abroad as ambassadors of the Kingdom of God. There was present an air of invincible confidence and optimism which swept many of the delegates out of their narrow and parochial lives and inspired them with a vision of a new heaven and a new earth. For those who were present, this conference in retrospect seemed like the glory of a golden sunset before black darkness descended upon the earth the following summer. It is tempting, in the light of all that has transpired since 1914, to regard those students of the pre-World War I generation as hopelessly naïve, misguided utopians. I disagree. They were right in their day to be carried away by dreams of a fairer world. If it had not been for them and students like them, much of the good that has been accomplished in American society during the past fifty years would never have been accomplished. They have served literally as the leaven in the lump. And the most heartening thing in the United States in recent years has been that thousands of students have responded to the world-wide appeal of the Peace Corps in much the same spirit that many of my generation responded to the appeal of the Volunteer Movement.

The second big event of the year was a religious campaign at Penn State to which I had been invited by Frank Buchman. A campaign of this kind in those days was quite an extraordinary affair. Nothing like it could occur now. The management of the campaign practically took over the college or university for a week. Every night a large mass meeting was held, attended by a fair proportion of the entire student body. After that there were small meetings in all of the fraternities. In the mornings the professors asked visiting workers (there were often scores of these) to speak to their classes and there were literally hundreds of personal interviews. I was fortunate in having been asked to stay during the campaign in the President's home and to share a room with David R. Porter, national secretary of the Student Y.M.C.A., who began talking to me while we were there about joining his staff.

The third big event of the year, which bulks much larger in my memory than the other two, was the "Mott Campaign" at Washington and Lee. It had been decided to invite my hero, John R. Mott, to come for a series of addresses that spring. He accepted and I was asked to take charge of plans for his visit. I had learned a lot about organization at the Penn State campaign and since I naturally liked administration, I set to work with a good heart to make our W & L campaign a model of its kind. Though I was only eighteen at the time, the records show that it was as good a job of organization as I have ever done. The committee structure worked well under competent chairmen, and I had an agent in each fraternity to distribute literature and get the boys out. Further, the administration and the faculty could not have been more co-operative. The result was that practically the entire student body as well as many townspeople attended the meetings. Mott was much impressed; he was even more impressed when mother gave him a photograph of Robert E. Lee which the General himself had autographed for her.

After the campaign was over we followed it up with study groups; we also launched a number of projects as an expression of our wish to apply our faith to life. One project, in which I was especially interested, was a survey of Negro housing in Lexington.

In spite of the fact that I had been more preoccupied with other things than with my studies during my senior year, I was awarded Phi Beta Kappa and graduated with honors. Immediately after graduation, at David Porter's suggestion, I went to the student conference at Northfield. While there he asked me to join his staff as secretary for preparatory schools and I accepted. During the conference, the assassination of Archduke Ferdinand occurred in Serbia and from then on we could hear at first faintly and then louder and louder the hoofbeats of the Four Horsemen as they rode across the darkening sky. Yet most Americans remained incurably optimistic. On the Fourth of July, 1914, in addressing that conference, Dr. Jefferson of the Broadway Tabernacle, New York, assured the twelve hundred students before him (including a group from West Point) that "war would never again cast its dark shadow over this fair world of ours. Women would refuse to give birth to children to feed them to the cannon's mouth." Such fatuousness was all too typical of many good people during the early years of this century. I have been haunted ever since by the fact that those who should have known better did not prepare us for what was coming.

After the conference at Northfield I attended a school for Y.M.C.A. secretaries at Williams College. Surely Williamstown, Massachusetts, in those days was one of the most beautiful spots on God's earth.

For the next three years I traveled among the private preparatory

schools of the eastern part of the country from Maine to Ohio and
as far south as North Carolina doing what I could to strengthen the
Christian societies that existed, organizing societies where there
were none, and speaking in the school chapels. During the latter
part of this period I was also college secretary for New England, and
I can still feel the thrill of a horse-drawn sleigh ride with jingling
bells in the north New England winter when that was the sole means
of transportation.

In this work I made the acquaintance of a number of school boys
and college students who in the course of time became friends in
the deepest sense of that word: Alexander C. Zabriskie of Groton,
later dean of the Virginia Theological Seminary at Alexandria, Virginia; Henry Pitney Van Dusen of Penn Charter School, later president of Union Theological Seminary in New York; Charles P. Taft
of the Taft School, son of President Taft, and later mayor of Cincinnati; Richard F. Cleveland of Exeter, son of President Cleveland,
and later a leading member of the Baltimore bar; and Henry Hobson
of Yale, later Episcopal bishop of Ohio. These men were among the
finest of their generation.

In the summer of 1915, I was at Blue Ridge, North Carolina, for
the Secretaries Summer School. One of the classes was taught by
Dr. Hutchins, president of Berea College and father of Robert May-
nard Hutchins who became president of the University of Chicago.
Our textbook was the book of the Prophet Amos, and Dr. Hutchins's theme was that the Christian faith demanded social justice.
His method of teaching forced us to think about the social injustices
prevalent in our own time and his moral passion supplied a powerful incentive to corrective action. The development of my liberal
outlook owes much to Dr. Hutchins.

Sometime during 1916—I do not recall the exact date—the first
major crisis in my personal relations occurred. Frank Buchman had
been very kind to me, and I realized that I owed him a great deal.
But as time went by I discovered that he did not want reciprocity in
friendship—he wanted control. Buchman had left Penn State by
this time and was headed toward founding a movement of his own.
I increasingly resented his acting like a petty protestant pope in our
relations. Further, the techniques he was beginning to use in dealing
with other people's personal problems were repugnant to me. We
met one day at Hartford Seminary; a sharp difference of opinion
developed; and our heated conversation ended by my telling him I
was through with him. I may be pardoned for adding that it is a

matter of some pride with me that at twenty-one I had sense enough to see through and break with the founder of one of the least attractive Christian heresies of our time.

Work among the private preparatory schools of the East led me to conclude that it would be wise to have a special summer conference for schoolboys separate from the conference for college men at Northfield to which they had been going. With the cooperation of the headmasters of all the schools involved I organized a conference which began to meet annually at Blair Academy, Blairstown, New Jersey. When we met there in June, 1917, I knew that I would be leaving for France in a few days. At the conclusion of the conference Richard Cleveland made a moving little speech of thanks for what I had been trying to do and presented me with the wrist watch which I wore during the First World War.

III ✍ World War I

When war was declared against Germany in April, 1917, I wanted to get to France as soon as possible and the Y.M.C.A. offered me that opportunity. The Plattsburg training camp was swamped with applications and I did not want to wait for months for an Army commission and then be assigned to duty in the States. So on July 9, 1917, I sailed as a civilian Y.M.C.A. secretary, bound for Bordeaux, to work under Ned Carter, head of the army Y.M.C.A. in France, while awaiting a chance to get into some branch of the service. In the work we did that summer we were subject to all the rules of the Army and thought of ourselves as a part of it.

Finally, on September 27, I left Paris for Besançon in eastern France where a truck picked me up to take me to Camp du Valdahon. There the field artillery of the First Division of the U.S. regular army was preparing to go to the front. We were not far from the Swiss frontier, just west of the Jura range which rimmed the horizon.

Impressions of my service with the A.E.F. are recorded in letters to my family. On October 8, 1917, I was writing from one of the Y.M.C.A. barracks of the American army in France:

I am a private in the army, officially known as Pvt. F. P. Miller of Battery F, Fifth Field Artillery, First Division, American Expeditionary Force assigned to the Signal Detail.

There had been no arrangement made for recruiting here, as naturally one would not be expected to enlist on this side. However, the officers in charge were extremely helpful and secured the necessary authorization for us to be enrolled—I say us, for another secretary came down with me. The colonel of my regiment was kind enough to talk to me about the place he intended to assign me, and I fancy the work ought to be very interesting after one has begun to master it. The Fifth Field Artillery is a regiment of horse-drawn guns which correspond to the six-inch pieces used in the States—though the French designs are being used here. There are usually six batteries in a regiment. Our battery has four guns—and about two hundred men on its rolls.

To tell you the truth I have felt more contented during the last few days than I have felt in a long time. This may not be a good sign. I fear it is an indication of utter intellectual stagnation and a reversion to a lower species. Be that as it may, for the time being it is a real joy to have physical tasks facing one. It is the first time in several years that I have not been conscious of some responsibility of an executive character which—however agreeable—always made me feel as if a burden were strapped to my back. In contrast to sitting behind desks, presiding at meetings, and talking to head masters imagine the sensation of spending an hour this morning cleaning horses in the stables, or tugging at an ammunition wagon yesterday which had stuck in the mud, or cleaning up one's own bunk and equipment.

My first night with F Battery was unusual. For some reason the top sergeant decided I was a good one and gave me a bunk in his room until I was assigned a straw mattress on the floor of the stone barracks. That same night two characters in the battery stormed up the stairs with knives in hand threatening to cut the heart and liver out of the top sergeant. They were subdued and were eventually sent back to Leavenworth. Before that happy event the sheer task of keeping them with us taxed everyone's wit, and it fell to my lot occasionally to guard them. Security was finally achieved by chaining each prisoner to a stone too heavy for him to carry. Otherwise, they would immediately have gone AWOL.

When I was assigned a place to sleep I found that on the mattress next to me was a lad who had murdered his wife and served his time at Joliet. There were many men in the battery who were illiterate—boys who had come to America from Germany, Austria, Italy, and Eastern Europe in the great migration of 1900–1914. A few knew no English—they merely understood orders. Most of them had joined up because they had nothing else to do. There was a popular ditty among us—"I'm hungry, and I'm dirty and I ain't got nuthin' to do—so jine the army!" But these men who had so little and who owed almost nothing to America made magnificent soldiers. They were willing to die for a country they hardly knew.

A month after I enlisted we began to move up to the front, and the following letter was to prepare the folks at home:

Nov. 4, 1917

There is no need for worry, but I feel about this exactly as I do about one's being ill—that complete frankness is the kindest friend in the long run. Millions of other men like ourselves have in the past three years and a half gone through this period of training, and then quietly passed up to that long line on which the whole world seems to be experiencing its Calvary. And if some day we too should find ourselves there, it will be of course to take our small part in bearing what others have borne and enduring what others have endured, in order that Peace may come again upon this suffering world. . . .

Our first tour of duty at the front was on a quiet sector and was relatively brief. My battery was in position east of Nancy and just south of Arracourt in the Vosges near a tiny hamlet called Barthlemont. While there I wrote a description of our surroundings which was put in the post after we had returned to the rear echelon.

In a little village at the ends of the earth
Thanksgiving Day, 1917

How I wish you could peep in on me, or better, for I'm afraid I could not find you hotel accommodations in the neighborhood, I wish my pencil could in some way draw for you a picture of my surroundings. Nothing could be more grotesque! I am reclining on some hay which I was lucky enough to get from the stables, and which spread out on the dirt floor makes a most comfortable bunk. It is nearly ten o'clock of a Sunday morning, but high as the sun must be overhead, we have to trust for light to a little candle stuck in a beam leaning along side of me. Our light and I are in a corner—to the right are other makeshift beds, and just opposite dusky figures move about at their work hardly distinguishable in the dim room. Right above me a flight of stairs leads up to where a bit of daylight can be seen, streaking through a distant opening, and overhead the stone walls of our rooms arch up like the roof of a subway system. You may think I am describing my prison. Not at all. Our home, so they say, was probably once upon a time a well-stocked wine cellar, and overhead there still remain the skeletons of what must have been quite a pretentious establishment; and in some better day when the ravages of war have passed, may be again, but is now emptied of everything except us, the rats and the lice, which fortunately have passed me by thus far.

They tell us that across the hills not so very far away is the Plague that we have come to help drive out. It's hard to believe, at that, for most of the time the country is as quiet and still as if there had never been any-

thing like war in the world. The landscape hereabouts is bleak with November chill, and only an occasional horseman or foot traveler can be
seen on the deserted roads. At night the mists roll up with a density and
dampness that make one seek his blankets early. It is a bleak, sombre,
dreary country, and one would really have to wonder what maniacal purpose could have brought us hither if it were not for the fact that now and
then from the dugout on the hillside one's ear catches a distant boom,
and then a purring, burring, whistling, rushing sound, coming, coming!
coming!! when all at once there is a sharp explosion of shrapnel in the air,
or the duller thud of a high explosive plowing up the ground usually at a
safe distance, and leaving in the field a pot mark along with other pot
marks, which makes it look as though Old Mother Earth had had smallpox. But by no means imagine that all the boomings come this way, for
though there are few enough on either side, far more go over the hill than
ever come back. Suffice it to say that I have looked across the valley and
seen a long black line among the hills. Within that line is the den of the
Beast and I have looked back of the line into what I was told was a bit of
the country that we shall one day smash for bringing this curse on us.

Because of the censorship I neglected to say that I would have
been the first American artilleryman killed in France if it had not
been for my corporal John Bowman. Shortly after we put our guns
in position I was stringing wires by the pieces when I noticed a
German observation plane over the crossroads to our left. Some
howitzer shells were coming over and the plane was evidently ad-
justing the fire on us as target. I kept on stringing wire. The howitzer
shells were so slow that you could hear them coming just before
they arrived. I heard one coming right at me and at the same in-
stant Bowman yelled, "Miller, take cover." I dived into the dugout
and the shell exploded where I had been. Three of our men were
killed by that shell and ironically enough one was named Miller and
another Risemiller. It looked as if my number had been up. I helped
carry away the disemboweled body of one of the men and then I
knew the meaning of war. After leaving the regiment the following year I lost track of Bowman and have been haunted ever since
by the realization that I have never done anything for the man who
was responsible for my being alive today. Because of confusion of
names mother learned that I had been killed and it was some time
before she was informed that I was very much alive.

During that first stay at the front I began to realize the true worth
of the men who composed the old regular army. They were wonderful fellows. At night in our dugout they loved to sing. Considering
their backgrounds it was surprising that the songs they preferred

were nostalgic songs about home. I never heard these men of the old regular army amuse themselves with filthy ditties like those common in World War II. They drank, ran after women, and swore with devastating variety and effectiveness, but they were not foul-mouthed in their songs. A tenor named Taylor led us in our singing. I can hear him now in the dark of a dugout as he led off with "My Little Gray Home in the West" or "Pack Up Your Troubles" or "Tipperary" or "There's a Long Long Trail A-winding."

From the front we went into winter quarters in the village of Lumeville. This was near Gondrecourt in the Joan of Arc country. About this time, since the battalion was temporarily without a sergeant major, I was assigned to duty in that office. The winter that followed was severe. Many of the men slept in the haylofts of barns without benefit of heat of any kind. A sergeant was found dead where he slept one morning—apparently from exposure.

In January, I was made a corporal which seemed at the time an event as important as being promoted to full colonel seemed in World War II. And on March 22, I became battalion sergeant major.

Around the first of April our division was pulled out of the Bois de la Reine in the Toul Sector and sent by train with as much speed as possible toward the northwest. The final German offensive intended to deliver the knockout blow had been launched under the eye of the Kaiser on March 18. The British Fifth Army had been destroyed, nearly half a million allied troops had been captured, and the French had thrown in their last reserves.

Before going into the line we were billeted for a few days in a village awaiting our orders. On Easter morning it was announced there would be a communion service for our battalion. It was held outdoors in a barnyard. Very few attended. But a bishop of the Episcopal church presided, standing with all his vestments in that filthy and unecclesiastical spot. As I knelt to receive the sacraments, he did not ask me what I believed or to what church I belonged. It was sufficient that I asked to receive them. Years later I learned that the name of the bishop was Brent, one of the fathers of the ecumenic movement. I have always cherished the memory of that communion service as my first vivid experience of the meaning of the Church Universal.

We went into the lines in late April. It was not a quiet front. Our battalion headquarters was under frequent and at times continuous shellfire. Around the first of May I was ordered to go to Saumur to receive training to become an officer. Thinking that the war would last a long time, I was happy with this assignment.

May 4, 1918

For the past four or five days I have been like a man in a dream. After being in the field for seven months the experience of returning for a while to a more civilized way of living almost overcomes one. The first night we had sheets I yelled and giggled by turn for the first five minutes after crawling between them. The sensation was wonderful. Think of bathing again in a tub, when I hadn't so much as seen such a utensil since last September. And then the novelty of eating on china, and sleeping on a cot—with someone to make my bed in the morning! The very idea of having anyone around to clean up one's room, makes the dreamlike character of it all the more certain.

Well the dream, if such it is, is simply this—that for the time being I am what is called a candidate at a great old military school which has been turned over by the French for the use of our forces. It is a place where noncommissioned officers who seem to give promise of having some ability are given instruction looking toward their being granted commissions. . . . Just imagine the privilege of being trained to ride by French officers; if one got nothing else it would be worth being here for that alone. . . .

On July 30, I graduated second in my class at Saumur and after being commissioned was asked by my instructor, Captain Dreyfus of the French army, to remain and become his assistant instructor. Captain Dreyfus was a nephew of the famous Captain Alfred Dreyfus and was the most brilliant teacher I have ever had. His invitation was attractive but I declined as I was anxious to get back to the front. Instead of being assigned to a combat regiment, however, to my disgust, I was ordered to Angers to attend a heavy artillery school. There I learned to shoot fourteen-inch railroad pieces by aiming them on the stars; I graduated first in my class without ever really understanding the mathematics of what we did.

Soon afterwards I wrote:

Oct. 6, 1918

The end is not yet, but that it is approaching no one can for a moment doubt. These are great days in which to be living. Would that we could be more fully aware of their significance, and prepare ourselves more faithfully for the great years that are ahead.

The most fortunate and happy men that ever lived will be those who will have a share in actually establishing a League of Nations, in organizing a world Police Force, in helping to rebuild and reconstruct the areas that have been ruined by the war, and who will give themselves to the task of recreating the spirit of Russia, and helping the other nations that have become disintegrated during the last four years to become reestablished again. If it is possible I should certainly like to find a little corner somewhere where I could be of use—deus vult.

Again, I was "rewarded" by not being sent to a combat outfit but to a dreary replacement camp, and this outraged me. The men who had the worst records in training schools received the best assignments at the front, and those who had the best records either received poor assignments in the rear or none at all. I was getting an impression of Army G-1 (Personnel) which was to be confirmed again and again over the years—that it was incapable of using the best human material available and tended to specialize in misfits. However, in due course I was assigned to Battery E of the 58th C.A.C. which was using tractor-drawn eight-inch British howitzers. When the end of the war came, we were shelling the forts south of Metz from our positions in the Bois de Prêtre west of the Moselle River near Pont-à-Mousson. I had had no sleep for the better part of ten days and when the guns fell silent I crawled into my dugout bunk and awoke twenty-four hours later at noon on November 12.

From my dugout in the woods,
Nov. 14, 1918

"The War Is Won!" This is the headline in largest type of the latest paper we have had from Paris. Strange words, are they not? One can hardly credit his senses. He feels as if the world had conspired to take advantage of his helplessness by playing a huge capital joke on him. Surely it is hardly true, and yet one's judgment tells him that it must be true. Since Monday noon no shells have come this way; for the first time since August, 1914, blood has ceased to flow along the front of the Armies in the West.

No more war. It is difficult for one to adjust himself overnight to the changed situation. It had lasted so long, the whole scene was being staged upon such an enormous scale, and the enemy still seemed so strong. They were nearer the end than we knew, and when the collapse came it was startling in its suddenness. How God has avenged the right. The British back at Mons, the French on the German frontier and the Americans in Sedan! But how much more has He punished the wrongdoer! The Kaiser abdicated, reports of the assassination of the Crown Prince, all Germany in revolt, the Empire overthrown, and the Allies to occupy the banks of the Rhine!

In early December I took my first leave in fourteen months.

December 8, 1918

What a different Paris it was from the Paris of August and September, 1917. Every hotel was crammed, the streets in the evening were full to overflowing, and the whole city a blare of light at night, every little lamp apparently doing its best to make up for four years of perpetual darkness. The Place de la Concorde and Champs Elysées were lined with captured guns, and the whole place had an air of irrepressible relief at being freed from the pall which the gathering burdens of endless war had thrown over it.

I fear, Buddie, that my failing is the same as yours; I am too deeply dyed in the wool to get away from conferences if one happens within striking distance of me. As you might expect the first two days in Paris were occupied with nothing less than a Y.M.C.A. conference—actually the much defamed, greatly censured Y.M.C.A. Dr. King of Oberlin was there and Dr. Mackenzie of Hartford. Dr. Stevenson of Princeton was expected, but did not arrive. I haven't been to very many religious services during the last year, and I felt the need of such an atmosphere a great deal. Of course it did me a lot of good. Besides I had the honor of being the Chief Fly in the Ointment—a very enviable distinction no doubt. Ned Carter had urged me to say something, but I had refused knowing that my tongue would be very faltering having had no practice for so many months, and further the only point I could well make was altogether critical. However, at the very close when everything had been going beautifully, and all the "brethren" were up among the mountain peaks, I stood forth and explained with much hesitation that as far as my men were concerned the Y.M.C.A. was a mercantile institution pure and simple, and they were bitter against it—much applause from the audience. It was a relief to get what I wanted to say off my mind even if it was done very ineffectively. After seeing so little except this mercantile atmosphere for such a long time, it did encourage me and somewhat alter my point of view to find such men as Dr. King at work, and to find the emphasis of the entire conference so thoroughly Christian and actively religious. The meeting had to do with plans for the next few months in Europe, and it was a relief to hear nothing of the canteen except that it was not to be pushed to the fore. . . .

One of the few pleasant recollections I have of the winter that followed the Armistice is of the attitude that ordinary French people had toward us as Americans and particularly toward President Wilson. I doubt if there have been many occasions in history when a people welcomed foreign soldiers with such genuine friendliness. And for a few brief moments the French put Wilson on a higher pinnacle than they have ever put any other American president. I shall never forget sitting one evening by the hearth of a poor and old peasant who wanted to talk about Wilson. To him Wilson was an emanation of divinity—the Savior of France—the Creator of a new world order of peace. It was a beautiful dream which soon vanished, but while it lasted it filled the heart of a young American soldier with pride to know that the common people of Europe felt about us that way.

But it was a dreadful winter. Every day orders were expected which never came. In early February we started toward Bordeaux where we spent two more months at Bassens waiting for a ship. That was a bad spell. An inspection of the regiment by General Pershing helped, but the men were becoming desperate to get home. They could not understand the reasons for delay, and blamed our Colonel for offering our services to stay behind and load other regiments. Rumors of a mutiny among Canadian troops in England accentuated the unease, and we officers slept with our revolvers under our pillows.

Finally, around the middle of April, we went on board a fruit ship, the *Santa Barbara*, and sailed for home. On May 12, I was discharged from Camp Upton on Long Island.

Shortly afterwards I returned to Lexington to see the folks and though I did not expect the community to give me a hero's welcome, I did expect a slightly different reception than I got from the dean of Washington and Lee. When I approached him on the campus, his sole greeting was: "Francis, have you learned any sense yet?" To which the only apt reply that occurred to me was, "No, Sir, I'm afraid I haven't."

IV ✐ Oxford

While I was growing up, the talk in my family made it seem natural to think of towns called Oxford as places to secure an education. My grandfather received his B.A. from Miami University at Oxford, Ohio, and my father received his from the University of Mississippi at Oxford, Mississippi. Between 1914 and 1917 I was constantly reminded of the advantages and glories of Oxford University, England, when on the staff of David Porter, who had been one of the early Rhodes scholars.

While on leave in France after the Armistice I had taken an automobile trip to Rouen with Ned Carter and my dear Irish friend Eleanor Cargin. As we drove over the scenes of recent fighting and talked about the future they urged me to consider going to Oxford, England, the following year. So upon demobilization my thoughts turned in that direction.

I knew that I would require a long period of quiet and of study to collect myself. It is difficult for the generations that came after World War I to appreciate what that war did to the minds and spirits of boys like myself who had been born in the mid-nineties and who had grown up in idyllic communities like the Valley of Virginia. It was not so much the destruction of the material world that troubled me as the destruction of my psychological world—the world of the spirit. Lord Grey had said in August, 1914, "The lights are going out all over Europe: we shall not see them lit again in our lifetime."

In the spring of 1919 the light had gone out in me. Could it be re-lit? After getting out of the army, I felt as if I were a discharged battery. Could I be recharged? Perhaps Oxford might supply the answer.

I naturally wanted to be with my family for a while after release from the army and so I went with mother and William to South Hero, Vermont, on Lake Champlain. William was interested in a girl who was summering there. Beautiful as the surroundings were and glad as I was to see my folks again, that summer could hardly have been less pleasant, and so I busied myself as much as possible with my own plans. I decided to apply for a Rhodes scholarship, and since I had established legal residence in New York before the war, it seemed sensible to apply there.

Years later Bishop Beverley Tucker, who in 1919 was chairman of the Virginia Rhodes Scholar Selection Committee, asked me why I had not applied in Virginia. I replied that as a graduate of Washington and Lee I had realized that my chances of receiving a scholarship in Virginia were negligible since the awards up to that time had usually gone to University of Virginia students and no W & L student had yet received one. "Why, Francis," the Bishop said in a shocked voice, "we always gave them to the best men." "Of course," said I, "men from *The* University would naturally be the best!"

So I applied to the New York Rhodes committee. Fortunately David Porter was a member of that committee and briefed me on its procedures. Because of the disruption caused by the war, the usual procedural timetable was not being kept and the committee, after reviewing the files of applicants, narrowed its choice to two candidates: Phillip C. Jessup of Hamilton College and myself. Both of us were asked to appear before a special summer meeting of the committee in New York City. During my absence in France, my mother, with characteristic generosity, had given away most of my clothes to Belgian Relief. Consequently I appeared before the committee in an old and ill-fitting suit and my heart sank within me when the perfectly groomed Phillip walked in.

The committee decided not to announce the award until autumn, but I, being of a rather hopeful and persistent disposition, determined to go on to Oxford anyway and stay as long as my money lasted even if I did not receive the scholarship. I had saved a modest amount from my lieutenant's pay, so I proposed to mother that she go with me since her income (provided by Uncle Harvey) was enough to cover her share of our joint expenses. In this way we would be able to see some of the beautiful things we had always wanted to see in Europe even if my funds, without the scholarship, would only carry us for part of a year.

This episode in my life seems thoroughly quixotic. The academic year which was about to begin was the first full academic year after World War I. Every room in every Oxford college had long since been booked, as well as accommodations in licensed lodgings in town. In spite of all this I had not written to any college, I had not taken any entrance examinations, and I had not made advance inquiries as to where rooms might be available. I simply got on a ship and went to Oxford.

On October 3, we landed at Liverpool and took the train to Oxford. The conductor treated us as if we were his personal guests and waved farewell as the train left us on the Oxford platform. We went to the King's Arms, a modest little inn at the end of Broad Street, where we found rooms were available though we had made no advance reservations. My friend, David Porter, had suggested that we get temporary lodgings there since it was near Trinity College of which he had been a member and where I intended to apply using his name as an introduction.

As soon as we were settled in, I walked over to the college and asked at the Porter's Lodge where the President, Dr. Blakiston, lived. The Trinity head porter, named Gillam, with his white hair, ruddy cheeks, and stately manner, was often mistaken by newcomers for the president himself. Gillam courteously indicated Dr. Blakiston's residence and I went to the house and rang the doorbell.

Dr. Blakiston was a shy old bachelor whose spiritual home was in the seventeenth and eighteenth centuries. In the Cromwellian period the college had been staunchly royalist and in the following century it could count both the Earl of Chatham and Lord North among its former students. Not only did "Blinks" (as the students called their president) prefer England as it was before the industrial revolution, but he regarded the latter as a regrettable intrusion upon his world. This made it all the more ironic that in his old age he should have been killed by a bus on Boar's Hill.

When I rang the bell the President himself came to the door. I explained who I was and said that I should very much like to be admitted to Trinity since it had been recommended to me by a Trinity man, David Porter, whom he no doubt remembered. Dr. Blakiston's astonishment was great. So great in fact that he did not tell me to go jump in the Isis, which was the retort I deserved; instead, to my relief, he told me to go see the Dean, Mr. Nagel. I did so the very same evening, tracking him down at his home. That kind man gave me a sympathetic hearing and said a decision would be made in a few days. At the end of a week he told me that if I agreed to live in town I would be admitted—adding that as a veteran I would not be required to dine in college. This arrangement suited me exactly —it was just what I wanted.

So all that was left was to find a place to live. Various inquiries produced the same answer—every room taken. Finally someone suggested that we scan the "ads" in the Oxford newspaper. The first issue contained an advertisement describing a flat for rent which sounded as if it would do. Then I had an inspiration. I realized that if an Englishman were interested he would write a note to the advertisement's code address which would be delivered the next day. Instead of writing a note I sent a telegram which was answered at once and within a few hours we had rented an agreeable apartment from the Misses Mowbray on Winchester Road. Mother and I moved in and shortly thereafter the autumn term began.

The method of instruction at Oxford was, for a person with my background and interests, incomparably the best in the world. After choosing a particular field in which he wanted to read, the student was referred to a tutor. He generally met his tutor for an hour once a week. At this meeting the student read an essay on a previously assigned subject and the tutor conversed with him about the views expressed, sometimes approving and sometimes acidly criticizing. But however caustic the criticism, the student knew that his tutor was his friend and also his defender when he needed one. In addition the tutor would suggest several lecture courses which he thought might benefit the student should the latter care to attend.

I wanted to read history. So I was told to go to see Mr. Weaver, who was a history don. When Mr. Weaver inquired what kind of history interested me particularly, I replied that I wanted to know more about the histories of Russia and China since my knowledge of these countries was very limited, and all the events of the previous decade had made me feel that they were the critical areas for the future. It so happened that I had been greatly impressed by a remark of Theodore Roosevelt when he came back from his world tour: John R. Mott reported that Roosevelt had said, "Russia more than any country holds the fate of the coming years." China fascinated me, too, primarily because of its ancient civilization and vast size.

This was not the reply Mr. Weaver wanted. "I am sorry, Miller," he said, "if you want to study about Russia and China you will have to go to some other university, since we have no facilities for reading in those fields. If you stay here, you will have to read Bishop Stubbs's *Constitutional History of England*." So we settled for Stubbs, and I chose the diplomatic history of the nineteenth century as my special subject.

The autumn of 1919 was a bleak time. Around the middle of November I received a letter from David Porter saying that Jessup had been awarded the Rhodes scholarship from New York. All my dreams faded—dreams of having time to recollect myself, dreams of seeing Europe, dreams of not having to count every penny. I was filled with gloom.

On top of that my bicycle skidded on a wet road and several stitches had to be taken in my head as well as in my clothes; then the following week I went to the Acland Home to have my appendix out.

In February, "Blinks" heard that the Americans in college were having a "thin" time and he generously invited Mother and me to have tea with him one Sunday. The afternoon was dark as it can be dark only in England in midwinter. The atmosphere of the unlit and unheated house was correspondingly dismal. We were the only guests. Dr. Blakiston was always abashed in the presence of women and on this occasion was more than usually silent. Though my mother's conversational ability could generally be relied upon, her resources appeared to me to be a bit overtaxed, so I decided to chip in. "Dr. Blakiston," I said, "I think it is wonderful that Lord Harmsworth has just endowed a professorship of American history in the University." My remark was occasioned by the fact that prior to that time no American history had been taught at Oxford. There was a pause and then the president, looking me straight in the eye, replied, "Miller, I do not think there is material enough for a lectureship." The word that cut was "lectureship." After that there wasn't much more to be said. In retrospect I prize the memory of "Blinks" as much as any other Oxford memory. How right Lord North would have thought Dr. Blakiston's appraisal of American history was!

On May 12, about halfway through the spring term, Mr. Francis Wylie (later Sir Francis), the Oxford Secretary of the Rhodes Trust, rode around on his bicycle to tell me that I had just been awarded a Rhodes Scholarship by the New York Committee. In those days Rhodes Scholars were not permitted to marry. But Phillip Jessup began to feel that if he went off to England, Lois Kellogg might not want to wait, so he resigned his scholarship and got married. Whereupon the committee, apparently impressed by my stubborn determination to go to Oxford anyway, took an action that was without precedent, and I believe has not been repeated. It transferred Jessup's scholarship to me. When this miraculous event occurred, my bank balance had fallen to five pounds, but now our financial worries were over. I could stay at Oxford for three years and we could travel where we pleased on the Continent.

Toward the end of the spring term Dr. Mott asked me to organize a group of twelve or fifteen Rhodes scholars to go to Germany and spend the summer helping with the repatriation of war prisoners. I was to be in charge with a budget of $50,000.00. I accepted at once and had no trouble recruiting the others. A year and a half after the end of the war there were still some sixty thousand Russian prisoners in Germany and a far larger number of Austrians and Germans in Siberia, many of whom had been there for six years. An exchange was taking place on ships that shuttled back and forth between Stettin in Germany and Narva in Estonia. Our assignment was to do everything that our limited resources permitted to make life slightly more bearable for these wretched human beings. I stationed S. M. Keeny at Narva and Douglas Miller at Stettin. This was the beginning of Keeny's very distinguished forty-year career of service to migrants and refugees all over the world. Our headquarters was in Berlin and I kept two of the group with me there. The others were stationed at prisoner-of-war camps in various parts of Germany. In each camp we organized a simple school for any who wanted to attend, selecting teachers from among the prisoners. Games were encouraged, music was provided and some supplies, like writing paper, nonexistent before, were made available. Our special concern was to secure food for a few of the most seriously ill men—since all were on a starvation diet—and we did this by finagling some provisions that the American army had left in Belgium.

I have two indelible memories of that summer. One of a camp in which the prisoners literally believed that, as a result of the revolution, a new heaven and a new earth existed in Russia. There was a look of ecstatic mystical satisfaction in the faces of some, as of men who had lived with their Utopian dreams so long that they mistook them for reality. But no one who saw those faces could doubt that the revolution had come to stay. Strangely enough, these prisoners reminded me for all the world of people in our Southland who have been through a religious revival.

My other memory is of a ship docking in Stettin. I had gone up to see some of the Austrian prisoners who were arriving from Siberia. That particular ship was completely full of men whose experiences had deprived them of reason. They had no minds left; they were not insane, as we think of that; and they were not violent. On the contrary they said nothing and they did nothing. They just stood and stared like cowed domestic animals. They did not know their own names or the names of the places from which they had come. This was the ultimate horror of war. It had drained human bodies of their human spirits and left them worse off than animals. And the contrast that haunted me was the contrast between these dumb creatures and the gay Austrian lads they had been only a few years before as they had gone out singing from their charming Alpine villages garlanded by their girls to fight for the emperor.

When I returned to Oxford at the end of September, 1920, I realized that only eight months and two short vacations lay between me and my final comprehensive examinations or "schools" and that consequently I had better get to work. This I proceeded to do.

June came very quickly that year and with it "schools." There was a different examination every morning and every afternoon for six days and each examination lasted three hours. When I walked in a kind of daze out of the last examination, I was more mentally and nervously exhausted than I had ever been in my life. On the basis of the quality of a student's papers written in "schools" and of his oral answers to questions put to him sometime later in a "viva," the examiners rate him as having received a first, second, third, or fourth class, or as "failed." It is naturally the ambition of every serious student to get a "first." I got a second.

Rhodes scholarships at that time were given for three years, so I had a year and a term left of my scholarship. Before using the remainder I was invited by Tissington Tatlow, general secretary of the British Student Christian Movement (the British affiliate of the World's Student Christian Federation) to join his staff for six or eight months to visit the universities of England, Scotland, Wales, and North Ireland. No American had ever served on that staff before and British students generally knew very little about the United

States. The idea of going about for a short time as an interpreter of
my country and also of the World Student Christian Movement
naturally appealed to me and I accepted.

The British Student Movement differed in many respects from the
American Student Y.M.C.A. with which I had worked before the
war. The S.C.M. was more interested in ideas than in programs and
more concerned with reading and discussion than with organization.
I had already begun to wish that we had more of the same preoccupation within our Student Christian Associations in the United
States.

After completing a family tour of the British Isles, I went to Holland to attend the first conference that it had been possible to hold
since the war of Christian students from countries on both sides of
that conflict. We met at the invitation of the Dutch S.C.M. general
secretary, Dr. Herman Rutgers, at Hardenbroek Castle near Utrecht
and I became acquainted with two students there who touched my
life for years to come.

One was a dark-eyed, black-haired Bavarian named Fritz Berber.
He was a Lutheran and a student of jurisprudence at the University
of Munich. He had been a Communist on the barricades in the civil
strife of November, 1918, but he was now a Social Democrat. In
the course of one of our conference discussions he said, with his
piercing gaze fixed on me, "You Americans are all hypocrites—tear
off your masks so that we may know what you really are." I was
not accustomed to hearing such language, and I thought it might be
interesting to try to find out what made this fellow tick. So I asked
him if we might have a talk the following afternoon—which was a
Sunday. He agreed and after lunch we met at a spot across the moat
from the castle wall where there were good stones on which we could
sit. We talked for two or three hours. As we talked we became more
and more preoccupied with the question: What is the basis of government? Berber insisted that the only possible basis was force,
while I maintained that the only right basis was consent, explaining
that though we in the United States still had some way to go, we
were moving steadily in the direction of government based genuinely on the consent of a majority of our citizens. Neither of us
budged an inch in our positions, but Berber became more and more
extreme in his statements and finally blurted out: "If the Devil himself ever came to rule Germany I would serve him." This outburst
proved to be prophetic. Occasionally one finds himself in a conversation which illumines the age in which he lives. This was such a

conversation. It revealed the supreme issue of our times and spelled out the irreconcilable conflict of assumptions about society that made a second world war inevitable.

The other student at the conference whose life became intertwined with mine was W. A. Visser 't Hooft of Leiden University. Our meeting was the beginning of more than forty years of collaboration and friendship.

Between September and the following April I visited colleges and universities in England, Scotland, Wales, and North Ireland, talking to student groups and speaking at public meetings. These college visits provided a rare opportunity to become acquainted with British life and thought. In referring to some of these visits the S.C.M. journal said: "Few travelling secretaries can have charmed the Christian Unions in Scotland so much as F. P. Miller has done. Both in Edinburgh and Glasgow he met group after group and made speech after speech, and each time he turned up bright and smiling and—charmed! His visit will be remembered."

My debt to the British Student Movement is great, but I owe most to its senior woman secretary, Zoë Fairfield. Zoë was in her thirties when I met her. She had a first-class intellect, a sensitive social conscience, and great wisdom. Few people have stimulated my mind as much as she did or so definitely influenced the direction of my interests and intentions. She contributed directly to making me a liberal, and her death in 1929 deprived me of a much needed counselor and friend.

The highlight of my term with the S.C.M. was a dinner given by Lord Pentland in the House of Commons on March 28, 1922, at which I was asked to speak about the Student Movement. There were three other speakers, and among the forty-five guests were: Viscount Chelmsford (former Viceroy of India), Lord Robert Cecil, the Archbishop of Canterbury, H. A. L. Fisher (Minister of Education), Ernest Barker, the Earl and Countess of Buxton, Lord Henry Bentinck, Lord Clwyd, Lady Denman, Sir Frederick and Lady Maurice, Lady Parmoor, the Countess of Portsmouth, the Rt. Hon. Walter Runciman, and the Viscountess Wolmer. It was quite an occasion. The lady who sat by me told me that mine had been the best speech —that she knew for she was a "sermon-taster." Since she was also a taster of good wine, I took her praise with a grain of salt.

When my work with the S.C.M. terminated, I decided to remain at Oxford until the summer of 1923, using the rest of my Rhodes scholarship to read theology. I did this not with a view to entering the church but with a view to rejoining the staff of the International Committee of the Y.M.C.A. and eventually entering public life. James Madison read theology with John Witherspoon at Princeton, and it is to be regretted that American politicians generally have not profited by his example. So for the next fifteen months my home was at 33A High Street.

That spring an event occurred which profoundly affected my whole life. I met Helen Day Hill of Lake Forest, Illinois, at a tea party. She had graduated from Bryn Mawr and was completing a year in economics and political science at Oxford. Our meeting was casual and my first attempts to see more of her were not too successful. She did not care much for southerners—their talk was chaff and their sincerity was dubious. When she departed in June, she left nothing with me but a favorable impression.

I had gone to Oxford hoping that study there would help to recharge my battery. That is exactly what Oxford did, and my gratitude is profound. But it was not so much the courses of study that helped me find myself—it was the quality of intellectual and moral life which I encountered while I was there and the leisurely assimilation of the values of life through conversation with friends. These were the things that made it possible for me to acquire once more a sense of purpose and some zest for living.

The art of conversation is one of the best gifts Oxford bestows upon her sons. It was a thrilling ecumenic experience to spend an evening in Bevil Rudd's rooms in Trinity College conversing with that great Jesuit, Father Martindale. He assured me that I would be saved, in spite of my being a Presbyterian. Then there was the evening with Yeats in the rooms of a Balliol student. In response to our skeptical inquiries Yeats affirmed categorically that he had seen fairies in Bagley Woods on Boar's Hill, and I believed him.

Most of the great men of the turn of the century spoke at Oxford while I was there. Among those whom I heard were Viscount Bryce, Lord Reading, and Herbert Asquith. I shall remember as long as I live Lord Robert Cecil concluding an address at the Union by affirming that "the things that are seen are temporal, but the things that are not seen are eternal." I also heard many of the coming men. It was the time of the "troubles" in Ireland and once while Winston Churchill was speaking in the Union, a heckler shouted, "Get your Black and Tans out of Ireland." This interruption flabbergasted Mr. Churchill to such an extent that he sputtered and was unable to complete his sentence. Bishop William Temple (later archbishop of

Canterbury) was also a frequent speaker in the University and profoundly influenced my thinking about religion.

However, there was one man to whom I owe more than to any other person or institution in Oxford. That was Dr. W. B. Selbie, the principal of Mansfield Theological College. On a Sunday morning when he preached, the Mansfield chapel was always packed. Many Americans attended and because they were usually late John Harlan (now associate justice of the Supreme Court) and Arthur Kinsolving (former Episcopal rector of St. James's, New York) frequently had to sit on the front row. Selbie was a small man but a giant in his spirit. Undergraduates called him "the bloody inspired mouse." His preaching was the single most important factor in recharging my spiritual and moral batteries. To him God was very real and He became real to me when Selbie cried from the pulpit, "In the black darkness of this world stretch out your hand, and you will feel a hand grasp yours, for at the heart of the universe there stands a cross."

So I returned to America ready for whatever was in store for me.

V ✒ American Interlude

When I returned to the United States in the summer of 1923, I resumed, after an interval of six years, my connection with the Student Department of the Y.M.C.A. David R. Porter had asked me to be his associate national secretary for student work, which meant visiting colleges and universities throughout the country in the interests of the Student Christian Movement.

This appealed to me. The United States had rejected the League of Nations and the prospects for peace were dim. A world-wide community of Christians seemed the only hope for the human race and I shared with André Philip of France the conviction that "though we could not make a new civilization we could make the men who in their day would make a new civilization." The student Y.M.C.A. offered at that time the most promising opportunity of preparing young Americans to meet with faith and vision the challenges of the coming years. So I bought a tiny apartment in New York and went to work.

In the summer of 1924, I went from New York to High Leigh, England, to attend a meeting of the General Committee of the World's Student Christian Federation of which Dr. Mott was still chairman. The Federation had fascinated me from the first time I had heard of it. Here was an expression of man's longing for the universal. Its motto "Ut Omnes Unum Sint" affirmed the ultimate moral and spiritual goal of the human race.

There were delegates at High Leigh from every continent and from all the principal ethnic groups. The delegates themselves were not persons of any particular influence, but the mere existence of a world-wide student movement seemed to me to be a symbolic fact of great significance because the representatives of that movement were bound together by a prayer and a dream against which the forces of Hell itself had never been able finally to prevail. This was the ecumenic movement in embryo. Visser 't Hooft whom I had met at Hardenbroek in 1921 was at High Leigh; also Pierre Maury of France, Hanns Lilje of Germany, and others who in later years were to provide leadership for that movement.

My education as a member of the world community had commenced long before High Leigh but the meeting there accelerated and formalized the process. I began to learn how other people think about us Americans. I also began to understand the hard reality of the differences that separate nations and races which cannot be ignored except at the risk of creating deceptive illusions. I came to mistrust equally the sentimentalist who overlooked differences on the ground that good will alone would provide an adequate basis for peace, and the simplicist who was convinced that peace could only be established by governments outlawing war.

In due course I also came to realize that the art of listening is the most useful and at the same time the rarest art in ecumenic activity. This is also true in diplomatic activity. I do not mean just maintaining courteous silence while someone else is talking. I mean rather the art of listening creatively—of listening so intently and sympathetically that the right questions can be asked and it finally becomes possible to begin to understand what the other fellow is trying to say. This is a very difficult art for most Americans to master.

During the 1920s several efforts were made to bring the United States into the World Court. All of these efforts failed. However, it was a good issue on which to educate the university community, and, during the summer of 1925, I took advantage of my Y.M.C.A. position to create as much interest as possible among students across the country. A national committee was organized with Henry Pitney Van Dusen as director and various foundations were asked to supply funds.

Early in June I planned to attend the Midwestern Summer Conference of Student Y.M.C.A.'s. That meant passing through Chicago. Why not stop off en route to see my Uncle Harvey McElwee in Lake Forest? It had been twelve years since I had rejected his invitation to join him and he had bitterly stricken me from his will. Perhaps time had mellowed him. At any rate he was growing old and this was an opportunity to try to re-establish proper family relationships, so I wrote and asked if I might spend the night. I was told to come.

My uncle lived in the last house on Deer Path Avenue before it ended at Lake Michigan. Just west of my uncle's home was the home of Mrs. Russell Day Hill, the mother of Helen Hill whom I had met at Oxford. I had not seen Helen nor heard from her since the spring of 1922. It seemed that during the intervening years she had been working for the National Women's Trade Union League and at the same time studying for a Ph.D. degree in political science at the University of Chicago. I telephoned and was invited to tea. As she came in the door I experienced an intuition that this was the girl I was going to marry.

My visit with Uncle Harvey, though outwardly pleasant, did not improve our relations very much, but I now had a new reason for wanting to visit Lake Forest again and was delighted that our National Student Council was planning to meet there September 5–11. During the course of this meeting I managed to see both Helen and Uncle Harvey several times but apparently did not impress either. Mother was visiting Uncle Harvey too while I was there and reported after she left that he still thought of me as "throwing my life away" because I had not accepted his invitation in 1913. When I learned this I wrote to mother:

> To do what he wants me to do—to be a success by the standards of Chicago Big Business would be for me the great betrayal—it would represent in my life the equivalent of Judas and the thirty talents. Of course he can't see this—and perhaps never will. He is interested in economic power. I am interested in the power of ideas. These are two different worlds, and there is very little intercourse between them.
> I never had more contempt than I have now for the sordid atmosphere in which most of America's big businessmen live.

However negative my feeling may have been about Chicago businessmen, I had an increasingly positive feeling about Helen Hill. She came to New York early in October and I suddenly became aware that at thirty and for the first time in my life I had fallen head over heels in love.

It took me more than a year to win Helen. I proposed by letter shortly after her New York visit and for three months wrote every day and sometimes twice a day. She did not say "yes," but she did not say "no."

After a visit to Lake Forest in April, I was elated: when Helen drove me to the station to say good-by, she astonished herself and me by leaning over and kissing me ever so gently on the cheek. For days thereafter I walked on clouds. But when I saw her again she had evidently had afterthoughts and had withdrawn into her shell. My elation turned into profound depression.

I spent the summer of 1926 with mother at Estes Park, Colorado, attending the usual student conferences and lecturing at a Y.M.C.A. Secretaries Summer School. Mother had a very thin time that summer. She found me extremely difficult and at times rather unbearable. The truth is that I was desperate. Would this girl have me, or would she not? If she wouldn't I was going to leave the country—going to live in Japan or India. Was there anything more I could do to soften her up a bit? I had ordered Turkish Delight from a little shop I knew in Pera, Istanbul. She did not care for Turkish Delight. I took to writing doleful poems. She thought they weren't very good.

In the autumn, Helen came on to do a job in New York and we saw a good bit of each other—riding horses in Central Park and taking walks in Westchester. Then on November 10, I wrote mother:

It's late at night and I'm very tired but before going home I must get this off to tell you that Helen has "gone and done it." I've known for a long time that it was useless for me to urge her further but that when she had arrived she would let me know. Well she did last night right in her own deliciously quaint way—we were taking a ride after a storm on the top of a Fifth Avenue bus—wet seats—blowing wind—sounds very prosaic, doesn't it? But it was the most glorious moment of my life—and afterwards!!

Helen and I were never formally engaged, but it was a mutual commitment deeper than any ring could symbolize. We decided to get married the following summer and began to make our plans accordingly.

Three days before my bus ride with Helen I had made a decision to leave the Y.M.C.A. and accept a post with the World's Student Christian Federation in Geneva, Switzerland.

This decision came at the end of months of growing frustration in my work, accompanied by an increasing sense of alienation from the general Y.M.C.A. movement.

My three years as associate national secretary for the Student Department of the Y.M.C.A. had been a very mixed experience. On the one hand it gave me a wonderful opportunity to become acquainted with the colleges and universities of the country and to talk to students about the things I believed in. I lived the life of a traveling salesman on the road for weeks on end, visiting educational institutions in every state of the union. In the course of these travels I acquired a reputation as a speaker and filled a variety of engagements; they ranged as widely as entering the pulpit as a lay preacher at Amherst College, conducting series of religious meetings at midwestern colleges and serving as a member of a team of speakers in a week-long campaign in Atlanta. The theme of the campaign was "what would happen if Jesus came to Atlanta" and I spoke twenty-five times during the week to groups of all kinds, young and old and Negro and white. Other members of the team included Raymond Robbins, Sherwood Eddy, Henry Crane, and Mordecai Johnson.

Though I had all the work that I could do and much of it was intensely interesting, I was becoming thoroughly dissatisfied with the Y.M.C.A. as the organization responsible for promoting and supervising the Student Christian Movement in the colleges. This dissatisfaction was caused by a fundamental difference of opinion as to the kind of Student Christian Movement the colleges needed. As a result of two years with the A.E.F. and four years in England, I had become convinced that if the Christian faith was to make the appeal that it should make to American students, the organization responsible for presenting that appeal should be oriented to campus interests and needs rather than to the interests of the big city Y.M.C.A.'s. This seemed to me to be axiomatic. It also seemed axiomatic to my close friend and associate, Henry P. Van Dusen, and to many of the ablest student leaders. But it did not seem at all axiomatic to the bosses of the Metropolitan Y.M.C.A.'s. They thought of the Y.M.C.A. groups in the colleges as an integral part of the whole Y.M.C.A. movement, carrying out the programs and policies of that movement and subject to its supervision.

The city Y.M.C.A.'s were essentially very conservative in their outlook. Their budgets were derived in part from the contributions of wealthy benefactors, most of whom viewed with intense alarm the increasing interest of student groups in the implications of their faith for American society. It was inevitable, therefore, that the supervision which these city associations insisted upon providing would make it impossible to develop a movement in the colleges alive to the vital intellectual currents of the day and deeply con- concerned with the issues of social justice, for though their veto power was usually held in reserve, its implicit existence was enough to inhibit and thwart imaginative campus initiatives.

Clearly, if the student Y.M.C.A. was to do the job that ought to be done on the campuses, it should seek to secure a measure of in- dependence from the general Y.M.C.A. organization.

Under the leadership of David Porter a National Council of Stu- dent Y.M.C.A.'s had been created, and Van Dusen and I began to think of this as developing into a policy-making body which at the national level would be affiliated with the general Y.M.C.A. move- ment but not controlled by it. At a meeting of this council in Lake Forest, Illinois, during September, 1925, its student members had been enthusiastically in favor of an effort to secure greater inde- pendence. Some of the salaried secretaries also supported such an effort, but others held back, fearful that their retirement arrange- ments might be jeopardized.

Agitation for greater independence had reached a point where the General Board of the Y.M.C.A. appointed a commission under Dr. Thomas Graham of Oberlin to look into the relationship of student work to the rest of the Y.M.C.A. Our hopes were high that this commission would favor the views of the National Student Council. As it deliberated, Van Dusen and I did all that we could to mobilize support for our point of view.

One day in February, 1926, Mr. Wiley, general secretary of the whole Y.M.C.A., called me into his office and told me that it was widely reported that I was exerting my influence to break the Stu- dent Department away from the general movement and asked me to make some kind of public statement denying this. I replied that on the contrary I was working for the only kind of adjustment of relationships that would save the student Y.M.C.A.'s for the general Y.M.C.A. movement. I explained that the student associations could not meet the needs of the universities if they were required to con- form to the policies of the general movement; that those needs could only be met by a student movement responsive to the life of the campus; and that if the general Y.M.C.A. continued to try to impose its methods and programs on the student associations, these latter would wither away and die. I assured Mr. Wylie that the student associations would survive only if they were given freedom to de- velop their own policies and that consequently my activities had been directed to insure survival in affiliation with the general Y.M.C.A. movement. In conclusion I told him that I was not a man to accept a salary from an organization while undermining it and that if I ever did initiate an attempt to break away, he would have my resignation in his hands immediately.

I continued to hope that the report of the Graham commission would give the National Student Council sufficient freedom in policy-making to insure its remaining in affiliation with the general Y.M.C.A. movement. But my hopes were in vain. On October 13, 1926, the commission adopted by a vote of 7 to 6 a report which from my point of view was as bad as it could possibly be. This vote was the death warrant for my dream of an American Student Christian Movement. The thing that hurt most was the knowledge that John R. Mott had sold us down the river.

In retrospect I have often reflected that though I have had many failures in my life, my inability to convert the student Y.M.C.A. movement into the kind of university movement required by the times in which we live and by my understanding of the Christian faith was in some respects the greatest of all. Such a movement would have contributed much toward revitalizing the Protestant churches and furnishing leadership for the ecumenic movement. It would also have helped prepare a climate of public opinion favorable to our government's playing an even worthier role, commensurate with our great resources and power, on the world stage. In the course of the following years, college Y.M.C.A.'s began to disappear quietly from the scene in every part of the country. Some remained here and there as useful service centers. But the job which should have been done was not done, and the loss to American society and to the Christian church as a whole was incalculable.

After this defeat it was obvious that I had to find another job and I was offered the post of administrative secretary of the World's Student Christian Federation in Geneva, Switzerland. On November 6, I cabled my acceptance and said I would leave for Geneva in January.

Before leaving New York for Geneva I was given a beautiful farewell dinner by my friends in the Y.M.C.A. Speeches were made about the great services I had rendered; joy and pride were expressed in the opportunity that had come to me for wider service. They presented me with gifts to remember them by—one was a very fine leather toilet case which is still adorning my dresser after forty years.

This send-off almost made ostracism seem sweet. But in my heart I knew that I had been rejected, and this sense lingers still.

I rented my little apartment in New York, packed my few belongings, and sailed for Europe on the *Aquitania* on January 15, 1927. The one consolation I had was that in six or seven months Helen would join me.

VI ✐ Geneva

On my way to Switzerland I stopped off in London to see my friends in the British Student Movement and arrived in Geneva on a February morning when the very air itself seemed to be frozen. The reception was as frosty as the climate since no one from the World's Student Christian Federation headquarters except an American came to the station to greet me.

However, my spirits were high. For a brief moment I was a free man again—free from organizational hassling, and free to work toward my dream of a World Student Christian Movement. The one human reality that had begun to possess me was the reality of the Church Universal. As yet it was not very visible. It had to be made visible. It had to be built, and the builders had to come from that generation of students. My long-range task was to announce the goal and help find the men who would begin the work of construction. But my immediate task was to act as administrative secretary of an organization with a very large name and a very small budget in an all too modest office at 16 Boulevard des Philosophes. My duties were to supervise headquarters, correspond with the national movements, and organize and attend various committee meetings and conferences. The general secretary was a Swiss, Henri-Louis Henriod, who planned to spend most of his time traveling around the world doing what he could to help the national student associations and societies.

After getting settled in a pension nearby and after receiving as much briefing as was available, I began to take stock of the office and small staff for which I was responsible. My greatest achievement of that spring was to find a building for our headquarters more worthy of our cause. In the old city, at 13 rue Calvin, was a spacious mansion with a courtyard, built by a M. Buisson in the seventeenth century. There was far more space than we could use, but it was for rent at a very reasonable rate. It had the dignity that I felt should be associated with the headquarters of a world student movement, and besides there was a gorgeous view of the Lake. So we moved in, and the Federation remained there for more than forty years.

As summer drew near I was naturally very much preoccupied with my approaching marriage. I rented an apartment in the old Hotel Beau Séjour overlooking the city. As Helen's mother was giving us a sport roadster for a wedding present, I had to learn to drive a car and to pass my driving test on the steepest hills under the eye of the world's most austere policemen.

Helen and I had decided to be married in Oxford on August 25, since that was where we had first met and since we wanted Dr. Selbie, who had given me a new lease on life after the First World War, to marry us in the Mansfield College Chapel. I went to Oxford on August 24, and stayed at the old Clarendon Hotel. We were married at eleven o'clock the following morning. There were only twelve persons present, including Helen's mother and my dear friend, Zoë Fairfield of the British S.C.M. Toward the conclusion of the service Dr. Selbie paused, departed from the prescribed ritual, and spoke directly to us for four or five minutes about the meaning of marriage. He mentioned the pain as well as the joy of two lives uniting and his words were so inspired that my eyes became moist as did his. He started us well on our pilgrimage together. I know of no more successful marriage.

The next two years were a rare mixture of delight and disappointment. There was the thrill of living with Helen. There was also the thrill of the job I had set myself to do while with the Federation, the possibilities of which fascinated me more and more. On the other hand, there was the beginning of ill-health which dogged me for the next ten years.

Helen was bitterly disappointed by not receiving an offer, which she had been promised, of work in the International Labor Organization. She told me before we were married that I must realize that her work would come before everything else, and I was made painfully aware of this one night when I wakened to hear her quietly sobbing because no job had come through. Her disappointment continued until she began to do foreign language book reviews for the *Saturday Review of Literature* under Henry Seidel Canby.

My work, on the other hand, was absorbing me more and more. It was growing upon me that the curse of European civilization and of the Protestant churches in Europe was the type of nationalism that had developed there during the nineteenth century. For millions of Europeans their nation was in effect their deity. This perverted form of nationalism bred universal mistrust and hatred between peoples and was the principal cause of war. I had seen it come near destroying Europe in the First World War and I could see the same hellish forces at work again, beginning to prepare the way for a Second World War. It seemed to me that the only way to counteract this false religion of nationalism was for men to be reminded that they had an ultimate loyalty beyond the nation. For me loyalty to the Kingdom of God was the ultimate loyalty and that could only be expressed adequately through the Church Universal. I was beginning to think of the Federation as a movement through which students might acquire a sense of their ultimate loyalty, of the fact that they themselves by faith were members of the universal community of believers. At the end of the Versailles Conference, Keynes had said that he had learned to become a European in his cares and outlook. I wanted to challenge students to act, by faith, as if they were already members of the Church Universal in their cares and outlook. A corollary of this was the conviction that only through a process of cross-fertilization of minds and spirits between citizens of different nations and races could man emerge from the intellectual and spiritual bondage of the nation-state.

The resources at my disposal were extremely limited. I could plan occasional international conferences, I could speak whenever I had the opportunity, I could use the quarterly magazine of the Federation, *The Student World*, to get the issues discussed, and I could encourage individuals I met to consider the reality of the Church Universal and commit themselves to that reality.

A first step was to organize a conference at Hardenbroek in Holland for the leaders of the European student movements. It was essential for them to form the habit of meeting together regularly, of thinking together about their common problems, and of planning together a common European strategy. This conference met the last week of January, 1928, in the ancient moated castle of Hardenbroek where I had attended a student conference in 1921. There was no fire in my stone-walled room and the mid-winter chill of northern Europe entered into my bones. On February 4, I wrote mother:

The conference was for the general secretaries of our European movements. Strangely enough never in the history of the Federation had these general secretaries met to discuss their common task as Europeans on this continent. I am so happy that as an American I could make this possible. . . . There were about twenty secretaries present. In the course of their discussions they decided to create a Council of European Student Movements to facilitate their acting together.

The difficulties which in those days confronted anyone who was trying to get Europeans to think as Europeans is well illustrated by an experience I had as editor of *The Student World*, in each issue of which I tried to include a variety of viewpoints. Dr. Karl Barth was at that time a relatively young man but he had already acquired a European reputation through his commentary on the Epistle to the Romans and I was eager to have him contribute an article to the *Student World*. When he received my invitation, he replied forthwith that under no circumstance would he contribute to "my international orchestra." I was hurt and shocked by his reply but I came to realize later that his view of the Christian life at that time and my view were almost diametrically opposed to each other and were in fact irreconcilable. Several years later I heard him in a lecture in Geneva define the Christian life as "flight from the world." My view was and is that it is "assumption of responsibility in this world." It is an ironic fact of history that it was because the Protestant Christians of Germany in the early years of this century felt little or no responsibility for human affairs that it was so relatively easy for Hitler to gain control. It is equally ironic that it was the Satanic forces released by Hitler and not the plain teachings of the New Testament that forced Barth and many others to change their minds about the nature of the Christian life.

In addition to my Federation work I became Geneva correspondent for the *Christian Century* and the *World Tomorrow*. Further, during the winter of 1928–29, I studied under Paul Mantoux at the Graduate Institute for International Studies. Mantoux had been interpreter at the Peace Conference and later served on a commission to establish the boundaries between Poland and the Baltic States. To illustrate the extent to which the average rural inhabitant did not care very much to which nation he belonged, Mantoux said that in his efforts to establish an exact line, time and time again when he had asked a farmer, "To what country do you belong?" the reply was, "I am from here (je suis d'ici)."

The question of my future was raised sharply in February, 1928, by Dr. Mott's asking me to attend the next meeting of the General Committee of the Federation which was to be held in the following December in Mysore, India. After praising my work highly he informed me that he wanted me to succeed Henriod as general secretary of the Federation. His suggestion troubled me. It was only a year and a half before, at Nyborg, Denmark, that Dr. Mott had asked Henriod to become general secretary, and it struck me as being unfair to remove him so soon. Henriod was far from being a world statesman; on the contrary he was a rather typical parochial Swiss. But he was a thoroughly decent person. Further, I was quite sure of one thing and that was that I was not going to be used as a pawn to force his removal. I became aware one evening that he sensed what was transpiring when, in a social gathering, we were diverting ourselves with an impromptu game as older generations of Europeans were so fond of doing. Each member of the group was asked to describe other members by telling what kind of natural scenes or phenomena he thought of when he thought of them. When it came Henriod's turn to describe me, he said he thought of a great mountain range with sheer cliffs and deep gorges and an absolutely straight road blasted out of the rock running up over the range on an even gradient. This analogy touched me deeply, and reassured me that I was handling our relations properly.

Having turned down Dr. Mott's offer, it was obvious that I had to begin at once to find something else to do when I left the Federation in 1929. For a time I considered looking for a teaching job, perhaps at Johns Hopkins, but by mid-1928 Helen and I were fairly clear that when we went home we wanted to live on the Virginia side of the Potomac near Washington with the idea of developing there an institution comparable to the Royal Institute of International Affairs in London. Meanwhile, we had decided to begin gathering material for a book on the impact of American influence on Europe since 1917.

That spring William Martin of the *Journal de Genève* asked me to write a section of a book he was editing. My part dealt with the Christian in international affairs. This assignment forced me to wrestle with some very difficult questions, such as: what relation should exist between the Christian citizen and the state? Has the

Christian citizen the duty *as* a Christian to reserve the right to veto the state's control over him?

The autumn of 1928 was an unusually busy time since in addition to my other duties I had just become treasurer of the Federation. I was also responsible for preparing for the General Committee meeting in Mysore, India, and Dr. Mott cabled again asking me to attend. But I was convinced that I should not, even though I still had no idea where I might be able to find a job when I left the Federation.

In September, I arranged a public Federation dinner at which the principal speaker was my dear friend, Salvador de Madariaga, the great Spanish liberal. Some two hundred people were present and considerable interest was aroused as it was an unusual kind of event for Geneva.

In November, I was in London speaking in All Hallows Church, Lombard Street, in a series of services for students. The speaker who followed the next week was the famous Dean of St. Paul's, the Very Reverend W. R. Inge.

On December 9, I was brought up with a start. I received a cable from India saying that I had been elected to be the new chairman of the Federation to succeed Dr. Mott, who was retiring. As I wrote that evening to my mother:

> I wanted to think very hard before accepting and this afternoon sent a cable saying that I accepted. As you know I have resigned from the staff to take effect next June. The position of chairman is not a salaried position and I can press ahead with the other plans Helen and I have in mind. It will require a good bit of time but I do not mind that. . . .
>
> It seems a very strange thing that I should be chosen chairman when an American has already occupied that post for so long. . . . Then to be the person who was chosen to follow Dr. Mott is a thing I can hardly realize when I think of those early conferences in which he seemed to me such a very great man, but I do not feel great at all. It has made me feel very weak all day. May God make me worthy of it. In some ways there is no post in the world to which I would rather have been chosen. It is the highest honour that could be bestowed on a Christian student—and that is enough to make me extremely humble.

For the next three months I devoted myself to a reorganization of the Federation which was long overdue. By the end of March my plans had been completed and when presented to the officers were approved. In spite of the Federation's tiny budget of around $30,000, it was possible to collect an unusually able group of officers and staff —co-opting some and using others for part time. This group in-

cluded T. Z. Koo of China, S. K. Datta of India, and W. A. Visser 't
Hooft of Holland. Bringing Visser 't Hooft on to the staff of the
Federation in the spring of 1929 is one of the moves made at that
time which in retrospect gives me most satisfaction. He eventually
became general secretary of the Federation and that prepared him to
become general secretary of the World Council of Churches when it
was organized in 1948.

Having done what I could to put the Federation in competent
hands, I then had to deal with my own problem. The incredible thing
to me was that though I had been elected chairman there was not
one cent in the budget adopted at Mysore for the chairman's expenses. Consequently, it was obvious that in addition to finding
some way to earn a living after going off the Federation's payroll in
June, 1929, I would have to find sufficient money to take care of
travel and office expenses if I were to continue to function as the
chairman of the Federation was expected to do.

Helen and I decided to stay in Europe until March, 1930, gathering
material for our book, in spite of the fact that all of our requests for
grants to make the writing possible were turned down. However,
my personal commitment to the task of the Federation was so complete that I was determined to explore every possible avenue of
support. David Porter had asked me to give a series of addresses at
the Y.M.C.A. Secretaries Summer School at Estes Park, Colorado, so
I went to the States to do this and to search for funds. This was the
beginning of nine years of continuous uncertainty. My living came
from seven different sources during those years, and there were two
periods of several months each when Helen alone supported the
family. It was not only a nomadic existence. It was also quixotic. But
in many respects they were the best years of my life.

We left Geneva the end of May, 1929, and did so without many
regrets. Upon arrival in New York I asked for an appointment with
Dr. Mott and was told I would find him in a conference at Williamstown, Massachusetts. So to Williamstown I went. As chairman of
the Federation Dr. Mott had had a special "Federation Fund" which
took care of his travel and office expenses incurred on behalf of the
Federation. I had supposed that since he had apparently chosen me
to succeed him at the Mysore meeting, and since he had access to
many wealthy people who had financed him over the years, he would
be interested in giving me some introductions to his friends and
perhaps even in aiding me to some extent out of his own "Federation
Fund." I could not have been more mistaken. We had lunch at the

Williamstown Inn, and when I explained my problem, I drew a complete blank. He would do nothing.

This was a shattering experience for me. Mott had been my hero in a very special sense—endowed with the qualities of a great Christian leader and a world statesman. Suddenly the illusion faded: he was no hero at all, but a mere mortal man. During the next twenty-five years I did not see him or talk to him more than two or three times. At the Evanston, Illinois, meeting of the World Council of Churches in 1954, when he was nearly ninety, he spied me in the audience and sent Tracy Strong down to fetch me. When I reached him on the platform, he said with some emotion, "Francis, I have believed in you all along." I thanked him, and remarked to Tracy as I went back to my seat, "I wish he had said that to me a quarter of a century ago."

In June, 1929, I found myself completely on my own. I was chairman of a world organization, disowned by my predecessor, without a budget and without wealthy friends to whom I could go for help. By any rational standards I should have immediately resigned and looked for another appointment. But the dream of a world student movement as the pioneering agency for the Church Universal had captured me and I decided to continue as chairman for as long as it was humanly feasible to do so. This turned out to be nine years. It was only possible to continue that long because of financial assistance during 1930–33 from the Hazen Foundation of New Haven, Connecticut, and subsequently from a Yale student named Luther Tucker (now rector of the Indian Hill Church in Cincinnati) who had also been captured by the same dream. My debt to Luther is as great as my debt to anyone.

My mood during those years is best portrayed by some lines from Browning's "Paracelsus" which in retrospect seem to be an excellent description of my whole life:

> I am a wanderer, I remember well
> One journey how I feared the way was missed
> So long the city I desired to see lay hid
> When suddenly its spires afar
> Gleamed through the circling clouds.
> You can conceive my transport.
> Soon the vapors closed again
> But I had seen the city
> And one such glimpse no darkness could obscure.

In speeches at the National Assembly of Student Secretaries in July, 1929, I set forth my purposes:

Our task is as gigantic as modern civilization. It is nothing less than the task of seeing to it that this tremendous economic outthrust from the United States to the rest of the world is supplemented or parallelled by another kind of outthrust—an outthrust rooted in the mind and spirit of Jesus Christ—an outthrust of ethical concern and spiritual interest—an outthrust which on the one hand represents a determination that no nation however weak shall suffer injustice as a result of our commercial invasion, and on the other hand represents a desire to exchange intellectual and spiritual values as well as to find a market for our goods. That is our task. It is a task much too big for us as individuals or for us as a movement. It will require the use of every ounce of intelligence that we may possess. And it is only in God that we dare go forth to begin our work.

I returned to Europe soon afterwards, where Helen and I began a six-months' journey to become better acquainted with the national Student Christian Movements, and to gather material for our book about America's share in the creation of a North Atlantic civilization. It was a journey that was to take us to most of the important capitals of Europe from London and Paris to Moscow, and to a deeper understanding of national attitudes and beliefs. Most of all it provided evidence of the enormous impact of the United States upon European civilization. When Helen and I had completed gathering our materials in the spring of 1930, I summed it up in a letter to my brother.

We are really getting excited about our book. I don't know whether I ever gave you the title. We are naming it *The Return of the Mayflower*. It will be a study of the enormous power American civilization is already having over the destinies of Europe and an attempt to emphasize the responsibility which this carries with it. The same thing is happening now around the shores of the North Atlantic that once happened around the Mediterranean. We Americans play Rome's part. We are creating an Americanized North Atlantic civilization. In other words just as the Roman roads and the Latin speech made Paul's great work possible so the American method of industry and commerce and the universal acceptance of the English language is creating a situation in which it will be possible once again to build a concept of Christendom. The real Christians are perhaps not much more numerous now than they were in the fourth century. I hope we will succeed where they failed and not allow our religion to become identified with the American administrative system as they did with the Roman system.

VII ✍ The Church Universal

After living in Europe for three years, Helen and I sailed from Cherbourg for our native land on the maiden voyage of the S.S. *Europa* in March, 1930. I had also decided to go to South Africa around the middle of May in response to an invitation from a Y.M.C.A. secretary to serve as chairman of a conference between Bantu students and Boers.

The brief interval between arrival and departure was one of the most hectic periods in a rather hectic life. I had just six weeks and a half to be in Washington, of which five weeks were to be spent writing my half of our book. We also had to find a home and I had to find a job. In addition I ran a fever for three of the five weeks, which kept me in bed one week. It eventually proved to be due to two abcesses in my jaw, which had to be carved out before I got on the boat, to prevent my dying on the Equator! How we came through it all I don't know. But the fever left me before I sailed and the last chapter of the book was finished. We also acquired ten acres of land at Fairfax, Virginia, on which Helen was to build a house while I was on the South African journey. Finally I was appointed a lecturer at Yale University, receiving $2,500 for three months' work in the winter; this in addition to a thousand dollar honorarium from the Federation solved my financial difficulties for the time being.

The book was sold to a publisher, William Morrow & Co., for publication in September or October. Though we wanted to call it

The Return of the Mayflower, the publishers eventually imposed the title, *The Giant of the Western World*.

On May 23, 1930, I boarded the R.M.S. *Balmoral Castle* at Southampton and fourteen days later landed at Capetown. My trip to South Africa began as high adventure and ended as stark tragedy for the work I was doing.

The conference, of which I was to be chairman, brought Bantu and European students together at Fort Hare in Cape Province on July 3, 1930. It was a notable event. Such a gathering had not been held before and it could not be held now. Fraternal delegates had come from Ceylon, Europe, and the United States. Boer and Bantu students lived in the same dormitory and ate together at the same tables. There were Bantu leaders and Dutch leaders—among the latter several eminent professors from the universities of Stellenbosch, Witwatersrand, and Pretoria. The most distinguished South African present was Jan H. Hofmeyr who gave the opening address and remained through the conference. He was a little older than I, had been a triple first as a Rhodes Scholar at Oxford, was a member of Parliament, and had at one time been responsible for five different portfolios simultaneously as a member of one of Smuts's cabinets. He was the most brilliant man South Africa had thus far produced. But when he was in his mid-forties, he dropped dead one day. Then the lights went out in that part of the world and the darkness has become denser with every passing year. I once asked another South African what had been the cause of Hofmeyr's death and he replied, "tribal murder," meaning by "murder" the mental and spiritual torture to which he had been subjected by his fellow Boers because of his liberal views.

The theme of our conference was the question of racial relations in the light of Christ's teachings. There were lectures followed by discussions on many phases of Bantu rural and industrial life, together with suggestions for an equitable economic order. One of the concluding lectures was on: "How Can Students and Others Work for the Victory of God's Cause in the World?" That was nearly forty years ago. There was still hope then that a way out for South Africa could be found, and that the young participants could lead the way.

At the conclusion I was thanked by the members of the conference through a spokesman who said that they particularly appreciated my chairing the meetings with "sweet authority." I cherish this phrase as one of the nicest compliments I ever received.

For several weeks thereafter the principal Dutch newspapers of the Union published strongly worded criticisms of the proceedings of the conference which were with equal force defended by the Dutch leaders who were present. In those days one could still speak out.

I was about to take my departure from Fort Hare when a conversation occurred which introduced me to a personal scandal within the organization whose ramifications eventually reached out to three continents and threatened the very integrity of the World's Student Christian Federation itself. The crisis continued for the next two years, involving American Negroes, British, and Indians who were all members of the inner group of the Federation. Eventually, it was resolved through the withdrawal of the main characters from Federation work.

I continued to serve as chairman for seven more years, but the Federation was never quite the same again. Whatever innocence I may have had about human nature when this sordid affair began, I had wholly lost by the time it petered out. In the summer of 1931, I felt I had seen it all.

In spite of the depressing events of the final days of my sojourn I carried away from South Africa a limerick which has enlivened many a dull moment since. Frank N. D. Buchman had invaded South Africa a year or two before I was there with his so-called "Oxford Movement" and after paying his respects to the local saints like Andrew Murray he had gained many converts in those parts. The limerick ran:

> There was a young man from Pretoria
> Whose sins became gorier and gorier
> Till he found out by prayer
> And some *savoir faire*
> How to live at the Waldorf Astoria.

This is the most accurate description I have yet heard of that rather phony movement—now called Moral Rearmament.

After returning from South Africa in August, 1930, I attended the meeting of the Federation's executive committee at Schloss Waldenburg in Saxony and then hurried home. As Helen drove me north out of Fairfax Village along the Chain Bridge Road, I caught my first glimpse in the distance of the house she had begun to build for us while I was away. The materials came from a tavern erected opposite Fairfax Courthouse when the county seat was moved to Fairfax in 1800. The building, a large one, was scheduled for demolition to make room for a bank when Helen came along. In return for clearing the site, she obtained most of the materials we needed—bricks by the thousand, oak beams, graceful stair rails, overmantles. We had drawn plans ourselves in the Colonial tradition; an architect made scale blueprints. The proportions were perfect. Outside, the brick walls were painted buff, the columns white, the shutters dark green. Inside, the wide hall ran straight through to a view from the east porch across lawn and pasture. For the stairs, we used a handrail along which Jeb Stuart's fingers must have moved many times during the winter of 1861–62 when the tavern was his cavalry headquarters. In the living room, a tavern overmantle framed a fireplace faced with purple Dutch tile. In the library, the bookshelved walls were topped by a ceiling beamed with the tavern's hand-hewn framing; for the overmantle there, Helen's mother gave us some pieces of ancient oak linenfold paneling that she had bought in England.

That summer Helen had worked as a construction boss: she hired the workmen, one by one, and superintended all they did. During the autumn we lived in a small tenant house at the bottom of the hill. By the end of November our home was complete and on December 7, 1930, we moved in. Joining our middle names together we called it Pickens Hill, and I have always thought of its graciousness as a symbol of the life we hoped to live. We were there for seventeen years, and, though I was not home more than a third of the time, I loved it as Mr. Jefferson loved Monticello.

During those years of long absences and intense activity, Pickens Hill provided the ideal base from which to operate. Neither Helen nor I could have done the work we did or lived the kind of life our work required if it had not been for Emma and Worther Smith and Jenny and Newton Kenner, who kept our home and made it not only secure but delightful.

Early in 1931, after returning from Federation consultations in Europe, I went to New Haven to begin a course of lectures at the Yale Divinity School. This course lasted three months and I was asked to deal with the very broad subject of Christians and international relations. The announced title was rather grandiose: "The Challenge of Contemporary Civilization."

My assignment in New Haven was repeated each winter for four years and was literally a godsend. A modest income was assured, and I also found the leisure to read and think and recollect myself during a very difficult period of my life. In 1934, I organized a seminar on the writings of Lenin for students preparing for the Christian ministry. It seemed to me to be essential for these students to be familiar with the beliefs of the movement that posed the principal threat to Christianity in our time if they were to give proper leadership to the church. I suspect that this seminar was one of the first of its kind in an American university. Now there are so many Russian studies in so many universities that such a seminar would seem a commonplace. Parallel to my seminar on Lenin I conducted another class on St. Augustine's *City of God*.

In addition to teaching at Yale, the years 1931–34 were chock-full of activities quite apart from my work for the Federation. In the autumn of 1931, Henry P. Van Dusen took the initiative to bring together a group of what he called "Younger Theologians" for a weekend at the Princeton Inn, Princeton, New Jersey, to discuss questions of major concern to them as theologians and to the whole Christian community. This group continued to meet twice a year for thirty years and then annually for three or four more. Among its twenty-odd members, in addition to Van Dusen, were John Mackay, both Reinhold and Richard Niebuhr, Paul Tillich, Wilhelm Pauck, Angus Dun, Alexander Zabriskie, Robert Calhoun, Roland Bainton, Walter Horton, Ernest Wright, George Thomas, and John Bennett. I was the only nonacademic type included. Over the years members of this group profoundly influenced the development of my understanding of the Christian faith and my conception of the role of the Christian in society.

The discussions in our meetings, which were usually held in the College of Preachers at the Washington Cathedral, were always informative, often stimulating, and occasionally afforded brilliant insights into eternal verities. It is not too much to say that the ecumenic outlook of the American Protestant churches today owes a great deal to the existence of this group. One of its useful by-products was the extent to which it stimulated its members to write books. Growing directly out of conversations at our meetings was a little volume published in 1935 entitled *The Church Against the World*, written by Richard Niebuhr, Wilhelm Pauck, and myself. The section I wrote dealt with the necessity of American Protestant churches choosing between becoming wholly domesticated within the framework of the national culture of the United States and growing out into the framework of Christendom. I suggested that if they chose the former they would forfeit their right to speak in the name of the Christian faith.

Previously, John Mackay, Henry Van Dusen, and I had contributed to another volume entitled *The Christian Message for the World Today.* My chapter on "The New Religion of Nationalism" was a critique of the totalitarian forces emerging in Europe which threatened the whole Christian community as well as the character of western civilization. The thesis of this chapter was that national Protestant churches would be no match for secular totalitarianism; that only the reality of a world-wide community of dynamic faith could effectively oppose it; and that the actualization in concrete social form of the Church Universal was our sole guarantee against international anarchy on the one hand and personal enslavement on the other hand. I am rather proud of that 1933 analysis of the world situation!

As the threat of totalitarian dictatorships increased in Europe, Van Dusen, Reinhold Niebuhr, and I launched a little magazine called *Christianity and Crisis*; I wrote the editorial in the first issue. This journal continues to flourish, but its viewpoint has changed.

During November, 1931, I visited colleges on the Pacific Coast. Even when I was lecturing in New Haven I spent a great deal of time on the road. In one letter I mentioned that for five weeks I had been away for an average of three days each week visiting places as far apart as Columbus, Montreal, and Boston.

My first Asian trip began in May, 1932. I sailed from Vancouver on the *Empress of Russia* to Japan, then went to China, and from there across the Trans-Siberian railway to western Europe. The purpose of my visit was to become familiar with the groups in the Far East associated with the Federation, to consult them about their work, and to do what I could to help.

When I entered the port of Shanghai, the magnificence of the water front and the prosperity of the European part of the city surprised me. I was unprepared for such a great metropolis. I was equally surprised to learn that a cholera epidemic was raging in China for which I was wholly unprepared as my Washington doctor had failed before my departure to inoculate me against it. In Nanking I saw dead people lying in the streets, but fortunately I did not get cholera. Among the missionaries in Nanking was Dr. Frank Price of Rockbridge County, Virginia; he handed me a copy of the *Rockbridge County News*, our Lexington weekly paper, to read the news from home.

Nanking was most impressive at that time as the capital of the New China and hope was in the air. Building was going on everywhere, and the vast American-sponsored experimental farms which

lay outside the city walls gave one the feeling that progress was being made in the right direction.

But when I reached Peking, Nanking in retrospect seemed like a
very small provincial town. I was overwhelmed by what I saw and
still think of Peking as one of the most glorious cities that was ever
planned and built. The view from Coal Hill out over the Old For-
bidden City and on to the Western Hills was a vision of imperial
grandeur unequaled anywhere else in the world. As I grow older
one of my greatest regrets is that I cannot take Helen to see this
reminder of one of the few truly great civilizations that men have
created.

In order to connect with the Trans-Siberian railway in Manchouli,
I traveled from Peking to Mukden and then north via Harbin. The
Japanese had occupied Manchuria, using the so-called Mukden incident as a pretext. They alleged that the railway line near the city
had been blown up by guerrillas and that occupation was necessary
to maintain order. The twisted rail that was supposed to have been
dynamited was hung in the waiting room of the Mukden Station
and was the most unconvincing evidence imaginable to justify a
step that helped prepare the way for World War II. It is appalling
to reflect that the fate of the human race often turns on such trivia.

During the summer of 1932, a famous Chinese cavalry guerrilla
named General Ma raided at will in Middle Manchuria and had attacked the last train to Harbin before ours. When our train from
Mukden reached Changchun, then called Hsinking, which the Japanese had chosen for their Manchurian capital, there on the platform
stood three little gentlemen puppets in striped trousers and black
coats who bowed and welcomed me in the name of their government.
They assured me that I need not worry for my safety as they were
putting a company of infantry on board to protect the train as we
entered Ma's territory. I was naturally touched by their concern but
during the night which followed there were moments when I would
have preferred Ma. Apparently it was Manchurian theory that the
best defense against guerrillas was the blast of bugles. Our soldiers
in Korea became all too familiar with the Chinese bugle preceding
attacks. Its sound is utterly unlike that made by a Western bugle:
it is loud, penetrating, terrifying as it floats out over the plains, making one think of a fiery dragon on the rampage. This is what I heard
throughout the night. Ma must have heard it too, because the guerrillas did not attack.

On the Trans-Siberian train the Russians were still using pre-

1914 Wagon Lits rolling stock divested of its formerly luxurious interior equipment. We had blankets in private compartments, and there was a dining car, with little silverware, but well-stocked with caviar, black bread, and tea. This was our diet five times a day for ten days. It's the only time in my life when I have ever become surfeited with caviar. A surviving bottle of French champagne was produced by the steward (he said it was the last) and we used that to celebrate the birthday of one of our passengers—a German engineer.

As we traveled west, train after train passed us, moving toward the East, chock-full of humanity beginning the great migration that has continued for a third of a century to settle the vast empty spaces of Siberia. I stopped off in Moscow for some hours between trains and for the fun of it hired an east-side New Yorker turned Russian guide to take me on a tour of the city. This superficial touristic view confirmed the impressions I had received three years earlier, namely, that the mass of the population had not yet begun to benefit by the amenities of the new regime but only the privileged class composed of party members and commissars. My guide showed me a beautiful new hospital. I asked whom it was for—the reply was "that is where the commissars go." And so with apartment buildings and other facilities. This is, of course, no longer true of hospitals, and it is decreasingly true of housing—but the privileged class remains.

When I arrived in Western Europe, I attended the Federation General Committee in Holland and it was there that we elected W. A. Visser 't Hooft as the Federation's general secretary.

The great event of the latter part of 1932 was the arrival of our first-born son, Andrew Pickens, on December 21. Robert Day came two years later on October 22, 1934.

The following summer I started out on my second Asian trip— this time going East. I joined Visser 't Hooft and his perceptive and highly intelligent wife, Jetty, in Geneva and we sailed from Naples the middle of August on a Dutch freighter bound for Batavia (now Djakarta) in Java. There is no more delightful way to travel than on a large slow freighter with first-class cabin space for twenty or thirty passengers all eating at the Captain's table. We passed through the Suez Canal and the Indian Ocean and in a little more than two weeks reached our destination.

The purpose of this trip was twofold. I wanted 't Hooft to visit the universities of China and Japan with me, and prior to going there we had organized an all-Asia student conference to be held in the big house of an old rice plantation at Tjiteureup, Java, September 6–14. After the Tjiteureup Conference ill health prevented 't Hooft from accompanying me to China and Japan.

Until 1928, the Federation had been largely a one-man show. Dr. Mott, as chairman, with considerable funds at his disposal, had roamed around the world, paying the expenses of delegates to meetings which he ran as he thought best. That method was necessary to get the Federation launched, but the time had now come for a change of strategy. Expense accounts were no longer available to the same extent, and I was resolved that in the future the Federation should not be so dependent on one or two people but should depend more for its vitality upon the initiative and leadership of the national movements. As part of this strategy the Federation, on my recommendation, had adopted a policy of encouraging area or continental activity. The Council of European Student Movements had been formed and we were now planning a Council of Asiatic Student Movements, looking forward to the possibility of establishing a regional Federation office in some place like Hong Kong or Singapore. This was why we had come to Java.

The Tjiteureup Conference was remarkable in many ways. There were about a hundred delegates from: Australia, Burma, Ceylon, China, East Indies, Federated Malay States, India, Japan, New Zealand, and the Philippine Islands. I look back on this conference with very mixed feelings. On the one hand, there is the satisfaction in realizing that 't Hooft and I had chosen the right goals in 1933. On the other hand, there is the tragic awareness of the extent to which the forces of history limited and thwarted those goals. It will be many a long day before the Christian students of India and Japan can freely meet and discuss common Asiatic tasks with the Christian students of China. In fact, it may be that for a durable stretch of time there will be no Christian students in China. History much resembles the cycle of the polar icecap. During a long winter the ships are frozen in. Then for a few brief days the ice cracks up under the summer sun and the ships can move out into the open sea. The years 1930–35 were such a moment in Asia—and in South Africa. The Federation tried with its tiny resources to take advantage of the then existing open floes and move out. We didn't accomplish much, but we did set precedents for the World Council of Churches many years later.

Speaking toward the end of the Conference on the Christian message in relation to society, I pointed out that we had to accept the vast and dynamic social forces that were working themselves out almost automatically in our time. The best that man could do would be to influence to some extent the character of the molds in which these forces would set. And after urging the students to go into public life and work wholeheartedly for a better social order, I warned: " 'The way of deliverance is narrowly conditioned,' as Sorel observed. If we forget our personal limitations and the conditions of our social heritage, we shall become mere utopian dreamers. Our first task is to find what the social conditions are, that we may influence them intelligently, realistically, and effectively."

At that time de Kat Angelino was considered the foremost Dutch expert on Asiatic affairs. He was in Batavia when we were there and in the course of a conversation one day he remarked: "The cry has gone out 'Asia for the Asians' and the European might as well realize that he can't do anything about it. The colonial period is finished." No man could have been a truer prophet.

Since 't Hooft's health prevented him from accompanying me I sailed without him on a Dutch ship from Batavia to Hong Kong. The captain had me at his table and my mind staggers in retrospect at the thought of the seventeen courses which were provided for his dinner menu. The size of the captain was in proportion.

The schedule arranged for me required my going on to Japan first and then back-tracking to China before sailing for home.

During both of my visits to Japan in 1932 and 1933, I talked to a wide variety of people in all walks of life, as well as to government officials. I was impressed by their eagerness to absorb quickly whatever might benefit them from Western industrial experience. Their standard of living was rising rapidly, and there was prodigious activity everywhere. But I found very ominous trends. In reporting my impression at the time I wrote: "The real conflict in Japan is not between a European brand of Fascism and a European brand of Liberalism. Both of these are inconsequential. The real conflict is the conflict for control of the state between the warrior class and the civilian class. For the time being victory is with the warrior class and will probably remain there as long as funds hold out."

The net impression I carried away with me when I left was that there was no nation anywhere more united or more formidable. Japan was a block of granite. But China was at that time a pile of sand. You put your arm in and pulled it out—and everything was just the same.

From the granite monolith I went into the sandpile. My second visit to Peking, like the first, was sheer joy, except for the fact that I had been scheduled to speak twelve times in three and a half days. Kiang Wen Han was my interpreter and friend on this China tour. He was a young Student Y.M.C.A. secretary who had become so attached to my way of thinking that he was known in the Chinese universities as "Church Universal" Kiang.

From Peking we traveled to Wuchang where I stayed nearly a week, busy with the same hectic round of meetings, some of which were attended by hundreds of students. I cherish the memory of one particularly delightful episode which occurred while I was there. A young British missionary named George Osbourn had invited me to stay with him and he had an excellent cook whose productions I greatly appreciated. It seemed that Osbourn had made inquiries as to who was the best cook in that locality and was referred to a man who turned out to be chairman of the local Communist Cooks' Union. Nothing daunted, Osbourn hired him and was more than satisfied with his culinary art. The day I was to leave we were given a truly royal feast on a table covered with Chinese characters made of different colored rice. I asked what this was all about and Osbourn explained that the Communist cook had taken a fancy to me and because he thought I was a "good fellow" the dinner was being given in my honor. "And the meaning of the Chinese characters on the table?" They were a saying of Confucius: "In the seven seas all men are brothers." This was the message to me from a Communist cook in the heart of China!

We went by steamer down the Yangtze from Wuchang to Nanking and at one of the ports of call where porcelain was made Kiang Wen Han went ashore and returned with a small figurine of Lao Sho Sin—the god of happiness and plenty. It was exquisitely made of the finest porcelain and is now one of my most prized possessions. He explained that he was giving it to me because the Chinese students had nicknamed me Lao Sho Sin. I asked, "Why?" He said because our heads looked alike. We were both very bald.

While recuperating from flu at Hong Kong I had time to reflect on what I had seen and heard in Japan and China. In my report of those visits I wrote:

1. The "thought-forms" in which Christianity is expressed in both Japan and China are almost universally the "thought-forms" of the Christian Community in America and Western Europe. No process of cross-

fertilization or assimilation has taken place comparable to the process that occurred during the first three centuries between Christian thought and Greek thought.

2. Christian groups in the cities of both countries are for the most part recruited from the capitalist middle classes and tend to be specifically identified with the point of view of those classes.

As far as Chinese students are concerned, there are two great religions contesting for their souls—the religion of Communism and the religion of the New Testament. Karl Marx or Lenin and not Buddha or Confucius are the alternatives to Jesus Christ in the mind of the young Chinese intellectual.

At the conclusion of my notes on China I find these sentences: "Will China's destiny be taken out of her hands even more completely than it has been in the past by some extraneous catastrophic event over which Nanking has not the slightest control, but which could change the face of the Far East as completely as Europe was changed by the [First] World War? If the war that everyone expects does come, everything in Eastern Asia will be thrown into the melting pot."

But we Americans appear not to have understood the gigantic social forces that were at work in China, and as a nation we had neither the wit nor the capability for channeling these forces in another direction. I found students everywhere only interested in national regeneration. They had received the impression from some Americans like Sherwood Eddy that if they accepted Christianity, regeneration would occur overnight. In all my addresses I tried to put the Christian faith in different perspective—that Christianity was not a magic by which a nation could short-circuit history and that the way of deliverance was narrowly conditioned; that the road would be long and hard but only through the Christian faith could they eventually achieve a society based on freedom and opportunity. However, that process was too slow for them. It was apparent even then that communism would win the race. It offered what it called "national regeneration," and it offered it quickly by force. What has happened to China is, next to the slaughter of the Jews, the greatest human tragedy of the twentieth century, and it does not reflect any credit on American foreign policy in that part of the world.

My friend Kiang Wen Han is for me the personal symbol of that tragedy. I continued to see him from time to time until 1939. He seemed to me to be the embodiment of the type of intelligent, progressive, competent Chinese young men who could lead in the reconstruction of their country. When Mao took over, I heard indirectly that Kiang had denounced several of his fellow Christians; then came silence. He had disappeared into the fiery jaws of the Red Dragon.

This was my last long journey because the great depression into which the country had slumped after 1929 made it impossible for The Hazen Foundation to continue its subsidy and Yale Divinity School wrote to say that it could no longer afford to have me after the spring of 1934. So I had to look for a salaried position. My new work enabled me to continue to serve as chairman of the World's Student Christian Federation (in the sense of chairing meetings) for four more years. During that period I was back and forth across the Atlantic once or twice a year, attending meetings of the Federation Executive Committee or of its officers. In addition there were the meetings of the General Committee at Chamcoria, Bulgaria, in August, 1935, and again at Bièvres, France, in August, 1938. After serving as chairman for ten years, I resigned at Bièvres and was succeeded by the best possible team of officers with Visser 't Hooft as chairman and Robert Mackie of Scotland as general secretary. I owe more to the Federation than any other institution: it taught me about the meaning of my faith and the implications of that faith for human society. To be associated with such a movement in his youth is one of the greatest boons that can come to a man.

As I look back on those years, I am well aware of how little was actually accomplished in comparison with what I had hoped to accomplish. However, during 1928–38 the Federation became a training ground for the young Protestant leaders who after World War II were the architects and master builders of the World Council of Churches. What they have achieved when taken together with the "updating" that Pope John XXIII initiated in the Roman Church makes the concept of the Church Universal seem less of a utopian dream now than it did forty years ago.

VIII ✐ National Policy

When I returned from my second Asian trip in December, 1933, I realized that another chapter in my life had come to an end. There would be no more such trips for the Federation, and I would have to find some other source of livelihood. Due to the very generous attitude of Dean Weigle of the Yale Divinity School I had received another appointment there for the spring of 1934. This gave me a few months in which to decide: What next?

At the Divinity School I had given a series of addresses to the whole school (I called them my Abelardian talks) which had interested the faculty and students so much that Dean Weigle had called me in afterwards and said that if I would come back again in 1935 he would somehow wangle the money from President Angell and that some day he hoped to tempt me back with a full professorship. I profoundly appreciated this offer but I knew by then that the academic life was not for me.

't Hooft and Maury had written from Geneva wanting me to come back there and give my full time to the Federation but I had become convinced that whatever I was to accomplish in life had to be accomplished in the United States—that my job was in America.

During that spring I was asked by responsible persons speaking for their institutions whether I would consider becoming president of Reed College in Oregon, or director of International House in New York. But neither of these possibilities appealed to me sufficiently to convince me that I ought to explore them seriously.

Finally, on May 17, Raymond Leslie Buell, president of the Foreign Policy Association, and I met in the Yale Club in New York and talked for more than three hours. Buell was the only American I ever met who was an authentic encyclopedist. He possessed a photographic memory for facts and vast knowledge over a wide range of human experience. His life was exclusively devoted to research but he was saved from becoming a slave to his profession by a genuine interest in politics. In fact he was an unusual mixture of political scientist and imaginative philosopher. His political views were always influenced by his philosophy of life which in turn was rooted in the Christian tradition. Buell did not have many friends, and I suspect that in time I became as close a friend as he had. Somewhat to my surprise we got along very well together.

During our talk at the Yale Club, Buell asked me to join the staff of the F.P.A. as his associate. He had had a big idea and he wanted me to put it into execution. He had become convinced that the country as a whole lacked a sense of general national policy. There was little or no discussion of policy among responsible citizens prior to its determination by Congress in the form of legislation. Neither the universities, the press nor the political parties were capable of preparing the people for the new society which was coming; a new agency had to be created to help develop a sense of national policy. He proposed that we create this agency, and he intended to use the budget of F.P.A. to finance the start of our activity since in his view foreign and domestic policies were inexorably interrelated. He thought my office ought to be in Washington, and he saw no reason why I should not continue to chair annual meetings of the Federation and keep my membership in the Theological Discussion Group. I was much excited by Buell's proposal because it not only coincided with my own estimate of the state of the nation but also offered me an excellent opportunity to begin putting my roots down again in American soil. I told him that his offer appealed to me and that if he could persuade his Board to ratify his plan, I would accept.

One week later I received from Buell the F.P.A.'s official invitation and so my immediate future was settled. It was agreed that I should be called "the field secretary" and that I should spend one-third of my time traveling over the country organizing "Committees of Correspondence" whose business it would be to consider questions of national policy.

In August, just before sailing to Europe for Federation meetings, I received a long telegram from Dr. Charles Clayton Morrison offer-

ing me a "full-time editorial position with the *Christian Century*."
But my course was already set and I wired my regrets. Our views on
many fundamental issues were so different that it would never have
worked out, and I am still puzzled by why he wanted me.

Beginning in September I developed plans for organizing our
Committees of Correspondence or Public Policy Committees under
the auspices of the F.P.A. In the ensuing months I traveled widely
and visited more than fifteen cities in the South, Southwest, Midwest, and Rocky Mountain areas. In thirteen cities as far apart as
Atlanta, Denver, and Cleveland, I found great interest in our proposal and either organized committees or established firm contacts.
In only two places did I fail, Richmond, Virginia, and Kansas City.
Richmond at that time was one of the most frustrating cities in the
country for anyone with a serious proposal that required thought
and willingness to consider change. I have lately been told that
when a corporation wants to test a new product in the U.S.A. it
selects two cities for tryouts: one that will try anything, the other
that will not try anything much. Richmond is usually chosen as the
city that will not try anything much. I was received with great
courtesy and spent hours in delightful conversation with the most
charming people. But I found no concern about the nation or the
world deep enough or serious enough to cause anyone to feel responsible for discussing national policy and recommending the development of new lines of policy. The general reaction was a whim-
sical look, followed by, "Why, Francis, you don't suppose anything
we said would make any difference, do you?" and my silent reflection was, "No, I don't suppose it would, because I don't think you
would have anything to say!" The upper classes in Richmond were
well satisfied with things as they were in the Old Dominion and saw
no reason to bestir themselves.

When I made my preliminary report to the F.P.A. Board in January, there was a clear indication of trouble to come. Apparently I
had been too successful. Some of the Board members had concluded
that the Public Policy Committees which I had organized might em-
barrass the F.P.A. by taking too much interest in domestic as con-
trasted with foreign public affairs. We were given permission to
proceed for the time being, but by the first of April the opposition
had triumphed. The Board reached the conclusion that the experiment should not be continued further. My salary would be discon-
tinued September 1.

But Buell and I were determined to go forward with our project.

Early in the spring we had already begun to feel our way toward a separate national organization. On April 25–28, 1935, twenty-nine representatives of Public Policy Committees from nine southern states met in Atlanta. In advance of the meeting I told the committees that we were beginning a process which would probably continue for a number of years and asked them to prepare statements on the following subjects to be discussed at the meeting: Crop Control in Relation to Foreign Trade, Agrarian Policy, Regulation of Industry, Democratic Institutions and Social Objectives, and International Political Relations.

I urged the Committees, when they drafted their statements, to be as realistic as they would have to be if they were formulating recommendations for a legislative program, and I added that where there were sharply divergent points of view the opposing positions should be noted. Consideration in Atlanta of the issues raised by the committees (land use, tenancy, and government production control) inevitably included assessment of the desirability or undesirability of bills currently before Congress, and acts recently passed by Congress. Consequently the line between self-education and political advocacy was rather frequently crossed; to some extent the reservations of the F.P.A. Board were justified.

Following the Atlanta meeting, I wrote to a select list of people in the cities I had visited, proposing the establishment of an independent national committee whose purposes would be: (1) To organize policy groups in every section of the country composed of citizens who anticipated taking part in public affairs as well as keeping themselves informed. (2) To consider public policy as a whole—domestic as well as foreign policy.

In my letter I made the case for the committee on the grounds that the nation had been losing its sense of direction, that neither of the political party organizations seemed equipped to provide the information or supply the intellectual stimulus that the country needed, and that there was "an enormous amount of intelligence and concern" among citizens which was not being employed because the existing political parties were incapable of facilitating the release and the use of such resources. There were in fact various citizens committees, but most of these were working for special interests of some one class or group. There were also competent staffs within the executive branch of the government, but the activity of experts in the executive sphere of government should be, I felt, paralleled by "a process of citizen activity out across the country."

In response to my letter thirteen persons met in Chicago on June
23–24, 1935, and organized the National Policy Committee. Those
present were: Richard F. Cleveland of Baltimore who became chairman, W. W. Waymack of Des Moines who became a vice-chairman,
Brooks Hays of Little Rock who became a vice-chairman, Raymond
Leslie Buell of New York who became research advisor, and I who
became secretary. Likewise: Henry Miller Busch of Cleveland, Ben
M. Cherrington of Denver, Walter T. Fisher of Chicago, George
Fort Milton of Chattanooga, Clarence Nixon of New Orleans, Win-
field Riefler of Princeton, David Wickens of Washington, and M. L.
Wilson of Washington.

All of the above accepted membership on the Committee except
Riefler and Wilson who were unable to do so because of their gov-
ernment connections. In addition, several others joined the Com-
mittee immediately after the Chicago meeting: Brooks Emeny of
Cleveland, Aryness Joy of Washington, Dale Miller of Dallas, and
Philip Weltner of Atlanta.

Our main objectives were to supply citizens with concise summaries of reliable research and of expert opinion on issues of regional, national, and international importance; to stimulate their
discussion of public questions in preparation for political decision;
and thus to work towards a national policy based on the "general
interest" rather than on special interests.

These objectives were chosen because we were convinced that
there was such a thing as "due process of policy-making" and that
national policy could not be either very wise or very sound unless it
originated out of this "due process." We laid great stress on a two-
way flow in the policy-making process of a democracy. Information
and enacted legislation would in any case flow down to the people,
but prior to the determination of legislation it seemed to us to be essential for the policy choices of the people to flow up to Washington.
The demands of special interests were being pressed most effectively
anyway. However, at that time, there was little if any informed
opinion flowing up to Washington which represented concern for
the *national* interest as opposed to the interest of some highly organized industrial, labor, or farm group. It was our aim to encourage
this kind of reverse flow.

We proposed to organize the kind of groups that would automatically insure consideration of "what is best for the nation" as
opposed to "what is best for my corporation" or "what is best for
my union." We insisted that groups which met to consider national

policy issues should consist of a cross section of responsible opinion—that insofar as possible each group should include persons
from industry, labor, agriculture, education, religion, finance, press,
law, and the other professions. For the first time in America labor
leaders and industrial leaders met with their peers to consider their
own interests in the light of the national interest.

Waymack was, in my opinion, the foremost American editor of
his day. His style had a trenchant punch unequaled in our journalism. He was a great liberal and a great internationalist. With his
Register and Tribune he defeated the isolationist and reactionary
Chicago Tribune in the plains west of the Mississippi and led the
way for that area to support a foreign policy of international co-
operation. Besides, he was the champion amateur candymaker of
the Midwest!

Brooks Hays embodied the humane and forward looking forces
not only of Arkansas but also of the Deep South generally. His association with the National Policy Committee set him on a path that
led to many years of useful service in the House of Representatives.

Philip Weltner of Georgia later served as chancellor of the university system in that state. Philip reminded me in many ways of
what Mr. Washington must have been like. He was a quiet man of
impressive stature. His very presence was reassuring.

A special group was called by the National Policy Committee to
meet at Princeton, November 16–17, 1935, to consider the relation
of government to industry and trade and to prepare a statement on
this issue for further analysis by the local committees. This was the
first of a series of eighteen national meetings held over a period of
the next seven years with informal summaries of the off-the-record
discussions circulated in printed form among the affiliated groups.
Between 1942 and 1946 forty similar meetings were held in Washington. The participants were protected by the technique of not at-
tributing any one point of view to a particular individual. The names
of those present were listed but the ideas expressed were stripped
of their sponsors and written up in the published summaries to stand
or fall on their own merits.

The following year a Southern Policy Association was organized
under the chairmanship of Clarence Nixon and held its first south-
wide meeting in the Lookout Mountain Hotel, near Chattanooga on
May 11, 1936. Annual meetings continued to be held until Pearl
Harbor. At one of these meetings a discussion took place about
whether or not a poll tax should be required as a qualification for vot-

ing. The Richmond journalist, Virginius Dabney, was present. Before this meeting he had supported the poll tax, but as a result of the discussion he changed his mind and went home to write editorials against it in the *Richmond Times-Dispatch*. The Southern Policy Association prepared "A Working Economic Plan for the South" and issued in co-operation with The University of North Carolina Press a series of studies on conditions in the South.

At the same time an offshoot of the Southern Policy Association was holding dinner meetings in Washington in the interest of farm tenancy legislation and other measures to benefit southern agriculture. Brooks Hays and I were the conveners. We called ourselves the Hall's Restaurant Group since it was at that famous old saloon that we foregathered. Among the regular habitués were Lister Hill and John Sparkman of Alabama and William R. Poage of Texas. Another Texan who came occasionally was Lyndon B. Johnson, but he was careful not to become too closely identified with our progressive views.

I was the responsible executive for these various enterprises, but my ever-recurring problem remained: Where could I find the money required for a living? After my F.P.A. salary stopped, Buell and I devised an alternative source. As a research scholar he was more interested in documentation than in organization. So he proposed that we begin to publish inexpensive pamphlets which we hoped would produce some income and at the same time supply our policy groups with needed information. So I organized the Public Affairs Committee to publish monthly Public Affairs Pamphlets, and while doing so continued to give direction to the work of the National Policy Committee. Both of these activities were carried on in the same office in the National Press Building in Washington which had previously been my F.P.A. office. One of the first Public Affairs Pamphlets dealt with the problems of consumers and it was such a success that the future of our publishing venture was assured.

A year later, Luther Gulick, knowing a good thing when he saw it, tried to take over control of the Public Affairs Committee. I had no heart for another organizational power struggle, and so, after putting the Committee on a sound financial footing through foundation assistance, I resigned in the spring of 1937, and turned it over to the very capable hands of Maxwell Stewart who has directed it ever since. He told me recently that between 1935 and 1971 the Public Affairs Committee had sold more than fifty million pamphlets —more I imagine than any other pamphlet series has sold in any country at any time. So the little acorn that Buell and I almost inadvertently planted in 1936 has grown into quite an oak. And we would not have planted it at all if I had not been in such urgent need of a salary.

It was also in 1936 that Helen and I together wrote a little book called *The Blessings of Liberty*, published by The University of North Carolina Press. Our thesis was that though our Constitution was adopted to secure for the people of the United States the blessings of liberty, the economic conditions of life in the 1930s denied to millions of Americans the liberty they were supposed to possess. Where there was no employment and no security, there could be no liberty. Unemployed men in the soup lines were not free men. But we went on to say that too much state-guaranteed security also threatened liberty. Consequently, we felt that the major task of statesmanship in our time would be to learn the art of ascertaining and maintaining the delicate balance between freedom and security. Since Helen was working for the Department of Agriculture it did not seem wise to list her as one of the authors, so I dedicated *The Blessings of Liberty* to "Helen Hill, whose share in this book is too great to be mentioned."

The months following my resignation from the Public Affairs Committee were a very trying time for me. I was thoroughly disgusted with the kaleidoscopic character of my existence. I knew what I wanted to do, but I could not find a secure financial base from which to do it, and my health had deteriorated under the strain. Years of effort made it quite apparent that I had no taste for and little skill in raising funds for my own personal budget.

Meanwhile I had been getting more and more interested in Virginia politics for which I felt that all of my life had been preparing me. It was, therefore, with a sense of great relief that I was elected to the Virginia House of Delegates in November, 1937. The Assembly met in Richmond for sixty days during January-March, 1938, and opened the door to a new and fascinating world, which is the subject of later chapters.

Before the Assembly adjourned I was asked by the Council on Foreign Relations in New York to come up in April to confer about the possibility of joining its staff. The proposal was that I should organize committees on foreign relations across the country, using the same method of operations that I had perfected in the Public Policy Groups and the National Policy Committee. I accepted with alacrity, and my personal problems were solved. For the next four

years I enjoyed a financial security that I had not had for the previous nine.

When I decided to join the Council, responsibility for the National
Policy Committee had to be transferred to someone else. I persuaded
Helen to give the N.P.C. as much attention as she could in her spare
time with the assistance of our extremely efficient secretary, Winnie
Turner. She kept it going on this basis for two years and then resigned from the Department of Agriculture to divide her time during 1940–47 between acting as executive director of the N.P.C. and
serving first as correspondent and then as American representative
of *The Economist* of London. The brilliant contribution which the
National Policy Committee, under her direction, made to the nation's life is a story which I hope some day she will tell. Scores of
meetings were organized in Washington and across the country and
reports of these discussions were published. The lists of people who
participated reads like a who's who of the brains of the nation at
that time. Further, it is the only Committee I ever heard of which
closed down when it had completed the job it had set out to do—
and closed down at the end of its most financially successful year.

The word "policy" itself was not only not in common use in 1934,
but even responsible and well-educated citizens often had only the
vaguest notion of its meaning. Further, in 1934, few people were
talking about *national* policy. By 1947, everybody was talking about
it. Again, in 1934, it was very rare to find a cross-section group of
citizens who were leaders in their respective communities meeting to
consider urgent issues from the standpoint of the interests of the
United States as a whole. By 1947, cross-section discussion groups
had become the customary pattern of community enterprise.

Over the years the techniques of the N.P.C. proliferated in many
directions. Raymond Leslie Buell used them to organize Round
Tables for *Fortune* magazine; W. W. Waymack employed them in
the National Farm Institute at Des Moines; Josephine Wilkins put
them to work in the Citizens Fact Finding Movement of Georgia and
there are many other examples. But for me the most perfect illustration of the use of the N.P.C. technique is to be found in the Committees on Foreign Relations of the Council on Foreign Relations.

By 1941, Committees on Foreign Relations had been established
in Cleveland, Denver, Des Moines, Detroit, Houston, Los Angeles,
Louisville, Nashville, Portland (Oregon), Providence, St. Louis, and
St. Paul-Minneapolis. In more than half of these cities success was
assured through contacts I had made previously in the work of the

National Policy Committee. Again the only city in which I could discover no interest in having a committee was Richmond, Virginia. This made me very sad. Twenty-five years later all of these committees were still functioning and twenty-two more had been organized. Only community leaders were invited to join and the cross-section rule was mandatory. Industrialists, bankers, merchants, clergymen, educators, journalists, trade union officials, lawyers, doctors, farmers, and public officials were all included as well as other persons who exerted influence in their own localities. In the Detroit Committee, for instance, there were at the same time the head of General Motors, the head of the U.A.W., and the Archbishop of the Roman Catholic Church. Participation helped to prepare various committee members for distinguished government service in later years. William L. Clayton of Houston became undersecretary of state; Mark Ethridge of Louisville served on the UN's Commission to Study Greek Border Disputes; William S. Knudsen of Detroit became director general of the Office of Production Management; Edward P. Warner became head of the International Civil Aviation Organization; and W. W. Waymack of Des Moines served as a member of the Atomic Energy Commission. When the committees were first established, they were thought of primarily as a means of educating public opinion in their respective communities. But as it turned out, they became in time much more than that. In additon to being useful listening posts to sense the mood of the country, they played a unique role in preparing the nation for a bipartisan foreign policy in the fateful years that lay ahead.

At the beginning of 1940, I became administrative secretary for the "War and Peace Studies" which were organized at the office of the Council in New York. As soon as war had broken out the previous September, Hamilton Fish Armstrong with his usual perspicacity had gone down to Washington and asked the Department of State whether there was anything the Council could do to help. Since the Department did not have funds available to organize adequate research and analysis on its own, it encouraged the Council to collect a staff and organize studies under the general direction of a Steering Committee whose chairman was Norman H. Davis, with Ham Armstrong as a kind of executive vice-chairman. Among the research secretaries with whom I worked were Philip E. Mosely, Grayson Kirk, Mose L. Harvey, Walter R. Sharp, and William Diebold, Jr.

We began our work with four groups studying: Security and Armaments Problems, Economic and Financial Problems, Political

Problems, and Territorial Problems. Draft statements were prepared and brought before the group concerned with them where they were thoroughly discussed, sometimes for several successive meetings. They were then revised in the light of the discussion and transmitted to Washington. A fifth group was subsequently organized to prepare data on the peace aims of the different nations.

In February, 1941, the Department of State found the funds to establish a Division of Special Research under the direction of Leo Pasvolsky. The secretaries working with the Council's "War and Peace" groups were eventually transferred to this new division in State.

IX ✑ The Fight for Freedom

The summer of 1940 was a turning point in human history. That spring Hitler had unleashed the forces of Hell to conquer Europe and eventually the world. He had said that the Nazi state would endure for a thousand years.

In May, 1940, the National Policy Committee was planning to convene a meeting on June 29–30, to consider "The Implications to the United States of a German Victory." Somewhat to the executive director's surprise she received a letter toward the end of May from Richard F. Cleveland, former chairman of the N.P.C., asking her to proceed as quickly as possible with plans for this meeting. Encouraged by Cleveland's sense of urgency, Helen called him on the phone and suggested that a small informal group be brought together at once. He agreed and seven people were hurriedly collected at our home, Pickens Hill, Fairfax, Virginia, on Sunday, June 2. There were present, in addition to Helen and myself: Richard F. Cleveland of Baltimore, Stacy May of New York, Winfield W. Riefler of Princeton, Mr. and Mrs. Whitney H. Shepardson of New York, Edward P. Warner of the Civil Aeronautics Board, Washington, and M. L. Wilson of the Department of Agriculture, Washington. Four of the above had been members of the small group which founded the National Policy Committee in June, 1935.

It was Dunkirk weekend. The sense of impending doom was so strong that we began our consultation by considering what the

United States should do in view of the appalling catastrophe that
had just befallen the French and British armies on the Continent. We
discovered to our amazement that each of us had, prior to our meeting, independently arrived at the conclusion that the United States
should forthwith declare war on Germany. As the afternoon wore
on, it was agreed that we ought to make our views public. We had no
illusions, at that moment, about our ability to influence national policy, but we found ourselves in the mood of a member of the British
Parliament who, earlier that spring, had cried out in anguish in the
House of Commons, "Who will speak for England?" There was
desperate need in that hour for someone to speak for America. Why
should not we? Perhaps if we did, others with more influence might
take up the cry.

So I asked Whitney Shepardson, who had a gift for felicitous
expression with his pen, to go into my office, sit at the desk on which
I am now writing, and try his hand at a draft. In a short time he rejoined us. The statement he had prepared expressed our views so
exactly that after making a few minor alterations, we adopted it
unanimously. It was called "A Summons to Speak Out" and read
as follows:

The United States has now undertaken to meet the formidable challenge of Nazi Germany. Our program of national defense has been touched
off by the invasion of the Netherlands, Belgium, and France, and it is
designed to repel any German attack on our territory or any invasion of
our vital interests. . . .

In the German view, the American defense program means that the
United States has already joined with Great Britain and France in opposing the Nazi drive for world dominion—in the American view, Nazi Germany is the mortal enemy of our ideals, our institutions and our way
of life.

The frontier of our national interest is now on the Somme. Therefore,
all disposable air, naval, military, and material resources of the United
States should be made available at once to help maintain our common
front. . . .

The United States should immediately give official recognition to the
fact and to the logic of the situation—by declaring that a state of war
exists between this country and Germany. Only in this constitutional
manner can the energies be massed which are indispensable to the successful prosecution of a program of defense.

The undersigned, as individuals, invite those citizens of the United
States who share these views to express them publicly through the free
democratic institution of the American press. . . .

Cartoon by Edwin A. Finch from the Louisville Courier-Journal
Photographed by Lowell A. Kenyon, Chevy Chase, Maryland

In order to give as much weight as possible to our "Summons" we decided to circulate it immediately to a selected list of people, inviting them to join us in signing it for release in the press the following Monday. The next day Helen and I prepared a list of a hundred names and, on June 5, I mailed the "Summons" to these people with a covering note which said: "The gravity of events moving at lightning speed can no longer be ignored. The threat to our way of life implicit in these events makes it impossible for us to remain silent. We believe that there are responsible citizens in every part of the country who feel as we do. We hope you will wish to join us in signing it."

The signers of the note in addition to myself were: Richard F. Cleveland, Baltimore; Stacy May, New York; Helen Hill Miller, Washington; Winfield W. Riefler, Princeton; and Whitney H. Shep-

ardson, New York. Because of their government connections War-
ner and Wilson were unable to sign. On Monday, June 10, there
were prominent stories in the *New York Times* and the *Herald-
Tribune* reporting that the following persons had issued a demand
for an immediate declaration of war against Nazi Germany: Herbert
Agar, Louisville, Kentucky; Burke Baker, Houston, Texas; John
Balderston, Beverly Hills, California; Stringfellow Barr, Annapolis,
Maryland; J. Douglas Brown, Princeton, New Jersey; Richard F.
Cleveland, Baltimore, Maryland; James F. Curtis, New York, New
York; Edwin F. Gay, Pasadena, California; Edward T. Gushee, St.
Louis, Missouri; Marion R. Hedges, Washington, D.C.; William H.
Hessler, Cincinnati, Ohio; George Watts Hill, Durham, North Caro-
lina; Henry W. Hobson, Cincinnati, Ohio; LeRoy Hodges, Rich-
mond, Virginia; Calvin Hoover, Durham, North Carolina; Edward P.
Hubble, San Marino, California; Frank Kent, Baltimore, Maryland;
Edward R. Lewis, Chicago, Illinois; George W. Martin, New York,
New York; L. Randolph Mason, New York, New York; Stacy May,
New York, New York; Francis P. Miller, Fairfax, Virginia; Helen Hill
Miller, Washington, D.C.; Walter Millis, New York, New York;
George Fort Milton, Chattanooga, Tennessee; Lewis Mumford,
Amenia, New York; Winfield Riefler, Princeton, New Jersey; Whit-
ney H. Shepardson, New York, New York; William H. Standley,
New York, New York; and William Waller, Nashville, Tennessee.

Almost all of these people had worked with the National Policy
Committee or had been members of committees on Foreign Relations. Several of the signers received threatening letters when the
story appeared in the press. Mr. Gushee of St. Louis was subjected
to the worst attacks, but the palm for the most devastating reply to
a detractor went to another signer, George W. Martin of New York.
On June 10, Frank Miles, the editor of the *Iowa Legionnaire*, wrote
Mr. Martin as follows:

Dear Sir: The Associated Press report that you are one of a group of
thirty persons who in a meeting at Washington on Sunday urged the
United States to enter the European war immediately moves me to ask:
  What fighting did you do in the last war?
  Are you now of an age and of physical and mental fitness which would
enable you to do military service?
  If you could not be in our armed forces, how many of your own sons
would be?
  If we go to war now, what would you have our men fight with?
  Kindly reply by return mail.

On June 13, Mr. Martin replied:

Dear Mr. Miles: I have your letter of June 10, 1940. Answering your questions: In the last war I enlisted in the United States Army in April, 1917, and was honorably discharged in March, 1919. I received the divisional citation for gallantry in action during the Argonne-Meuse offensive. Is this enough, or will you have it inch by inch and minute by minute with a full box score?

Owing to the fact that I have supported myself without the assistance of the taxpayers ever since being discharged from the Army, I am now of an age and of a physical and mental fitness which will enable me to do military service. The only possible question of my mental fitness arises out of the fact that I am a member of the American Legion.

It is written in the Scriptures that Samson inflicted immense loss on the Philistines with the jawbone of an ass. If you will be good enough to send me your lower maxillary, I will forward it to the War Department in the full confidence that the country will hardly need more than this.

I have been sustained in many a trying moment through the years by recalling that last paragraph.

For a few days after the publication of the "Summons" there was a pause. Something ought to be done, but no one knew what. Then Henry Van Dusen, who was teaching at Union Theological Seminary, phoned to express his surprise and slight annoyance at not having been asked to join the sponsors of the "Summons." He rejected my explanation that I had not supposed a minister would wish to have his name associated with such a warlike statement and insisted on my telling him what we were going to do next. Since I did not know, I countered by suggesting that we ought to ask someone to convene a small group to find the answer. We were in the midst of a presidential campaign and it was essential that what we did should be bipartisan. So I proposed to Van Dusen that he go to see Lewis W. Douglas and ask him to invite a few of us to foregather at dinner. Douglas was then president of the Mutual Life Insurance Company and it had seemed to me that he would be an ideal convener not only because of his ability and known views, but also because though a former Democrat he was now supporting Willkie's candidacy for the presidency. Henry replied that he did not know Douglas. I then asked whether he would be willing to go anyway, provided I made the appointment for him. He agreed to this. Douglas consented to see him and after hearing our proposal issued an invitation to a number of individuals whose names I supplied for dinner at the Columbia Club on the evening of July 11. Thus was born what became known later as the Century Group since there-after we met for dinner at the Century Club. I have always felt that Henry Van Dusen was co-founder of this group because if it had not been for his stubborn insistence, I am not sure what the next move would have been.

There were eleven of us present at the dinner on July 11. In addi-tion to Lew Douglas and myself—Herbert Agar of the *Louisville Courier-Journal* and chairman of the N.P.C.; W. L. Clayton, cotton broker of Houston, Texas; Dr. Henry Sloane Coffin, president of Union Theological Seminary; Henry W. Hobson, Episcopal bishop of Ohio; Ernest M. Hopkins, president of Dartmouth College; Henry R. Luce of *Time, Life,* and *Fortune;* Whitney H. Shepardson, vice-president, International Railways of Central America; William H. Stanley, admiral, retired; and Henry P. Van Dusen of Union Theological Seminary.

Our group was extremely informal. We invited those whom we thought could help do the job, and several invited themselves when word got around. During the weeks that followed there were some twenty others who either attended dinners or worked with us in one way or another. They were Dean Acheson, attorney, Washington; William Agar, author, New York; Robert S. Allen, columnist; Jo-seph Alsop, columnist; John L. Balderston, script-writer, Hollywood; Ulric Bell, reporter, *Louisville Courier-Journal;* Barry Bingham, pub-lisher, *Louisville Courier-Journal;* Ward Cheney, manufacturer, New York; James B. Conant, president, Harvard University; Elmer Davis, news commentator; Allen W. Dulles, attorney, New York; George F. Eliot, columnist; George Field, member of staff of William Allen White Committee; Harold Guinsburg, publisher, New York; George Watts Hill, banker, Durham, North Carolina; Geoffrey Par-sons, editor, *Herald-Tribune,* New York; Frank L. Polk, attorney, New York; Robert Emmet Sherwood, playwright; Walter Wanger, movie producer, Hollywood; and James P. Warburg, banker and author, New York.

Taken all together no better group could have been assembled. Some were for Willkie and some were for Roosevelt. But everyone was deeply conscious of the fact that there were national and world interests than transcended the partisan interests of presidential cam-paigns and we were able to work together in complete harmony for these broader objectives. I look back upon my association with the Century Group as having given me a chance to do what was prob-ably the most useful work I have ever done and in addition as having made possible the most satisfying experience in my life. It was thrilling that summer to realize what it meant to be an American and to have some part in turning the tide against tyranny.

The fact that Henry Luce was willing to identify himself with us at the dinner on July 11, and to serve as one of the conveners of the group was, of course, a tremendous asset, but he was a strange person. Though he proved to be a genius in founding his great periodical empire, when participating in group discussions he was one of the most inarticulate men I have ever known. It was very painful to listen to his halting and sometimes incomplete sentences. At one of our dinners in midsummer he insisted on forcing a discussion of what were a publisher's moral responsibilities at such a time. He would not drop the matter, and the rest of us became increasingly wearied as we did not consider it our business to help Harry Luce make up his mind as to what his moral duties were in the midst of a world crisis. We knew what our consciences required us to do, and we wanted to get on with the job. Luce sensed that we did not care to play the part of serving as his group confessor and as I recall it he did not attend another dinner.

The most useful members of the group were Herbert Agar, John L. Balderston, Ulric Bell, Ward Cheney, Lewis Douglas, and Henry Van Dusen. Agar was absolutely magnificent that summer. He was our Old Testament prophet. Whenever our mental and spiritual batteries ran down, he recharged them, and whenever our vision grew dim, he restated and clarified our goals with passionate conviction. Ulric Bell was our contact man in Washington and toward the end of the summer John Balderston made a unique contribution through his wire service to newspapers. Ward Cheney was the principal financial underwriter of our activities. Without him we could have done little or nothing. Lew Douglas as our chairman and our bridge to Wendell Willkie played a decisive role in assuring the success of our efforts.

Discussion at the dinner on July 11 affirmed several obvious facts: that the world-wide threats to our way of life all stemmed from Nazi Germany, that the survival of the British Commonwealth of nations was important for the United States, and that the survival of the British fleet was essential to our defense. We recommended that our government provide the British immediately with food, credit, and munitions and that the planes and ships of our Navy join in the protection of the British Isles and the British fleet. However, we adjourned without having agreed upon the precise task on which we should concentrate. It was two weeks before we discovered exactly what we wanted to do.

Meanwhile, it was obvious that we ought to ask someone to open a small office and prepare to administer our activities. The lot fell to me as the Council on Foreign Relations was willing to give me extended leave while no one else could get free. Due to Cheney's generosity resulting from Agar's solicitation we were able to open shop. I doubt if any great enterprise ever operated on such a modest budget. Our total expenditures that summer amounted to around ten thousand dollars.

I rented Room 2940 in the Albee Building just west of Fifth Avenue on 42nd Street. Hitler had boasted that the Nazis would rule the world for a thousand years—until A.D. 2940. So we felt that the number of our office was a good omen for free men. When we moved into the office we found ourselves ironically next door to an office of the German Fellowship Forum—a cover for German intelligence. This was a fortuitous bit of luck because it enabled me before the summer was over to supply the F.B.I. with a certain amount of information about the activities of that office which was useful later when they picked up the man in charge as he was about to leave this country.

The staff of our office consisted of myself and two secretaries. The function of the office was to serve as a clearing house, a co-ordinator, and an initiator of ideas and action.

In order to reach wise decisions regarding our concrete goals it was obvious that we required fuller and more precise information about the most pressing British needs. Joseph Alsop agreed to provide this for us. The memorandum which he prepared presented detailed data derived from the most authoritative resources. When we met to consider our next steps on July 25, twenty-four of us sat down to dinner. As a result of our deliberations that evening the following statement of principles was adopted, including this:

The most vulnerable sector in the American defense line is the North Atlantic. Consequently the primary immediate responsibility of the Government is to insure adequate defense in that area.

If Germany wins control of the North Atlantic the period to the completion of our own two ocean navy will be a period of acute danger for us. During that period the United States could be invaded from the Atlantic.

In order to remove the risk of invasion the Government should take all possible steps to prevent German control of the North Atlantic.

The most certain preventive (until our two ocean navy is built) is the continued existence of the British fleet. And the fate of the British fleet will be settled by the battle for the control of the North Atlantic which is about to begin on the shores of England, Scotland, and Ireland.

The British chances of success are at present doubtful; but responsible British officials believe that they could successfully withstand invasion if they had 100 more destroyers.

The United States (it is understood) has more than 100 over-age destroyers recently recommissioned.

American naval experts believe that:

1—British crews could take these destroyers to England immediately and without special training.

2—British naval crews could learn to operate them in the discharge of all their naval functions in two weeks' to one month's time.

In the interest of its own national defense the United States should put a hundred of these destroyers into British hands at once....

However reliable Alsop's information might be I felt the need of opening a direct channel to the British ambassador which I could use when needed. The ambassador at that time was Philip Kerr, the Marquess of Lothian. Helen and I had known him in England where he had been head of the Rhodes Trust. Prior to his appointment we had mistrusted his close association with the appeasers of the Cliveden set and also the effects upon him of his Christian Science religion. But it had already become evident that he was on the way to becoming one of Britain's greatest ambassadors to the United States. Consequently I asked Helen to hand him a slip of paper with a question on it. She did this on July 28, and in return received the following:

MEMORANDUM ON BRITISH DEFENSE

In 1918 the British had 433 destroyers. In 1939 they had 176. It is understood that approximately one fifth of these (36) were stationed in other parts of the world. This left around 140 for home defense. There are those who are in a position to know who are convinced that only about one-half of this number (70) now remain in active service.

Since destroyers and torpedo boats are the only naval craft that can be used effectively in the Channel to repel an invasion the British Government views this situation with the utmost gravity. The situation is so serious that if the facts were known they would not be believed.

The British have asked for 48 destroyers. If this number could be augmented to one hundred the chances of successfully repelling an invasion would be greatly increased.

More important than destroyers or sea planes are *flying boats*. There is the most urgent need for 100 of the PBY5 type. The American government has this number on order now from the Consolidated Aircraft Company of San Diego, California.

Helen continued to relay information as circumstances required.

Shortly after our July 25 dinner, Henry Luce and others from our group consulted the president about the urgency of transferring the destroyers. He told them that for the moment it was politically impossible. *We sent him word that we were going to make it politically possible for him to act.* On August 1, Herbert Agar, Joe Alsop, and I converged on the cabinet in Washington. We knew which cabinet members already shared our convictions so we concentrated on those whose views were as yet unknown. I went to see the vice-president to be, Henry Wallace, and was delighted to find him sympathetic. When we had finished our rounds, every member of the cabinet had declared himself equally in favor of dispatching destroyers to England.

But we knew that the principal job we had to do was to create a climate of public opinion throughout the country which would make it possible for the president to transfer the destroyers without too great political risk. We felt that he was unduly hesitant, but we realized that we had to accept his judgment on that point. It was obvious that he was not going to move until he could move safely. To prepare the country and to reassure Roosevelt, several dramatic steps had to be taken that would appeal to the nation as a whole. There was need for a series of radio addresses by eminent and influential citizens and particularly a nation-wide address by a universally respected elder statesman who had no political axe to grind and could speak on defense matters with the greatest authority; there was need for a convincing statement issued by several of our ablest lawyers to the effect that the Constitution gave the president the authority to take such action; and finally it was absolutely essential that we secure Mr. Willkie's assurance that he would not attack the president for transferring the destroyers.

One day shortly after we had opened our office, Walter Mallory of the Council on Foreign Relations called me in Room 2940 to say that he had heard Frank Altschul suggest the evening before that General Pershing ought to be asked to address the nation supporting the transfer of destroyers. I said it was a marvelous idea but that I had no entree to the general nor did I know anyone who did since the last time I had seen him was when he had inspected me as a young lieutenant on the docks of Bordeaux in February, 1919. I asked Walter if he knew of anyone who might approach the general. He said he did and explained that an elderly retired gentleman whom he knew named George A. C. Christiancy was one of the general's closest friends. The two had become acquainted when both of them were living in the southwest because of poor health. Christiancy was now living permanently in a suite in a New York hospital where he could be near his doctors. Through a relationship that was never clear to me Walter called him "Uncle George." He said that since Uncle George left the hospital occasionally for special engagements, he would try to arrange for him to have lunch with us at the Yale Club the following Monday, July 29, adding that though Christiancy was a close friend of several Latin American dictators, he was at the same time a fervent patriot and he felt sure that he would help as much as he could.

Mr. Christiancy accepted our invitation and during luncheon I made a supreme effort to secure a sympathetic response to our appeal for help. His interest mounted as we talked on and finally he said he would be willing to go to Washington to see General Pershing who was then living at the Carlton Hotel, but that he did not wish himself to ask for an appointment. However, he said he knew the very man to make an appointment for him and that was General James Harbord of the R.C.A. He was sure that if Harbord made the request it would be granted. So we rose from luncheon and traipsed over to the R.C.A. offices nearby. The general was in and saw us at once. Our mission was explained and Harbord immediately got General Pershing on the phone. It was a bizarre conversation because both generals were a bit deaf and from the amount of yelling at our end I was never quite sure how much of what got through. However, when he hung up Harbord said that Pershing would be delighted to see Christiancy two days later (Wednesday, July 31). That was all we wanted to know. Now it was up to me to deliver "Uncle George" in Washington at the appointed hour. If General Pershing agreed to make a statement to the country, I was sure that Herbert Agar would be the best man to work with him on a draft provided he requested such help, so I phoned Herbert in Louisville and asked him to come to Washington and stand by until we heard Pershing's decision. Then I went to work on arrangements for Mr. Christiancy's trip.

On the next day (Thursday, July 30), Mr. Christiancy decided that he wanted to consult me about something and left his hospital room unattended to come to my office in the Albee Building. But he had forgotten to make a note of the number of my office which was not listed on the Building Directory in the entrance lobby. As a result he wandered around without finding me until he was exhausted. Some-one in the hospital had phoned that he was coming down, and when he did not show up I began to be worried. Then it occurred to me that a tired old man who had lost his way in that part of town might very well think of sitting down to rest in the waiting room of the Grand Central Station. And there to my enormous relief I found him. We were going to make that appointment after all!

I went on to Washington ahead of Mr. Christiancy to be sure that everything was in order. He wired me "arrive Eastern Airways one twenty." I met that plane but he was not on board. My heart once more sank within me. Had something gone wrong? There was noth-ing else to do for the time being but to wait at the airport, checking every plane that came in, and finally he emerged from one. I took him to the old Cosmos Club, and we phoned General Pershing's suite at the Carlton Hotel. The sergeant in charge said that the gen-eral was taking his afternoon nap but was expecting Mr. Christiancy and that he would call us back as soon as the general was ready to receive him. While waiting I explained to Mr. Christiancy the im-portance of his persuading General Pershing to invite Herbert Agar to come to see him at once. In due course the call came and we went over to the hotel where I waited in the lobby while he went up. When he came down he reported that the general had agreed to make a statement and was willing to see Agar, but it was not yet clear whether the general preferred to issue a statement to the press or to make a radio talk to the nation. I sent word to Herbert to make an appointment with General Pershing immediately. Before the hour of the appointment arrived, Agar went to see Mr. Roosevelt who asked him to tell the general that the president wished him to speak to the nation. This message was decisive. The general agreed to speak on a nation-wide hookup the following Sunday evening, Au-gust 4, and requested Agar to secure the collaboration of Walter Lippmann in preparing a draft of his speech.

I did not see Mr. Christiancy again. He was only on the stage for a brief moment, but he played his part splendidly, and great good for the free world resulted from the use he made of that moment.

Joe Alsop had an excellent entry to the various radio networks and I asked him to make arrangements for Pershing's speech. He did this so well that on August 5 I wrote him "you have done a per-fectly superb job on the Pershing broadcast. You deserve your country's thanks if there were any way of giving it, which there is not."

In the course of his address to the nation on the evening of Sunday, August 4, the general, after describing the gravity of the world crisis that threatened us, said:

I say to you solemnly that tomorrow may be forever too late to keep war from the Americas—We must be ready to meet force with stronger force—And I am telling you tonight before it is too late that the British Navy needs destroyers to convoy merchant ships, hunt submarines and repel invasion. We have an immense reserve of destroyers left over from the other war—If there is anything we can do to save the British fleet—we shall be failing in our duty to America if we do not do it. If a proper method can be found, America will safeguard her freedom and security by making available to the British or Canadian governments at least fifty of the over-age destroyers.

He concluded by referring to the war which Hitler had started as a war against civilization—"A revolution which denies the dignity of men, and which banishes the hope of brotherhood and comradeship on earth." His final sentence was an appeal to the nation to face the threat with daring and devotion—"We must make ourselves so strong that the tradition we live by shall not perish from the earth."

In retrospect we realized that General Pershing's speech was the turning point in our efforts to create a public opinion favorable to the president's taking action. Less than ten days had elapsed between Walter Mallory's phone call and the general going on the air. It had been quite an operation. But much more needed to be done, and I arranged a series of radio broadcasts at regular intervals:

August 10—Admiral William H. Standley
August 17—Colonel William J. Donovan
August 26—Robert E. Sherwood

Then there was the all-important question of the constitutional powers of the president. Did he have the authority in the Constitution to transfer units of our fleet, under certain circumstances, to a friendly foreign nation after the secretary of the navy had certified that the vessels in question were not essential to our national defense? One day around the first of August Benjamin Cohen and Felix Frankfurter happened to be talking and in the course of their conversation this question was raised. Cohen agreed to study the matter and prepare a memorandum for the consideration of the White House. When this had been done, it was decided to ask several of the country's most eminent and respected lawyers to examine the memorandum and if they agreed with its conclusions to use it as

the basis for a letter to the *New York Times*. It happened that prior
to that summer Dean Acheson had drifted away somewhat from the
administration and the president was eager to woo him back. So
Cohen asked Acheson to work with him on the final draft of the
letter which was published in the *New York Times* on August 11,
and was signed by: Dean G. Acheson, Charles C. Burlingham,
Thomas D. Thacher, and George Rublee.

The letter argued the matter at considerable length and concluded
that the president had the authority under the Constitution to transfer the destroyers. I was told that this letter carried great weight with
the president when he was considering his final decision.

Toward the end of August John Balderston's wire service and
news letter operation went into high as we prepared to bring matters
to a head. About the same time the propaganda of the America First
people was getting shriller and more personal. One of the principal
advocates of their line of reasoning was Garret Garrett of the *Saturday Evening Post*. Since his articles revealed no understanding of
what we were trying to do and complete misunderstanding about
the nature of the world crisis, I decided to visit him and attempt to
explain why we were acting as we did. The only thanks I got for my
efforts was that he accused me of being a British spy!

One final step had to be taken. We knew that Roosevelt would not
act until he had been reliably assured that Willkie would not attack
him for giving away part of our fleet. If the Republicans had
launched an all out attack on the president for doing this, their candidate would have attracted hundreds of thousands of America
First isolationist voters who otherwise might not go to the polls.
The political stakes were high and the temptation great. But there
were two weighty factors in our favor. Our chairman, Lew Douglas,
was one of Willkie's most ardent supporters and trusted advisers.
Further, Willkie himself was a great patriot. During the course of the
summer both Douglas and William Allen White had discussed this
question with him and toward the end of August we realized that the
time had come to ask him for his answer. On the evening of August
30, Herbert Agar, Ulric Bell, Ward Cheney, and Archibald MacLeish
met with me in a room at the Hay Adams House just across from the
White House. MacLeish was a trusted friend of Russell Davenport
of *Fortune* magazine who was serving as head of Willkie's campaign
"brain trust." The purpose of our foregathering was to place a telephone call from MacLeish to Davenport in Colorado Springs to receive Willkie's decision. While we waited for the call to go through,

the suspense was terrific because so much depended upon the answer. Finally Davenport came on the line and told MacLeish that Willkie would not attack the president for transferring the destroyers. We were jubilant. The summer's work had paid off and the green light for which we were waiting had been given. Ulric Bell immediately passed the word to the White House. The president had got what he wanted; it was now politically possible for him to act. On September 3, at a press conference on his train while returning from an inspection of defense plants he announced that fifty destroyers were being sent to Great Britain in return for bases in Newfoundland and the West Indies.

British naval power may not have been greatly augmented by the addition of these old destroyers, but many of them did essential convoy work in the North Atlantic and saw our first American troops safely across. Moreover, the significance of the president's action could not be estimated primarily in military terms. Its value was also psychological and moral. In that sense it had an immense impact on freedom loving people everywhere. Notice was served that we would not stand idly by while Hitler tried to conquer the world. It was a historic moment, for this act publicly marked the turning of the tide in the United States from isolationism to increasingly active participation in the world-wide struggle against the forces of tyranny.

In the memo Lord Lothian had given Helen on July 28, the statement was made that "more important than destroyers or sea planes are *flying boats*. There is the most urgent need for 100 of the PBY5 type." These were long-distance patrol planes of which the British had none. Actually only two or three had been completed by that time in this country. But we gave what we could to the British and long afterwards I was thrilled to learn that it was one of these flying boats with an American naval officer on board that spotted the *Bismarck* in the North Atlantic on May 26, 1941, thus making possible its destruction the following day by the Royal Navy and the Royal Air Force.

During the autumn of 1940 in addition to my full-time job with the Council to which I had returned, I participated actively in the work of our Century Group as its members and members of William Allen White's Committee joined to evolve into a Fight for Freedom Committee.

There was a joint discussion on November 20 of how to counteract Ambassador Joseph Kennedy's activities in Hollywood where he was advising motion picture producers to cease making anti-Nazi films and to prepare to do business with a victorious Germany. In the winter we worked for the passage of Lend-Lease legislation. Finally, in March, agreement was reached upon the purpose and structure of the Fight for Freedom Committee; it was established in April. The committee called on all American citizens to join it in doing whatever was necessary to insure Hitler's defeat. "We must throw our full weight now into the fight for freedom, knowing if this means war, it also means the surest and swiftest road to peace." As finally constituted the committee elected Senator Carter Glass of Virginia honorary chairman, and Bishop Henry W. Hobson, chairman, with Mrs. Calvin Coolidge and me as vice-chairmen. The committee, under the direction of Peter Cusick, continued to operate effectively until Pearl Harbor.

Early in May, on the occasion of President Roosevelt's visit to Staunton, Virginia, to dedicate a shrine to the memory of Woodrow Wilson, Governor Price of Virginia presented to him a petition which I had drafted and which was signed by many Virginians asking the president to declare a state of full national emergency in order that our own armed forces might be employed under the American flag to establish control over the whole North Atlantic area and to convoy supplies to British ports.

During that spring there were stirrings in the Northeast as well as in the South. Sinclair Weeks and Henry B. Cabot invited me to come to Boston on May 14 and speak to sixty of the most influential citizens of New England on the nature of the crisis that confronted us. All six of the New England states were represented. There were governors, businessmen, editors, and educators. I have seldom addressed a more distinguished audience or one that was more sympathetic. It was obvious that Joe Kennedy did not represent responsible opinion in that part of the United States.

And so we worked on until December 7.

X ✍ World War II–OSS

News of Pearl Harbor reached me at Culpeper Station on my return from a meeting of the Southern Policy Committee at Farmington, Virginia. I wanted to get into active war work at once. Early in January, Robert Sherwood phoned me from the White House to ask me to serve as chairman of the Board of the Foreign Information Service, one of the many activities initiated by Colonel William J. Donovan under the Office of Strategic Services. Sherwood had become director and he had collected several able people for his board, including Edmund Taylor and John Wylie. This organization eventually became OWI but it had just been established and was still a very modest affair. Sherwood explained that our function would be to issue policy directives determining the selection and character of news items and comments for broadcasting to foreign countries. He added that I would be assisted in my office by Miss Evangeline Bell. I accepted and went to work for OSS in February. Upon arrival I understood why Sherwood had mentioned Miss Bell's name. Her father had been a U.S. foreign service officer and her mother was English. She knew both London and Washington and besides was, and still is, one of the most beautiful women of her generation. Her presence gave great distinction to my office.

FIS was floundering like every other newly created war agency, trying desperately to discover how to function. My trouble was that I could never find Sherwood. He was director. It was his responsibility to establish a channel to the State Department through which we could learn what our foreign policy was in particular instances. It was also his responsibility to come around occasionally to see what we were doing and give us an opportunity to seek his counsel. But there were times when for days on end I could not reach him on the phone. I was usually told that he was doing some work for the president and my calls were seldom, if ever, returned. Nor did he attend the regular meetings of our board.

In desperation, Edmund Taylor and I decided that if we could not get anybody to tell us what U.S. government policy was in particular instances, we would have to assume responsibility ourselves for saying what it was. We did so. After a few weeks of this improvisation, the State Department woke up with a start to the realization that one of Donovan's impertinent little offices was making policy for it and so a high level council was called of twenty or thirty people from State and OSS to discuss establishing better liaison. Meanwhile, representatives of the British Ministry of Information were also arriving to co-ordinate their work with ours.

General Donovan expected the board of FIS to wait on him once a week, but we rarely had a chance to report or to discuss questions of policy. He did nearly all of the talking and the impression grew on me that he had little interest in ideas as such, but was exclusively interested in action. At these weekly meetings, his aide would bring in a pile of papers and place them before him. He would thumb through the papers, commenting on points that occurred to him, apparently quite oblivious of the fact that the function of our board was to make policy for the people who were in charge of overseas broadcasting. What, for instance, were we to say to the people of India who were in the throes of their independence movement—and independence from Great Britain, now our closest friend and ally? This sort of thing did not interest him. He spoke to us about what did interest him, usually guerrilla warfare.

Once while he was going through the papers before him at one of our meetings, he came across a note from the president which evidently pleased him very much. It went something like this: "Dear Bill: A Mr. Adams from Harrisburg, Pa., has invented an incendiary capsule small enough for a bat to carry. He suggests that if a sufficient number of bats armed with these capsules were let loose over Tokyo it would set that city on fire. Will you investigate and report? (signed) Franklin." As Donovan read this note, I could visualize the president dictating it with his cigarette holder tilted up at an exceptionally high angle. That was a sure sign, as General George Marshall once told me, that the president was up to mischief. But Donovan sensed no mischievousness. He was deadly serious and turning to me said: "Francis, this is in your area. Prepare a staff paper." Incendiary bats in my area!—and I thought my responsibility was for ideas on air-waves. The only connection I could see was that both bats and ideas operated through the air. But it was not for me to reason why, so I said, "Yes, Sir," and reached for the president's note.

As soon as I got back to my office I phoned Mr. Adams and asked him to come down immediately. Then I inquired at the Smithsonian as to who was the leading bat authority in Washington and was referred to a Mr. Monroe who in turn referred me to a number of books. I learned that at that time of year (it was March) millions of bats were dormant in the Carlsbad Caverns of New Mexico. Mr. Adams's idea was that several thousand of these should be taken from the Caverns while still dormant, have the capsules attached to them, be packed into suitable crates, put aboard long distance planes and released over Tokyo. He anticipated that as the bats fell through the air they would wake up and as they lit on the wood-and-paper houses, the capsules would ignite. There you were!

At the end of two days I had completed my intensive study of bat lore and had written my staff paper—a one-page discussion of the proposal giving pros and cons and making a recommendation, with appendices attached. My recommendation was that the Air Force be required to catch the bats, attach the incendiary capsules, and experiment with them over the desert on our side of the Mexican frontier.

I sent my staff paper forward through channels and heard nothing more about it for more than three years. After the fighting in Europe was over and SHAEF had moved to Frankfurt, I entered the officers' mess one day and sat down by an Air Force Colonel. We were in a reminiscent frame of mind and were regaling each other with old soldiers' tales. Finally to amuse him I began to tell him the story of Donovan and the bats. As I proceeded his face grew darker and darker and his mien less friendly. When I had finished he blurted out, "My God! Did *you* write that staff paper? *We* had to do it!"

Later in the spring I became thoroughly weary of working under the direction of a man whom I could never find. At that time David K. E. Bruce was head of SI/OSS. He asked me to take charge of his British Section and I was delighted to accept. I invited Miss Bell to move over with me, but she declined as she wanted to go to London. William Phillips, our former ambassador to Italy, was then head of OSS London, and I arranged for her to be sent over to work for him. When Bruce succeeded Phillips, she continued in the same office and after the war became Mrs. Bruce, gracing our embassies for many years in Paris, Bonn, and London.

Some weeks after I joined SI, Donovan sent down word that he wanted me to secure for OSS copies of the "Bermuda Intercepts." The British were intercepting mail and telegrams from Europe and the United States destined for Latin American countries and these were collected and sorted out at Bermuda and Trinidad. The information they provided was of great assistance in breaking the Nazi network in that part of the world. Our government was already receiving copies of the intercepts for economic warfare purposes, and I never understood why Donovan himself did not ask the British for another set instead of instructing me to get copies furtively. We had a sharp cookie from New York working for us who seemed to be just the man for the job. I explained to him what was wanted and told him to get busy.

A day or two later a truck rolled in with bales of intercepts. We stored them in the basement of one of our buildings. During the days that followed trucks continued to roll in until our basement was nearly full. Donovan had given no instruction for distribution and unless the trucks were stopped, we were going to have an overflow of material. So I sent for the New Yorker and told him that I had to know where he was getting the intercepts. He was very reluctant to tell me, but finally the truth came out. The intercepts were those discarded by the Office of Economic Warfare over on Q Street of which Fowler Hamilton was the director. I jumped in a car and sped to that office. As I entered I asked: "Fowler, after your people have finished with the Bermuda intercepts, what happens to them?" "Burned, of course," he replied, "They are classified material." "You are mistaken," I said acidly, "I have them." I made my profuse apologies and swore it would never happen again. The smart cookie had given a small bribe to the man responsible for burning papers and that was enough for him to get the lot. I reflected how easy it must have been in those days for German agents operating in Washington to pick up a good bit of useful information.

My New Yorker was obviously quite an operator, so I assigned another job to him which he carried through with great competence. It occurred to me that it would be a good plan to collect authentic

French clothing—suits, shirts, underwear, socks, shoes, hats—everything that a person would need who was being dropped into occupied France. The clothes were to be a little worn, but current. New York was an ideal place to acquire such a collection from Free French visitors and refugees. My friend amassed an enormous wardrobe which was eventually shipped to London and served as a veritable haberdashery goldmine when we began operations from there a year later.

Among the various duties I had in Q Building nothing intrigued or interested me more than general supervision of the work of George Merten and Donald MacLaren. Merten had been a civil servant of the Prussian government, but though a Prussian he was a liberal. Because of his liberalism he had escaped to America in the early thirties, and after war broke out in Europe, worked in New York along with MacLaren for "the quiet Canadian," Bill Stephenson, until Pearl Harbor. Both of these men were then transferred to Allen Dulles who, in turn, transferred them to me. Their job, through using the Bermuda and Trinidad intercepts and by other means, was to uncover the Nazi network in Latin America. This network used I. G. Farben as a cover and also as a transmission belt for receiving funds through the good offices of various American companies with Latin American connections. In a pamphlet called *Sequel to the Apocalypse* Merten and MacLaren exposed the extent to which the money of American consumers was helping to pay for Hitler's war. Merten was an expert operator and from his office in New York he was able to trace and stop the flow of funds and messages so effectively that Nazi agents found it increasingly difficult to function. He rendered a service of very great value to the Free World, and my association with him was the beginning of a warm friendship which has continued ever since.

In the autumn of 1942, I flew to London for several weeks to become acquainted with the British service and to talk about intelligence preparations for the eventual invasion of Europe.

Later I began to make plans to go back to London for good the following year, as I was determined to have some part in the invasion of Europe. I applied for a commission which eventually came through. There was vague talk of the possibility of an OSS operation to gather strategic intelligence. I thought I could help. So I collected a small group of able officers, among whom the ablest was the late Justin O'Brien of Columbia University, and we arranged to leave in the summer. Before I left, Helen and I asked Alexander and Mary Zabriskie (he was dean of the Episcopal Seminary at Alexandria) to bring up our boys in case neither of us survived the war. We admired and loved them both and felt we would rather entrust our children to them than to anybody else.

At that time OSS men bound for the European Theater did not have high transportation priority, so we fussed and fumed around during one of the hottest spells on record and did not get seats on a plane until early September.

In London I lived at Brown's Hotel for nine months. It was perhaps foolish but I never went to the air-raid shelters. At times the warnings came almost every night, but sleep meant more to me than overhead protection. The night a string of bombs fell near St. James's Palace the old building really shook, and it sounded as if they were coming down right on top of us.

During the autumn of 1943 the British were so delighted that the Americans had arrived that all of us in OSS received frequent invitations to meals and parties. As soon as the word got around that Eisenhower might be the supreme commander, everyone I met was immensely pleased. They took it for granted he was a man who would cause them no trouble and who would probably allow them to have pretty much their own way.

After some pulling and hauling I was assigned staff responsibility for planning, organizing, and mounting an operation called "Sussex." The purpose of this operation was to gather strategic military intelligence through agents placed behind the enemy's lines prior to D-day and during subsequent operations. Strategic intelligence meant information regarding enemy reserves (the location and redeployment of particular units), indication of targets for bombing such as munition dumps, bridges, and railway yards, and any other data which might be of value to our offensive operations. Organizing such an operation was a complex undertaking. It involved recruiting agents, training them for months in field techniques and skills, endowing them with new personalities, furnishing them with appropriate clothes and gadgets, dropping them in at designated spots, and above all insuring that they would be met by competent reception committees who would take them to three different "safe" houses on successive nights so that the Gestapo would lose the trail. The British had been doing this sort of thing for years and were professionals in every sense of the word. They were also mounting an operation under the same code name and our work had to be carefully co-ordinated. This was done through a committee of three:

Campaign picture for senatorial race of 1952.

Francis (right) and William (left), with friend, at Rockbridge Baths, ca. 1900.

Member of Harry Lee crew, Washington and Lee University, 1913.

Executive Committee of World's Student Christian Federation, Chamcoria, Bulgaria, 1935. Front row from left: Helen Morton, U.S.A.; Augustine Ralla Ram, India; W. A. Visser 't Hooft, Holland; Francis P. Miller, U.S.A.; Pierre Maury, France; Suzanne de Dietrich, France. Back row: Enichi Kan, Japan; Luther Tucker, U.S.A.; Jaroslav Simsa, Czechoslovakia; Robert Mackie, Scotland; Ambrose Reeves, England; and H. P. Cruse, South Africa.

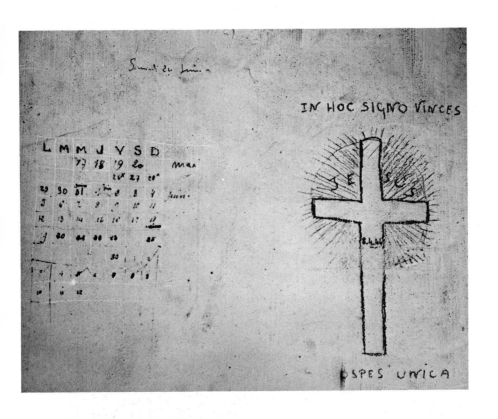

Graffiti of Allied agents on walls of Gestapo prison house in Avenue Foch, Paris.

Decorated with Legion of Merit (the second such award) by General Lucius D. Clay, Berlin, 1945.

Portrait by Walmsley Lenhard, 1947.
Photograph by Lowell A. Kenyon, Chevy Chase, Maryland.

Family picture for gubernatorial campaign of 1948–49.

Commander Kenneth Cohen, a British naval officer, Colonel Roulier (the famous "Rémy") for the French, and myself. Roulier, who was a past master at the art of underground organization, was responsible for giving general advice, for contact with the French networks, and for arranging for the "Reception Committees." His own network was responsible for one of the most brilliant intelligence feats in the European Theater—the delivery in London of the German army's own map of the defenses on the Normandy coast where the invasion was to take place.

I was the complete amateur and had everything to learn. The British were marvelous. They opened all doors to us—shared the knowledge of their techniques and put their school at our disposal to which I assigned Henry Macy with several assistants. Macy and his fellows learned quickly and did a magnificent job of instruction and training. The first major difficulty we encountered was in the recruitment of agents. No matter how perfect their spoken French, American boys could not be expected to perform as well as native Frenchmen on a job of this kind. But there were not enough French youth of the right type in England. Consequently we arranged through the OSS offices in North Africa for the recruiting to be done there among the numerous Free French who had escaped from occupied France. This plan worked well and in the end we secured an adequate number of high grade candidates.

An operation of this kind required an impressive variety of equipment. The British were far ahead of us in the invention of tools for espionage, and among other things had perfected a ground-to-plane phone which they allowed us to use. The Germans had become expert at locating ordinary radio transmitters, but the radio waves from this phone went skyward in a cone and the Germans could not pinpoint the source with their regular "direction finders." Mosquito planes based in England, with receiving sets installed, flew out over the channel to listen to the reports of agents who used these phones.

Only once was there a crisis of confidence with the British. In midwinter the naval officer who was my opposite number arrived one day accompanied by a colonel of the guards to say that it was Montgomery's wish that my Sussex agents should send their messages back through British channels. I was becoming enough of a professional to realize what this meant. It meant control. By that time we had our own radio receiving station, and I replied that I regretted that the request had been made because we intended to have our own independent operation. I added that if Montgomery insisted I would carry the matter to Eisenhower. There the subject was dropped and none of us ever referred to it again.

As D-day approached I felt rather proud of Sussex. I had set out to prove that even in OSS it was possible to have a well-planned, efficiently organized, and smoothly launched operation. My staff work was nearly finished and I was conscious that I had attained my goal, so that it was with a certain amount of pleasurable anticipation that I heard that General Donovan was coming to inspect us toward the end of May. I was particularly proud of our top-secret Sussex war room with maps indicating where our agents had been dropped. Justin O'Brien was in charge of this room since he supervised the agents' final briefing and dispatch. Consequently, when the general arrived, I asked O'Brien to show him the maps and explain the individual missions of different agents. When Donovan had finished looking around, he turned to me and said, "Francis, tell David Bruce to call a meeting of the staff as soon as they can be assembled." I rushed off and in a short time all the top OSS officers in London had come together to hear what the general had to say. Though I took no notes, I will never forget his words. A brief and accurate summary of his remarks would run like this: "Gentlemen, I find that here in London you have been doing too much planning. Plans are no good on the day of battle. I ask you to throw your plans out of the window. If I had been in command at Anzio, we would have been in Rome within three days. It was the plans prepared by the army in advance that were responsible for the invading forces getting bogged down." He had just inspected the "Sussex" war room and it was clear that my careful planning had triggered this outburst. I knew at once that I could no longer work for such a man. So as soon as the meeting was dismissed, I went to David Bruce and asked him to help me get a transfer out of OSS to some other branch of the service, and he very generously found a job for me at SHAEF.

Donovan may not have been impressed with Sussex but others whose opinion I valued more highly were. It was one of the few operations with which I have had anything to do that was carried through to a wholly successful conclusion. I glow with a bit of pride now when I think about it. Fifty-six agents dropped behind the enemy lines with not a single miscarriage in reception arrangements: a thousand messages received back from those agents, and only three of them were caught in the line of duty and executed by the Germans.

Four more of them were executed, but it was not in the line of duty. These four, including one girl, were so intoxicated by news of the liberation of Paris that they ignored their orders, came up out of cover, and started off to Paris with all of their equipment in a small truck, ignorant of the fact that the Germans still controlled some of the territory between them and their destination. When they arrived at the town of Vendôme, a German sentry halted their truck and ordered them out. As they were dismounting with their suitcases, one of these fell open, revealing a radio set. They were immediately lined up and shot without any semblance of a court martial. I made it my business to trace the Germans responsible for this breach of the rules of war. They were located, and I preferred charges against them, trusting that an allied tribunal would give them the punishment they deserved.

Of the three agents executed in the line of duty, none, as far as we could tell, revealed any information about other agents during torture prior to execution. One of the three had been dropped at Chartres. He was equipped with a ground-to-plane phone and before D-day reported that the Panzer Lehr Division was being held in reserve in that area. When reporting his voice indicated stress of emotion and we feared for him. A few days later he was caught. The Panzer Lehr Division was the best equipped division in the German army and its presence in France had not been known to either American or British headquarters. Montgomery's chief of intelligence remarked later that spotting that Division alone was worth the entire Sussex operation. It was the Division that stalled Mongomery at Caen and continued to fight on until it was surrounded in the Ruhr the following spring.

The compliment that pleased me most came from the Air Force. They said they liked to bomb the munitions dump targets supplied by Sussex agents because whenever they did so there was a big explosion proving the accuracy of the reporting.

I cannot close my account of Sussex without paying a tribute to those marvelous Free French boys and girls from North Africa who volunteered for this hazardous enterprise. Of them the world is not worthy.

The success of Sussex was due to many different factors woven into a relatively harmonious pattern of operational activity. There was the ability and devotion of Justin O'Brien and the other American officers on my small staff; the complete co-operation and assistance of the British Service; the perfect direction and control of the reception committees by Colonel Roulier; and the ingenuity and courage of the indomitable French peasants who formed the reception committees. Finally, the skill of the American airmen assigned the duty of delivering the agents was beyond all praise. They never missed a rendezvous. A certain Colonel Heflin was in charge and to my great regret I never met him. He was magnificent, for when the weather was foul he would fly in himself rather than send one of his men.

It was unfortunate for our Army that as our troops moved northeast toward the German frontier, no operation had been mounted comparable to Sussex. If there had been, we might have been better prepared for the Battle of the Bulge. But that would have required planning, and according to Donovan the time for planning was past.

I did not know Donovan intimately but I believe I understood him tolerably well. In limited areas he was a genius, and this was certainly true of his ability to pick men. Since he did not pick me, I feel no embarrassment in making this comment. The roster of individuals who served in OSS during 1942–46 is a remarkable one. I doubt if anyone in the history of our country ever assembled an abler or more competent group. Donovan was also somewhat of a genius in his imaginative invention of things that needed to be done.

His greatest weakness was his limited understanding of the nature of collecting information through secret intelligence operations. That is a strange thing to say about the founding father of our present intelligence service, but I believe it to be true. Donovan thought of intelligence in terms of doing something. His passion was for action—any kind of action, and his heart was in SO (operations). As I observed his direction of OSS, I came to the conclusion that he did not consider the covert collection of information to be his primary business. It did not excite his imagination and consequently he gave less thought to the skills and techniques required for that than to those required for his other activities. The CIA inherited from Donovan his lopsided and mischievous preoccupation with action and the Bay of Pigs was one of the results of that legacy.

A day or two before D-day Roulier came into my office and said that General de Gaulle wished to know where the landing would take place. He went to my map on the wall, pointed to the Normandy Coast, and asked if that was the area. Our orders were strict, and I was mum, but he had been of such tremendous help that it hurt me not to tell. He was equally distressed when I withdrew into my shell, but he told me later that my face had remained completely enigmatic —that even my eyes had revealed nothing.

XI ✍ World War II—SHAEF

Toward the end of June orders came transferring me from OSS to SHAEF. Brigadier General T. J. Betts, who had asked for me, was the senior American intelligence officer on Eisenhower's staff. He was born in Virginia, brought up in Baltimore, attended the University of Virginia, and married Elizabeth Randolph—a direct descendant of Thomas Jefferson. After World War I he had remained in the service. General Betts had many of the qualities I have always associated with General Lee, and when I was working for him I felt at home. Richard Collins, for positive intelligence, and H. Gordon Sheen for counter-intelligence, were the senior American colonels in G-2 and both became friends. Collins has had a remarkable career. Prior to the war he had been a gynecologist in Boston and at the same time was an officer in a national guard artillery unit. When war came he secured an intelligence assignment, discovered he had a natural talent for that work, and retired as a permanent major-general after occupying the highest intelligence posts in the army.

When I reported for duty early in July, SHAEF still maintained part of its headquarters at Bushy Park, near Hampton Court on the Thames, and remained there until the liberation of Paris. One evening when I was walking on the bridge over the river, returning to my billet, I heard something I had never heard before—a very loud, very sharp crack in the distance with no warning sound in advance of its arrival. It was the first V-2 to hit the city. The V-1 traveled much more slowly and could be both seen and heard some time before impact. Not so the V-2. This was Hitler's secret weapon, and the sound was ominous.

Around the first of September I crossed the channel to our newly established headquarters at Versailles from which the Germans had recently departed. One of the first things I did there was to take one of our army cameramen to a house on Avenue Foch and have him photograph all the walls in the rooms on the top floor. This had been where the Gestapo had kept captured English and French agents prior to execution. Every room had the British royal coat of arms drawn on the wall, and every room a cross with the motto "in hoc signo vinci." Most poignant of all were the sketched calendars with dates crossed out. The crossings out ceased on the day of execution.

I had heard many horrible things about the Nazis, but in order to know the truth at first hand I went to the death hall just outside of Paris. At one end of the hall was the execution post with a white cloth soaked in blood still clinging to it. That man must have been shot just before the city was liberated. But this was not the horror. The horror was the hall itself. It could be hermetically sealed and was lined with thick asbestos. There in the asbestos were the imprints of human hands and bodies as they had vaulted in their frenzy and flung themselves against the walls in the agonizing throes of some awful death. The sight filled me with a nauseous loathing and an eternal hatred for all tyrants and for their totalitarian systems.

My assignment in G-2 was responsibility for intelligence in connection with our anticipated occupation of Germany. But I soon found that no one label would cover all the chores that found their way to my office. I asked the navy to send me an ONI officer expert in Japanese intelligence since we were sure to find, as we moved across Germany, some information about the Japanese that might still be of use in the Pacific. A young scientist was assigned to me to take care of all scientific questions that were referred to SHAEF. I also had to make policy in regard to collecting the mountains of German government documents that would fall into our hands—and for conserving libraries and art treasures.

At various times I served on staff groups organized to give advice to the supreme commander. One group was asked to consider where headquarters of the military government of Germany should be located. Another was responsible for recommending the style we should adopt when going into Germany—whether with colors flying, bands playing, and a general display of smart military discipline, or quietly and without fanfare.

Occasionally serendipity enters one's life with a moment of un-alloyed pleasure—which is entirely unexpected and could not have been planned. These are the best moments. One such occurred to me during that winter. I was standing in the garden of the Trianon Palace Hotel at Versailles, in which our offices were located, talking to my sergeant. As I looked up two generals of the army were coming down a path that ran near where I stood. One was the su-preme commander, the other was a visitor. I froze to attention. Ike's companion was General George Marshall, whom I regarded as our greatest general, and also, in many respects, as one of the greatest Americans of his day. When he came opposite to me General Mar-shall left Eisenhower, and came over to ask me how things were going. It was a precious encounter.

Because of my interest during 1942–43 in I. G. Farben as the prin-cipal provider of funds and cover for Nazi agents working in Latin America, I felt it was important for us to question some of Farben's top executives whenever we could lay our hands on them. Conse-quently, after General Patton's columns broke loose and were roar-ing across southern Germany toward Austria, I sent his headquarters a telegram asking his G-2 to keep an eye out for these gentlemen and send them on to me whenever anyone picked them up.

Several weeks later a travel-stained major appeared at the door of my office, saluted and reported that he had brought in Max Ilgner, Willie Schmidt, and August von Knieriem, members of the Farben board of directors. They had been found hiding in the cellar of a hotel in Wuerzburg and he said he had driven them 450 kilometers in a jeep. I was overjoyed. But we had no detention place as yet at SHAEF. "Dustbin" was to come later. So I phoned John Oakes (now in charge of the editorial page of the *New York Times*) who was then with OSS in Paris, knowing that he had accommodations in Paris for persons in whom the U.S. had an interest, and inquired if he would welcome some additional guests. When I explained who they were, he said he would be delighted to receive them. So I sent them down.

A few days thereafter there was a knock at my door and a civilian entered. He said, "I am Philip W. Amram, from the Department of Justice. Did you get my cable?" I replied, "No, Sir, what was it about?" (As a matter of fact that cable never did arrive.) Amram then proceeded to explain the purpose of his mission.

He was in charge of one of the greatest of all wartime lawsuits between Standard Oil of New Jersey and the Alien Property Custodian, then pending in the federal court in New York City. The stakes were the United States patents for synthetic petroleum, artificial rubber, and other petro-chemicals. Standard claimed to be the owner of these patents; the government claimed that they were actually the property of I. G. Farben and that Standard was holding them for Farben during the war to protect them from vesting by the Alien Property Custodian. The Standard-Farben relationship went back to the 1920s and in September, 1939, just a few weeks after World War II broke out, agreements were entered into at The Hague between Standard and Farben. Von Knieriem, as the head of the patent department of Farben and its general counsel, knew more about these than any man in the world outside the Standard organization.

Very early in the war enough suspicion was generated so that the Alien Property Custodian tentatively seized all these patents in March, 1942. Standard claimed ownership and brought suit for their return, which effectively restrained the government from the fullest utilization of the patents.

The famous John W. Davis represented Standard, and Amram, for the Department of Justice, needed all the evidence he could unearth to prove the agreement of concealment.

By some uncanny coincidence (things like this don't happen very often) the people who had picked up von Knieriem and his associates in Wuerzburg sent a cable to army headquarters in Washington, giving their names and asking if anyone in Washington had any interest in these "ordinary businessmen." John McCloy immediately notified Francis Biddle, the attorney general, who sent Amram to Paris by the first available plane to take advantage of this incredible piece of luck.

"The man I particularly want to see," Amram said to me, "is von Knieriem. We have to interview him, and I will wait as long as necessary and go wherever he is." Amram, of course, had no idea that von Knieriem was already in Paris. I looked him straight in the eye and asked, "Would you like to see him at three o'clock this afternoon?" Amram, naturally resenting what he considered to be my frivolous attitude, flushed, and snapped: "Colonel, this is no joking matter." "I am not joking," I replied. "When would you like to see him?" Then I explained that von Knieriem, with the other Farben executives, had been driven in from Germany and were being held at a detention house in Paris. So I phoned Oakes that a Department of Justice official wanted to interview the men I had sent down. There followed a comic interlude of two or three days before Amram was given a chance to see them. Donovan was so proud that he had these gentlemen in his possession and he was so eager to exploit to the full the opportunities for interrogation which their presence offered (with all the credit that would accrue to him as a result), that, even though it was I who had found them and entrusted them for safekeeping to OSS, he ordered Oakes not to return them to me. So we had to cable Washington to get the secretary of war and the attorney general to order Donovan to release them to Amram.

The sequel was even more dramatic. Von Knieriem told Amram everything, adding some details entirely unknown to the Department of Justice. He also told him that, for safety purposes, he had secreted, at his country home near Heidelberg, the original files of his office with all the original papers involving the Standard-Farben deals and all the original correspondence on the matter between Farben and the Nazi authorities. He agreed to find all of these and to come to New York to testify as a government witness.

Amram arranged through me with the Paris military authorities to send von Knieriem to Heidelberg in the next few days with a military guard to get these files together. Then Amram flew back to New York to begin the trial, which opened May 21, 1945, and lasted three weeks. During the second week, he received word that von Knieriem had arrived at Ellis Island with the needed documents. Upon arriving, von Knieriem, a great German lawyer and world-renowned corporate executive, begged Amram to buy him a clean white shirt and tie (he was dressed in rough clothes) since he did not wish to see his former friends and associates so shabbily dressed.

Standard's lawyers and executives had no inkling of what was happening. Amram told me that von Knieriem's entrance into the courtroom that last week in May, 1945, was one of the most dramatic moments of his entire career at the bar.

I should like to have been there myself to see the faces of the Standard executives as the door opened and von Knieriem, in his new white shirt and tie, walked in with his files under his arm. They knew the case was lost. The trial judge decided every issue in favor of the government and his decision was affirmed on appeal.

It is seldom in intelligence that one can foresee and plan long enough in advance to have the right man or the right bit of information available at the right moment. But in this instance I had managed to do that, and it was a thrilling experience.

One day in March, 1945, General Betts called me in and told me to get a civilian suit over from London, have a passport made overnight, and have a plane laid on. He explained that it had been decided to send me on a special mission to Madrid. It seemed that a German agent with a message for us had been waiting in a Madrid hotel for several weeks hoping that someone would appear to hear what he had to say. The Vatican attached such importance to this message that it had been urging our government to send someone down to receive it. I had been selected as the man to go. I made my preparations immediately. The suit arrived, the passport was made overnight, and the plane was ready. Then several puzzling days went by with no orders to depart. At length Robert Murphy informed me that the decision had been reversed and that no one was to be sent down. Since the war was so nearly won, it was felt that there was no point in making contact with the Germans or in receiving a message from them. I was bitterly disappointed—all the more so subsequently when I read some of the testimony given at von Ribbentrop's trial in Nuremburg. Evidence given there seemed to indicate that the man who was waiting in Madrid might have been Fritz Berber.

Fritz Berber had been the German law student at the European student conference at Hardenbroek, Holland in 1921 with whom I had a famous argument as to whether "consent" or "force" was the proper basis of government, in the course of which he had said that if the Devil himself ever came to rule Germany, he would serve him. The following year Berber had visited me in Oxford and then stayed on for some months with the Quakers at Selly Oak near Birmingham where he perfected his English. Having been a Communist in the autumn of 1918, he had become a Social Democrat in 1919 and after receiving his law degree served as a judge for some time in the criminal court of Munich. He then joined the faculty of the Hochschule für Politik (Graduate School of Politics) in Berlin where I saw him on several occasions. After Hitler came to power Goebbels offered Berber a job and he accepted. Then he joined von Ribbentrop in the German Foreign Office and wrote the White Papers justifying the foreign policy of the Third Reich. Toward the end of the war he turned up from time to time on intelligence missions in Geneva, attempting to exploit his connections with the English Quakers.

After the German capitulation he was reported to have served for a while as denazification director of the French Zone in Germany and then went to India to act as an adviser to Nehru. As recently as 1966 he was professor of international law at the University of Munich. I should like to hear his lectures. But what would have given me infinitely more pleasure, provided Berber was the man waiting in Madrid, would have been to have opened the door of his hotel room and said, "Hello, Fritz, how does it feel to have served the Devil?" When I reflected on the tortuous story of this man's life, it seems to me to have been a parable on the tragedy of our time—of the intellectual confusion and moral bankruptcy which continues to threaten Western civilization.

Toward the end of the war American troops pushed rapidly eastward into Austria. Many notable Germans were picked up on the way, including a few whom Hitler had detained in concentration camps. These were joined by others who had fled into northern Italy and this combined group of VIP's was taken to the island of Capri for temporary rehabilitation. It was then decided to bring them to SHAEF for sorting out and interrogation. I was ordered to do the staff work in connection with arrangements for their reception and detention. We took over a vast and pretentious villa on the grounds of the Versailles Palace, surrounded it with barbed wire, and installed cots and a kitchen. Our VIP prisoners were to receive exactly the same fare as the American soldier, the best fed soldier of any in the world. American supply sergeants are superb at making arrangements of this kind, and almost overnight the reception center was ready. We dubbed it "Dustbin."

When the group for whom we were waiting arrived, it turned out to be a very mixed bag—all the way from Pastor Martin Niemoeller to Ohlendorf, who had been assistant to Himmler and was one of the worst war criminals. Among others were more respectable citizens like Krupp von Bohlen, Thyssen, and Speer. The last had been Hitler's architect and minister of industrial production. He was still in the prime of life and one of the most magnificent looking men I had ever seen. Toward the end of the war Speer realized that all was lost, and he determined to kill Hitler, Goering, and Goebbels. His scheme was ingenious. He planned to pump poison gas down the air vents of the bunker in the chancellery courtyard when the three of them were below. But he was never able to produce a gas heavy enough to stay down. Then he planned to have them shot as their cars moved down a Berlin street, but the cars were never in the right place at the right time. Though these efforts failed, the fact that he had made them helped to save Speer himself from execution. In a strange way I rather admired the man—partly because when he designed Hitler's office, he made the walls and the desk of cheap veneer!

Pastor Niemoeller resented being treated, during this preliminary detention period, exactly like the other Germans. He thought that since Hitler had put him in a concentration camp, an exception ought to have been made of him. It is true that Hitler had done this, but it is also true that as concentration camps went, he had been unusually well taken care of. I had no intention of making an exception of him, because after Pearl Harbor he had written Hitler offering to become a submarine commander to fight again as he had done in the First World War.

While Niemoeller was waiting at Capri before being brought up to Versailles, he was interviewed by the American journalist, Dorothy Thompson. She told him how shocked his American friends were when they learned of his offer to Hitler and asked him why he had made it. He replied, "Because my soul belongs to God, but my body to the Reich." This reply is the most perfect statement I know of the heresy that cursed European Protestantism in the early part of this century and which led to its ethical bankruptcy. The truth is that both soul and body belong to God and we are as much responsible to Him for the use of the body as we are for the use of the soul. I was so flabbergasted by Niemoeller's reply that several weeks later, after we had moved up to Frankfurt, I requested Francis Harmon, who had come over as a civilian for the Federal Council of Churches to contact German Protestants, to ask him if Miss Thompson had correctly reported his views. Niemoeller replied, "Yes, that is exactly what I believe." In view of this man's record it has seemed to me nothing less than a scandal that some American Protestants lionized him during the years after the war.

Once, in the course of inspecting "Dustbin," I inspected Ohlendorf, and I am glad I did, because when I had seen him I had seen the essence of the Nazi movement. As I entered his room, he came to attention with all the precision and smartness of a perfectly trained Prussian officer. His face was well-structured but hard as steel; his eyes were an icy-cold green and looked straight at me. He stood there proud, arrogant, and as contemptuous as the circumstances permitted, embodying more fully than anyone I had previously seen the ruthless, merciless spirit of the Nazi killer. His execution was well-deserved.

The British officer who was my immediate superior, Brigadier R. J. Maunsell, was extraordinarily intelligent, resourceful, and energetic—a fellow brigadier described him as "heavy and slow in appearance but alert and quick-witted in mind." He was also extremely considerate of his staff and in due course we became fast friends. Maunsell had brought with him from the Middle East several officers who had served with him there in the tough school of counterintelligence. One of these was Lieutenant Colonel Joseph Spencer, a seasoned regular. As we moved into Germany, our troops began to overrun concentration camps and it was essential to have accurate reports of conditions in these camps as the troops entered. Spencer was the very man for the job and I asked him to accompany the outfit that was about to overrun the camp at Ohrdruf which was one of the worst of the lot. Several days later he appeared at my door to report. He was so changed that I hardly recognized him. His face was ashen as if he were seriously ill. When I looked up I exclaimed, "Joe, what has happened to you, are you not feeling well?" He replied, "Colonel, I have seen things which the eye of man was not intended to see and heard things that the ear of man was not intended to hear. I beg you not to send me into that accursed country again." After he had finished making his report, I not only understood his reaction, but I felt very much as he did. It is happily impossible to convey in words the horror of those camps. Hell had come to earth, and there the will of Satan reigned.

On June 14, General de Gaulle was to bestow on General Eisenhower the Cross of Liberation, the highest decoration that could be awarded by the French government. That day was chosen because it marked the fifth anniversary of the capture of Paris by the Germans, and the ceremony was to take place under the Arc de Triomphe. It so happened that de Gaulle had recently been very much annoyed by the attitude of the British General Edward Spears in Syria toward French interests in that area. Consequently, the day before the ceremony was to take place he had phoned our headquarters and expressed the wish that no British officers should accompany General Eisenhower on the morrow. Eisenhower replied that as supreme commander of Allied headquarters, he would naturally bring with him appropriate officers from his staff—both British and American. De Gaulle understood this but explained that the dinner he was giving Eisenhower in the evening was a private affair to which no British were being invited. Ike had no alternative but to accept that explanation. However, de Gaulle felt that he had been rebuffed by Eisenhower and since his nature was such that he could not tolerate the thought of not having the last say, he reserved his retaliation for the next day.

The ceremony was to take place at two o'clock. If either party is late for an affair of this kind, it is a mark of discourtesy and the greater the ceremony the greater the discourtesy. My friend Roulier was still very close to de Gaulle at that time and he had invited me to witness the ceremony with him after having lunch together at the Hotel La Pérouse. Roulier had an entree everywhere and so he took me within the charmed circle of the Arc where we could see the show at close quarters. It was a marvelous June day and one had the impression that the whole population of Paris was lining the streets and standing on the roof tops. General Eisenhower arrived ahead of time with the British Air Marshal Tedder, General Bedell Smith, and other members of his staff. Two o'clock came, but there was no de Gaulle. Two-two, two-four, two-six, the minutes passed. At about two-eight Eisenhower recognized General Giraud, de Gaulle's bitter enemy, standing near the Arc and stepped over to embrace him to the delight of the Parisian crowd. It was not until about two-twelve that a car slowly came up the Avenue and out stepped de Gaulle. He strolled toward the Arc in a manner so leisurely that it would appear he thought two o'clock had not yet struck, and the ceremony began.

De Gaulle's tardiness was not due to chance. It was an act of calculated discourtesy. He wanted to keep the allied supreme commander waiting for him for twelve whole minutes before the people of Paris so that they would know who was top dog in France. He had had the final word, and that is all that mattered to him.

In due course SHAEF was moved from Versailles to Frankfurt. G-2 offices were in the adjoining town of Hochst and I was billeted nearby in the village of Hofheim.

While at Hochst R.J. Maunsell and I went up one day to the Saalburg. It was on the crest of the low ridge running east and west to the north of Frankfurt. There, almost as the Romans left it, was a section of the great earthen wall facing north with ditch in front which the Romans had built from the Rhine to the Danube as a defense against the barbarians. In the days of the empire this was the outer limit of the civilized world. After eighteen hundred years we found ourselves back on the same frontier and wondered how much progress the human race had made in the interval.

As I looked out toward Frankfurt from my billet on the hill in the village of Hofheim, the I. G. Farben works seemed to stretch endlessly over the valley below. From that distance they appeared to be completely intact, yet the residential areas in much of Frankfurt had been reduced to rubble. This could not have been by chance. Why were the German people made to suffer so much more than I. G. Farben, which had been one of the principal agents of Hitler's infamous rule? I understood the British theory of "de-housing" the German cities, but it seemed to me strangely ironic that so few of our bombs fell near that vast plant. Would not destroying Nazi industrial potential have been a quicker way to end the war and with far less loss of civilian life?

While waiting at Hofheim, one of the loveliest things happened to me that has ever happened in my life. General Betts issued orders putting me on duty in London for a week. Helen was coming there for the London *Economist* which she represented in the United States. It was a little taste of paradise. Brown's Hotel gave us the large suite that had been occupied during the war by a prime minister of one of the governments-in-exile and we had a glorious seven days going to the theater and seeing our friends. Rémy came over from Paris, and I introduced Helen to the various British officers with whom I had worked. But best of all was just being with her again. When I left Washington in 1943 her hair was dark. Now it was turning grey, and this changed her appearance. It was for me evidence of what she had been going through.

After returning to Hochst I soon received my orders to report for duty to the Office of the Director of Intelligence, Office of Military Government (U.S.), Berlin.

XII ✒ Berlin, 1945-1946

And so toward the end of July, 1945, I set off for Berlin in a weapons carrier. We were in no convoy and we had no escort. We were going alone through the heart of Germany, but there were no incidents of any kind.

As soon as we crossed the Elbe, we began to meet Russians. Five times between the Elbe and Berlin as we passed Russian posts, a Russian soldier rushed out into the road and stopped my car. Each time I pulled out my orders for him to see, and each time he paid not the slightest attention to them. Instead the soldier would grab my left arm, point to my twenty-five dollar wrist watch, and indicate with his fingers that he would give me for it "occupation marks" worth one hundred, two hundred, or three hundred dollars.

I discovered after getting settled in Berlin that the glittering world of ours fascinated and attracted the Russian GI's so much that they were wandering over into our zone not only to buy, but in some instances even to stay. On two occasions when I descended from my billet in the morning, I found a Russian soldier asleep on the floor below—gone AWOL and hoping to find refuge with us as a halfway house to reaching that Utopia in the west called America. Each time I had no alternative but to send the soldier back under guard to the Russian Zone.

Free contact with American GI's in Berlin was in itself the most powerful anticommunist propaganda that could be conceived—far more effective than words on the air-waves. Unorganized and uncontrolled subversion was at work in the Russian army as a result of the Russian soldiers' lust for American cigarettes, watches, and other gadgets. It was evident to the Russian High Command that this must be stopped at once and that the only way to stop it was to prevent fraternization between Russians and Americans. There must be no free access to the American Zone. And so the fateful step was taken. The Iron Curtain came down—not only in Berlin but all the way from the Baltic to the Alps, dividing Europe in two.

General Lucius D. Clay was the over-all commander of U.S. Military Government in Germany. Our intelligence office was in the former Max Planck Institute, at 9 Boltzman Strasse where the Germans had had their only atomic reactor before the Russians swept through. The reactor had, of course, been carried off, and every metal object or fixture in any way related to the building had also been ripped out and carted away—everything from doorknobs to toilet fixtures! Some officer had been told to "get the works," and he had taken his orders literally. One of my first targets in Berlin was the Japanese Embassy which had not been destroyed and which to our mystified surprise had been entirely ignored by the Russians who got there first. All the safes were completely intact so we scooped up the lot.

In the early days of our occupation of Germany our chief preoccupation was with the Russians. To what extent were they willing to co-operate with us? We hoped against hope, and did everything that was humanly possible to convince them of our good will and of our desire to work with them. But it was all to no purpose. Military government consisted of a series of committees. It was an awkward method but the only one possible under the circumstances. At that time each committee included representatives of the four occupying powers—American, British, French, and Russian—with the chairmanship rotating. Brigadier General Bryan Conrad, head of intelligence, asked me to go with him to the meetings of the Four Power Intelligence Committee and in his absence I represented the United States. The British representative was Major General J. S. Lethbridge, who personified the finest traditions of the old Indian army. A perceptive and sensitive man, he became one of my closest friends and remained so as long as he lived. The Russian representative was Major General Sidnev of the MVD.

At our meetings the American, the British, and the French spoke freely without reservation. But the Russians always asked that the question under consideration be postponed until the next meeting. We soon realized why this was so. They were afraid to speak without being told by the Kremlin what to say, so they had to ask for instructions. But the bureaucracy in Moscow was either too swamped with requests for guidance to reply or else it did not know the answers itself. At any rate no replies ever came, so no business was ever transacted by our committee. In due course we met less and less frequently and then not at all. Four power government never got off the ground. We persisted in our efforts to exchange intelligence with the Russians, but as I recall it, we never received but two documents from them—the first was an innocuous tidbit and the second was the album of personal photographs of poor Eva Braun, Hitler's mistress, which was passed around at one of our committee meetings.

The condition of Berlin's population—psychological, moral, and spiritual—was worse than the condition of the parks and buildings. There were thousands living in basements, short on rations, often alone, and always tormented. The poignant symbols of this misery were the informal bulletin boards that appeared on trees and walls covered with notices of every conceivable kind from articles for exchange, to food and clothing wanted in return for specified services. The most poignant of all were the offers of girls to give their bodies in exchange for room and rations. Berlin in 1945 represented the ultimate degradation of the human spirit.

One of the junior officers who had joined us as we moved to Berlin was Captain William H. Crosson, Jr. He had seen action with the Sixty-third Division and brought with him one of his sergeants, Ben Carb of Pittsburgh. Carb was a powerfully built young Jew, had shown great fearlessness in combat, and reminded me of what the Maccabeans who fought the Seleucids must have been like. Carb naturally hated Hitler with a perfect hatred. It occurred to me that it would do his soul good to see the ruin of Hitler's office and the bunker where Hitler had spent his last hours, so one day I arranged to take him down. The Wilhelmstrasse was in the Russian Zone but at that time there was nothing to prevent an American officer from going back and forth, and there was no Russian guard to forbid entry to the chancellery. We went first to Hitler's office and I was amused to see what a cheap job of construction Speer had done. Since there had been no direct hit, the walls were still standing, but the veneer which covered them had collapsed. Even Hitler's desk was a veneer affair. The ceiling had fallen on it but a good bit remained. Suddenly Carb had an inspiration. A Russian soldier was lolling nearby with a sledge hammer. Carb went over and borrowed it. When he returned he went to work on that desk with all the pent-up fury of his race. I did not stop him because it seemed to me to be a fitting end to the desk from which had been issued the most evil orders that ever cursed the human race. Further, I could not resist taking a few splinters away with me as a memento.

We then went down into the bunker in the courtyard and saw a sofa with blood on it; we wondered if it was Hitler's blood or Eva Braun's—or if it was from both. Here was where the Rat had been cornered and where he had written his will in which he blamed all his troubles on the German people—his master race. In it there was not the faintest intimation of any touch of nobility in his death—he died as he lived, a despicable, loathsome, demonic character. We came up out of that foul place to look around the courtyard and there we found a small hollowed out area where there had obviously been a fire. In my opinion it was almost certainly the place where Adolf and Eva's bodies had been burned.

In the autumn the commanding general of the French Zone awarded the Croix de Guerre to seven American officers: Richard Collins, H. G. Sheen, T. F. Bogart, Murray Black, Haakon Lindjord, T. Nichol, Jr., and myself at a gala occasion, outdoors, and the November cold was piercing. But the military music, and the embrace of a French general, together with the refreshments offered afterwards were enough to warm one's heart. We were the first American officers decorated by the French in Berlin. Sheen and Black are dead and I haven't seen Bogart since that autumn, but Collins, Lindjord, Nichol, and I with our wives have annual dinners together.

As the fall wore on, I became increasingly disturbed by the conditions which prevailed among our troops. The rapid disintegration of a great army is not a very pleasant spectacle. When the fighting ceased in the spring, we had the finest army in Europe that any nation had ever fielded. A few months later, elements of the same army stationed in Berlin were little more than a well-housed, well-clothed, and well-fed rabble. What had happened? Occupation duty among the ruins of a great city is in itself demoralizing enough, but that was not the chief cause. The chief sources of the disintegration were to be found in the attitudes of Generals Eisenhower and Clay and in the political pressures generated by the "Moms" of America. I doubt if there is a comparable instance in history of such damage being done to a nation's interests by the massive sentimental female cry of "bring the boys home."

The cry "bring the boys home" was a powerful contributing factor to the disintegration, but even then it could have been prevented to some extent if Eisenhower and Clay had taken the situation in hand. That is exactly what General Pershing did at the end of World War I. For some months after the Armistice he spent most of his time inspecting the divisions left in France. One never knew when the general was coming. For weeks on end in my regiment we "spit and polished" and maintained our discipline, for we knew that the eye of the general was on us. Finally, the great day came and he walked down every rank of us, even inspecting first lieutenants like me.

But after World War II the eye of General Eisenhower was not on his troops, nor was the eye of any other general. Eisenhower himself seemed to be preoccupied with high level diplomatic activity in Paris, London, and Moscow, and General Bradley had no responsibility for occupation troops. As far as Berlin was concerned, that responsibility was General Clay's. Clay was a first class administrator but was supremely disinterested in the psychological and moral welfare of the Americans under his command, and the general who was his chief administrative officer not only did not set a good example for his troops, but was known to everyone as setting a very poor example. The men knew that the eye of the general was not on them.

On Thanksgiving Day a regiment was paraded and General Clay addressed the troops. That speech provided the key to his attitude. It sounded like an old-fashioned Fourth of July oration. He said one thing that at first I did not understand, but suddenly I realized that it was the heart of his message. As I recall it, he said, "In thirty years' service I have never known the escutcheon of our army to be smeared or stained." In view of what was going on in Berlin at that time, one's first impulse was to laugh. Was the General so deaf or so blind that he did not know? Of course he knew. His message to the GI's as we understood it was not that he did not know, but that he did not intend to know.

Our office was naturally a place where one heard a great deal. But little of what we heard was mere gossip or rumor. Most of what we heard had a basis of fact. There were continuous reports of what was going on in the black market—of officers and men making thousands of dollars selling government property and of huge accounts being opened in Swiss banks. One indication of the size of the trade was the rapid rise in the volume of dollars being sent home via postal money orders. Our postmaster laughingly remarked to me one day that I was the only officer he knew who received any money via postal money order from home. I had arranged to have my entire pay remitted to Helen except for $25.00 a month which was all I needed. The demand for goods to sell on the black market was so great that one party of racketeering GI's actually stopped the supply train coming up to Berlin from the south and raided it.

What outraged me most was the disappearance of ordinary military discipline. Our building was guarded by a unit of the famous Eighty-second Airborne Division. There were times when I entered the front door in the morning to find the sentry asleep, or seated with his jacket open, reading the "Funnies," with his rifle on the floor. I reported such incidents in writing but it did no good, for no one was ever disciplined. Were these vagabond boys members of the great army I had known six months before? Some might have been replacements, but in any case the fault was not so much with them. The fault was with their commanding officers. Since these guards were our only protection, there was obviously little security for the office of the director of intelligence. That did not matter too much, as I doubt that the Russians would have found anything in our files that would have been of much use to them. What did matter was that the sleeping sentry symbolized the disintegration of the army.

In the course of the autumn, Bogart, the Executive Officer of ODI, had been transferred and I was designated to succeed him. I was extremely dissatisfied with the flow of intelligence into our office and prepared a major staff paper at General Conrad's request, making a series of recommendations intended to increase the quantity and quality of the flow and to effect other improvements in our structure and procedures. General Clay vetoed all of my recommendations. I was so concerned by his veto that on January 6, 1946, I went to discuss the intelligence situation with Robert Murphy, the State Department's representative at OMGUS. While we were talking, General Clay came in and I explained to him the reasons for my concern. My point was that we did not know what was going on in the Russian Zone. After a long discussion he said, "Why don't you ask the Russians?" and I realized that it was futile to pursue the matter further. As a result of my experience during that first year of occupation, I was not surprised when I learned years later that American officials in Berlin in August, 1961, had no advance warning that a wall was going to be built. The first intimation they had was when they learned that workmen were building it. Apparently General Clay's attitude of complete disinterestedness in doing whatever had to be done to establish an effective intelligence network in East Berlin had been inherited by his successors.

One of the principal preoccupations of our office that winter and spring was the staff work involved in the collection and sorting out of the vast piles of German government records and documents that our troops had overrun. The salvaging, assembly, and preservation of these archives was one of the great achievements of military government.

One of my concerns upon arrival in Berlin was to try to find trace of the father of an officer who had been one of our interrogators at "Dustbin." This man, Waldemar Hoeffding, an economist, had worked many years in our Berlin Embassy and had been transferred to the Swiss Embassy when it took over United States affairs at the time our relations with Germany were broken after Pearl Harbor. The problem was that Hoeffding had spent his childhood in Russia, where his father was employed as an engineer, and had come out on a Nansen passport after World War I. We ascertained that when the Russians came into Berlin he had gone into their headquarters to report his presence, and had never emerged.

Repeated high-level representations to the Russian general who headed the MVD, and finally an inquiry from General Clay to the top Russian commander, after a long silence, produced a report that they had never heard of the man. Shortly afterwards, in the fantastic way that things sometimes happened, a message reached us from Hoeffding: he was in a concentration camp near Dresden. The letter indicated a desperate plight; we decided to tell the Russians that we knew, and demand his release. Nothing happened.

Imagine our amazement when, some two years later, Helen looked up from her desk in the National Press Building, Washington, to find a little man in the doorway. The stranger said simply, "I am Hoeffding." He had come to thank me for my efforts.

His story was a melodrama. Our efforts apparently convinced the Russians that Hoeffding was important enough to figure in negotiations for an exchange. He was moved to a detention house in Potsdam. There, one evening when his guard was out of the room, Hoeffding pinched enough pfennigs for carfare into Berlin. He climbed out the window, dropped into the garden, scaled a high wooden fence whose cleats were inexplicably on the inside, walked to the nearest tram station, paid his fare with the stolen pfennigs, and twenty minutes later was in Berlin, a free man.

When I offered in the summer of 1945 to serve in Berlin for a year in order to help see the job through, it occurred to me that it would be a good idea to assemble a small group of young regular army officers and review with them some of our intelligence experiences in World War II so that they would be better prepared next time than our senior officers had been this time to appreciate the value of intelligence and to insure that it was properly organized. Our army had not in the past attached much importance to intelligence. The regimental intelligence officer was usually the sports officer and that was symbolic of the attitude throughout the service. No brilliant West Pointer ever thought of intelligence as the natural career for his talents. So I cabled my proposal to Washington and requested the assignment of several of the ablest available young regulars. In reply to this request a number of officers arrived, among whom were Henry Beukema (subsequently killed in a plane accident), the son of Colonel Herman Beukema of West Point, William A. Knowlton, and Michael J. L. Greene. A group consisting of these and several officers already members of our staff, including Haakon Lindjord, Wm. H. Crosson, Jr., and Thomas Nichol, Jr. formed a little seminar which met from time to time during the winter. Collins, Sheen, and I took turns describing, in the light of our experience during the war, what we considered important for them to know and to be thinking about.

It was very informal, with interruptions, questions, and a good bit of discussion. Apart from technical know-how, I stressed that the essential qualification of a good intelligence officer was a sense of priorities. In retrospect, I believe the organization of this seminar was the most useful thing I did in Berlin. I have lost track of some of the other officers but I know that both Greene and Crosson feel that they owed something to it. Greene is now a brigadier general and after serving as deputy commandant at the Army War College at Carlisle is presently on duty in Vietnam. Colonel Crosson, who before leaving the service was director of military intelligence at General Westmoreland's headquarters in Saigon until the spring of 1966, was generous enough to say that it was because of our little seminar that he knew what to do in Vietnam. Major General Knowlton is now superintendent at West Point.

While in Berlin I resumed contact with some of the churchmen I had known between wars. The first was Otto Dibelius, the Protestant bishop of Berlin. There was no place to eat except our officers' mess; it must have caused him some embarrassment to be seen fraternizing with the enemy so soon after the occupation of the city. As a result of the relationship thus established, I was able to help members of the Christian community in Berlin from time to time.

Among them was Reinold von Thadden, a Prussian Junker from Trieglaff in Pomerania. In 1929, Helen and I had made a strange visit to him and his wife Elizabeth, daughter of a Bavarian general, on their estate northeast of Berlin and just south of Stettin, where Reinold's Teutonic knight ancestor had settled in the eleventh century. Trieglaff (the place was named from a three-faced Slavonic god) bordered the lands of the Bismarcks; the two families were linked by a close friendship. Five hundred Slavs lived and labored on its acres. The farming was very primitive and reminded me in many ways of what a southern plantation would have been like before the Civil War. And we found that for these people Germany was not at peace in 1929 and had not been for more than fifteen years. During conversations, the words "in peacetime" occurred frequently; they meant the years prior to 1914.

I wrote my brother at the time:

The world in which these Prussian Junkers still live is so absolutely antithetical to ours that our whole experience there seemed to authenticate the war to me. Sooner or later the kind of democracy we believe in would of necessity clash with that. The world is not big enough to hold both.

First of all these people are intensely pious. As much so as our most pious fundamentalists at home. But Christ (as it seems to me) has just taken the place of one of their old pagan gods. They believe in authority over their fellow men which they have received and inherit by divine right. As a result their great estates are just about like the old southern plantations with white men instead of black as slaves. Further they believe that righteousness can be advanced by the force of arms—Mussolini is Dr. von Thadden's great ideal. The fact that one and the same person could have Mussolini as his hero and Jesus Christ as the object of his faith is evidence enough that the teaching of the New Testament has made little or no impress on the mentality of the Baltic peoples.

It was a most exhausting experience because they are so very cordial and we had to maintain an attitude of outward courtesy—while *boiling* within.

We boiled most during a conversation at the breakfast table where five small sons had joined us: Frau von Thadden remarked at one point that the proudest day of her life would be the day when her boys fell on the field of battle fighting for the Fatherland. Two decades later, three of those boys had been killed on the Russian front. A fourth had become a Roman Catholic priest, which for old-fashioned Protestant parents could seem far worse than falling in battle. Yet from this family and others like it came the only effective resistance to Hitler. Reinold's sister, headmistress of a girls' school in Frankfurt, was a member of the July 20, 1944, conspiracy to assassinate Hitler; garroted when it failed, she was the only woman in Germany condemned to suffer this horrible form of death.

After serving as military governor of Louvain, von Thadden went back to Trieglaff in the spring of 1945 to await the war's end; he had been unheard from since the Russians overran his castle.

Then one day Bishop Dibelius phoned me to say that von Thadden was at a certain Christian hostel. I immediately drove to the address and found a person who before the war had been a stockily built man weighing over two hundred pounds stretched out on a cot, too weak to stand. Little more than skin and bones, he weighed less than a hundred now. But he was alive.

Against orders, I supplied him some nourishing food; under Elizabeth's care, he regained strength, and told us his story. The Russians had taken him to Archangel and left him in a concentration camp there. He became desperately ill. For some reason known only to them, the Russians then turned him loose. By a series of miracles, he found his way back to Berlin.

When he was able to travel, I smuggled him and Elizabeth and their son Rudolph out to West Germany under a truckload of furniture; when the sergeant driver got to the British Zone he parked for the night in an official British army parking lot. There one of those poignant personal tragedies happened. The von Thaddens had with them in suitcases a few of their most precious possessions—the family Bible, photographs, mementos of Trieglaff and some jewelry. It never occurred to me that I would have to caution a Prussian officer to keep an eye on his luggage; as a Prussian officer, he probably felt that this was the sergeant's responsibility.

The von Thaddens left to sleep in a bunker; I never found out where the sergeant slept. But in the morning the suitcases were gone. Since it was an American truck, supplied by me, I felt that in some way the von Thaddens held me responsible.

Von Thadden's Pomeranian estate with its castle now belonged to Poland; the Poles had taken all his personal possessions including his large library. But one thing he had not lost: his faith. In the concentration camp, the Christians had improvised ecumenic services. The idea came to him to organize occasional Church Days (Kirchentäge) for all German Protestants. This he proceeded to do, drawing attendance from both sides of the Iron Curtain. Over the years, these occasions have been attended by millions and served as one of the important factors in the renewal of the German Protestant Church.

I have told Reinold jokingly that though he may be the father of the Kirchentäge I am the foster father, since if I had not been in Berlin in 1945 he might not have been around later to have the idea.

As spring came I realized that I had done all I could in Berlin, which was little enough, and that I could do no more. I had been told that I would be returned to the States in June and began to prepare for my departure.

While there had been a few pleasant moments during my year in Berlin, on the whole I felt that no one, thereafter, would have to tell me what Hades was like, for I had been there. What could Hades offer more than a scene of complete ruin and devastation of what had been one of the world's proudest capitals, together with the degradation of its surviving population as well as of the army that occupied it? I never wanted to go back to Germany again, though I realize now that the recovery and survival of West Berlin over the years has undoubtedly been a miracle due as much to the stoutheartedness of the Berliners themselves as to the firmness of the American, British, and French commanders toward the Russians.

When I think of General Clay, I think of a man who would have made one of the best of the Roman emperors prior to Constantine. My idea of a good general had been derived from men like Lee and Jackson. The comparison of these men with men like Clay was a measure of my disillusion with our performance in Berlin.

With the passage of time I had become more and more outraged by conditions in the Berlin command—little or no discipline, general demoralization among the troops, scandalous black market activities, and wholly inadequate intelligence available to our office. We knew that there was no point in calling these conditions to the attention of the local representative of the inspector general. He knew the situation as well as we did and had no intention of doing anything about it. Colonel Sheen saw the zone inspector general but could arouse no interest in his office. Then one day my friend, Dr. Thomas Parran, the surgeon general, showed up in Berlin. He asked me how things were going and I told him. When he returned to Washington, he reported what I had said to Senator J. M. Mead of New York who had succeeded to the chairmanship of Truman's committee on the National Defense Program.

The ship on which Collins and I were sent home was the *Victory Williams*. It was carrying a nondescript cargo of returnees. There were no officers' quarters and we shared a small room which looked as if it had been the ship's jail. I spent my time reading *Moby Dick*.

It was wonderful to be with Helen and the boys again, but my home-coming was marred that autumn by an aftermath of Berlin which in some respects was as distasteful as Berlin itself. Shortly after my return to Fairfax, George Meader, the chief counsel of Senator Mead's committee, phoned and asked me to come in to see him. After our talk he said that he wanted me to appear before the committee, that it would be a secret executive session and that he would clear my appearance with the Pentagon. This was done and my testimony was subsequently published in Part 42 of the report of that committee. One of the members of the committee who heard me was Senator Owen Brewster of Maine. Without asking the permission of the committee and without asking my permission (which he would not have received), he took my sworn testimony given in secret executive session and published it as an article over his own name in the issue of *Liberty* magazine for November 9, 1946. I had never experienced a more complete breach of faith. Up to that time I had thought of senators generally as persons of somewhat superior virtue. Now I knew better.

The reaction of the army was what might have been expected. Regulars never like to have their personal conduct and their management of affairs criticized, but it is especially obnoxious to them to have this done by a civilian officer like myself. So the fat was really in the fire. The inspector general, a man named Cook, questioned me for three hours. It was as much like a Gestapo interrogation as could take place in this country. Cook could not conceive of an officer reporting the conditions I had reported solely because of his love for the good name of the United States. He was convinced that, by giving my testimony, I was serving some sinister purpose. Consequently he was determined to "get me," and his interrogation was conducted with that sole end in view. His questions were not framed to elicit or clarify facts but were intended to trap me into making a damaging admission that could then be used against me. As there was nothing damaging for me to admit, the inspector failed

to achieve his purpose. But if he could not "get me" through interrogation in Washington, he concluded that he might still succeed in
"getting me" if he went to Berlin.

I have often wondered what it was that I came so near exposing
in my testimony to the Mead Committee. Whatever it was, Kenneth
Royall, the secretary of war, acted as if exposure of something or
other must at all cost be prevented. In the course of a few days he
sent Howard C. Petersen, his assistant secretary, and Cook, the
inspector general, to Berlin while George Meader went along to
make his own inspection. It was an impressive mission. Cook's investigation of me in Berlin was as thorough as his interrogation in
Washington and was conducted in the same spirit. Again he was
disappointed. He learned that I did not have a mistress living with
me in my billet, that I had not engaged in black market activity, that
I was anti-Communist and that I had a good record as executive
officer of ODI. It was all very puzzling. But he still had to "get me."
So when he issued his report, he said that I had made statements
which raised questions regarding my integrity as an officer, without
saying what the statements were, and without preferring charges.
This was the final insult and indignity. It was the first time in my
life anybody had questioned my integrity, and I considered asking
for a court-martial in order to bring the entire matter out into the
open. But I was thoroughly sick of the whole business and wisely
decided to turn to affairs in Virginia. Besides I had the satisfaction of
knowing that, as a result of my testimony, the chief administrative
officer in Berlin, whose policy of permissiveness had contributed so
directly to creating the mess there, had been summarily relieved of
his command, put on a plane, and shipped home.

Further, I felt that subsequent events more than vindicated me,
both personally and officially. The U.S. Military Academy at West
Point, over the strenuous objection of Kenneth Royall, asked me to
come up and speak to the Corps of Cadets on April 27, 1947. The
subject assigned me was "Military Government in Occupied Areas,"
which gave me an excellent opportunity to talk about character in
the army. Royall could not afford to press his objection too far, because the Academy had taken a dim view of Royall's efforts to
bring to the attention of the cadets, while he was secretary of war, a
life insurance company in North Carolina in which he was interested.

Later I had an even more impressive vindication. At the time of
the football scandal at West Point, President Truman appointed me
and Father John A. Flynn of Brooklyn to the Academy's Board of

Visitors. It was hoped that we could find out what went wrong and recommend measures that might help to avoid a repetition. The cause was clear enough. Earl Blaik was both football coach and director of athletics. The combination of these two posts in the hands of one person gave that person more power over the lives of the cadets than any other individual not excepting the superintendent himself. Blaik's natural ambition was to have the best team in America—and in any event to beat Notre Dame. To accomplish this purpose he required so many hours each day from members of the football squad that they did not have time left to prepare their classwork. The academy's academic standards were high. If a cadet could not maintain the grades required, he was dismissed. So several members of the squad were faced with the alternative of probably having to leave or cheating in the classroom. They chose to cheat, and the cheating spread until it involved ninety-one cadets. Then a glorious thing happened—one of the finest hours in the history of our army. One day, two or three cadets asked permission to see the superintendent. They reported to him what had been going on and said that the corps had decided that unless those ninety-one cadets were dismissed, the whole corps would leave West Point. The honor of the academy had been saved by the cadets themselves.

The Board of Visitors upon completion of its inquiry, recommended two things: (1) that the posts of football coach and director of athletics be separated and given to two different individuals and (2) that a simple course in ethics be given to new men on their arrival at the Academy.

These recommendations had an amusing aftermath. When Eisenhower became president, he appointed Lucius Clay to the board and sent Clay a letter expressing the hope that the board would rehabilitate Blaik. Since it had not occurred to us that we had done anything to make rehabilitation necessary, we ignored the letter. During the course of that same meeting, Clay asked us to rescind our action regarding the establishment of an elementary ethics course since he said that he did not see what that had to do with the training of an officer. I acidly replied that some of our greatest generals (I was thinking of Lee and Jackson and Marshall) had attached importance to an officer's familiarity with ethics. In retrospect it has always seemed to me that this incident threw quite a bit of light on the reason for conditions in Berlin while General Clay was in command there.

XIII ⟋ The Gentleman
from Fairfax

During the decade of the thirties before World War II I led a double life. I went all over the world in the interest of the ecumenic movement and thereafter went pretty much all over the United States, first on behalf of the National Policy Committee, and then on behalf of the Council on Foreign Relations, organizing committees on foreign relations from my office in New York. At the same time I was also leading a full life in Virginia. Interweaving the latter with my activities abroad in the interest of maintaining chronological sequence would be very confusing to the reader. Hence, at the risk of defying chronology, it seems preferable to tell about political activities in Virginia consecutively, and so we will now retrace our steps and pick up threads of the other half of my existence.

I had always been a Democrat. When I settled in New York in 1923, I registered to vote and voted the straight Tammany ticket as long as I was there. At that time, my interest in politics was that of a fascinated spectator, but two experiences left impressions that affected my later life.

In the summer of 1924, I secured a gallery ticket in the old Madison Square Garden where the Democratic National Convention was exhausting itself in the contest between the Catholic "wet," Al Smith, and the Protestant "dry," Senator McAdoo, eventually resolved by the nomination of the Wall Street lawyer, John W. Davis, whom Calvin Coolidge annihilated in November. But likewise at stake was the policy of the Democratic party in regard both to the League of Nations and to the Ku Klux Klan, and the consideration of these produced two unforgettable episodes.

The first was the plea of Newton D. Baker for adoption of a resolution favoring entry into the League of Nations. Baker, as Wilson's former secretary of war, felt that the dead president's mantle had fallen upon his shoulders. I have heard five or six truly great speeches during the past fifty years—among the greatest were Franklin Roosevelt's "The only thing we have to fear is fear itself," Alben Barkley's call to action at the Philadelphia Democratic convention in 1948, and John F. Kennedy's inaugural. But from the standpoint of moral and emotional content Newton Baker's was the greatest of all. As he approached the podium, he knew that the Democratic party was going to reject Wilson and the league, but the only effect of that knowledge was to endow him with almost superhuman powers of speech. I can still feel the thrill that passed through me and through that vast throng at his opening sentence. "As I stand here the shadow of one of the greatest men of all the ages falls across this rostrum." Most convention speeches are thoroughly unreal—prepared by ghost writers to create ghost images. This one was real; the soul and conscience of a man crying out to the American people like the prophets of old "mend your ways before it is too late." I doubt if there has ever been such a moment in a convention. Irish politicians who shortly thereafter would be casting their votes against the resolution, stood with tears pouring down their cheeks. My friend, Whitney H. Shepardson, a former Rhodes scholar who had been a young secretary at the Versailles Peace Conference, was sitting in Walter Lippmann's box and when Baker concluded, the emotional tension was so great that Shepardson fainted dead away. The Democratic party could kill Baker's resolution but it could not kill the idea which he embodied that day. Twenty years later, after another world war and infinite human suffering, its time came.

The second episode of high drama was even more important in a domestic sense and reflected, as if in anticipation, the soul-searching of the nation that would take place during the next half-century. Some Smith supporter had introduced a resolution denouncing the Ku Klux Klan. The McAdoo forces were opposed to it since they were relying on white Protestant support. A preliminary vote had indicated that the resolution could be passed by a narrow margin and so McAdoo persuaded William Jennings Bryan to take the platform in a last-ditch attempt to defeat it. It was my first experience of complete political disillusionment. Here was the great Populist leader, the man my father had so much admired, the man whom Wilson made his secretary of state, and here he was appealing to the bigotry and race prejudice of his audience through a smoke screen of dishonest sophistry. The spectacle nauseated me. But Bryan knew his audience and he accomplished what he had been assigned to do. The curtain, however, had not been rung down. The play was not yet over. There was to be one more act—the greatest and most thrilling of all. The applause had scarcely died away when a young man named Andrew C. Erwin of Athens, Georgia, was seen climbing onto the platform. Since he was a member of the Georgia delegation, it was assumed that he would continue the attack on the resolution. However, as soon as he began to speak, it was obvious that his purpose was the exact opposite. He rose to support the resolution and to deliver the most scathing and devastating attack on the Klan I had ever heard. The effect was electric. When he finished it seemed certain the resolution would pass. The northern delegates became delirious in their enthusiasm and a spontaneous march of the standards was organized. The standards moved toward the Georgia delegation to honor the courage of the young southerner from Athens who had dared to reply to Bryan, dared to defy the convictions of many of his fellow-southerners, and dared to appeal to the conscience of the nation. Then just at the moment of triumph disaster struck like a bolt of lightning. The Yankee band broke into "Marching Through Georgia." This was only sixty years after Sherman himself had actually marched through Georgia laying it waste from end to end. The hearts of the southern delegates froze. Then the roll was called and you could hear the shift taking place. In every southern state a few votes here and a few votes there that had been cast for the resolution were changed to "No." When the results were tallied, out of approximately 1300 votes the resolution was defeated by something like 1½ or 2½ votes.

These impressions stayed with me as I became an active participant in politics.

Shortly after settling at Fairfax in the autumn of 1930 we were introduced to R. Walton Moore, then Congressman from Virginia's old Eighth District, and the members of his extensive family. He was a bachelor but he had numerous sisters and nieces, one of the latter being married to Shield McCandlish, an attorney, who became my closest friend shortly before his premature death. Mr. Moore himself was universally regarded as Fairfax's most distinguished citizen, and there was a saying around the county that everyone in that neighborhood was either "Moore or less." At the time of the Civil War, Mr. Moore's father, Tom Moore, was an ardent Confederate and had been equally dominant in the area. However, along the Chain Bridge road to the north of our house, people in those days were more apt to be in sympathy with the Union. Some of them even read Horace Greeley's *New York Tribune*. As the prospect of war grew more menacing, Tom Moore had told these people to stop subscribing to the *Tribune* or to "git out." They refused to "git" and that established the line in our county between North and South. It ran practically through our dining room table with Helen, of course, seated to the north and I to the south.

Mr. Moore was an ardent admirer of George Mason, author of the Revolutionary Bill of Rights, and as Congressman had been on what was then considered the liberal side of the Democratic party. He was not a member of the political organization controlled by Harry Flood Byrd and became increasingly unsympathetic to Byrd's views. In 1930, Mr. Moore decided not to offer for re-election and shortly after the inauguration of the New Deal his close friend, Cordell Hull, who had become secretary of state, appointed him to the post of counselor of the State Department which he held until shortly before his death.

"Uncle Walton," as I like to think of Mr. Moore, was no ordinary politician. He was one of the last figures of the "ancient regime" in Virginia—trained in the classics, well-read, sophisticated, and wise, with the manners of a courtly gentleman. Shortly after we moved into our new home at Pickens Hill, a note was left at the door. It was from Mr. Moore, welcoming us to the community, and the note contained a quotation from Pliny on the beauties of friendship. Fairfax County then had only 25,000 inhabitants, and newcomers like ourselves were rare and welcome. Now with a population of almost 500,000 a new person moving into the county is a "nemo" lost in the faceless mass except to the realtors who profit by his arrival. Years later I was much moved when I was told by someone who had read Mr. Moore's diaries that he had thought of me as his political heir apparent. I did not realize that at the time, but I was well aware that when he died there was no one left in Virginia of his stature whose advice and assistance I could seek.

It would be difficult, if not impossible, for a recent suburban settler in Fairfax County to realize what that county was like only forty years ago. In 1930, it was almost as rural as it had been at the time of the War between the States. The few main highways had been hard-surfaced for less than a decade, and asphalt tops had been put down on the old roads just as they were with little straightening out or grading. Because of the winding and lolloping character of these ancient rights of way the legal speed limit for cars in those days was thirty-five miles an hour. Most of the side roads were still plain dirt, and where the dirt was clay they were impassable for cars during much of the winter.

The arable area of the county south of the Potomac and west of Falls Church was an important part of the Washington milk shed— dairy farming was the most profitable form of agriculture—profitable in terms of that day, not ours. As a result, the most influential citizens in the various local communities were apt to be dairy farmers. They exercised a decisive influence on politics—particularly in the choice of members of the county Board of Supervisors and of the county's single representative in the House of Delegates of the Virginia General Assembly. The more prosperous farmers of the northern part of the county belonged to the National Grange, which was considered an elite organization.

Helen had always been interested in farming and so she shortly acquired sixty additional acres adjoining our original twenty-acre plot, and using this land and the barn which came with it she raised purebred guernsey heifers to sell to neighboring dairymen as replacement stock for their herds. Worther Smith, the husband of our cook, was her farmer, and her venture succeeded so well that she made a slight annual profit as long as we lived there. Our boys, as they grew old enough, had responsibilities for chickens, garden, animals, and a small milk route, and learned much from their experience of success and failure.

But all this is now a thing of the past. The farm is gone; there are eight houses on what was once one of Helen's pastures, and what happened to her farm has happened to thousands of others. Where cattle once grazed, high-rise apartments have risen and "new towns" have obliterated woodlands. The Washington milk shed has been pushed west and south into adjoining counties which in their turn are beginning to be cannibalized by the spread of megalopolis.

The fantastic change that has taken place in the character of Fairfax County is best illustrated by Springfield. Forty years ago there was a tiny station of this name on the rail line that passed through on its way south. The only important residence that I remember was the home of Mr. Brookfield, the rural mail carrier, who dressed like a nineteenth-century country gentleman with his spectacles on a black silk ribbon around his neck; his wife was the sister of Congressman Howard Smith. Now Springfield has a huge shopping center and a population approaching 60,000—it has registered a gain of 500 percent in the past ten years.

The whole south part of the county, which used to be marginal land covered with a tangle of scrub, is now a rapidly developing region where tens of thousands of suburbanites live while working in Washington. The old narrow winding dirt roads have given place to massive thruways that even threaten the lands of George Washington and George Mason.

In 1930, Fairfax City was a sleepy little town whose principal business centered in the Court House. The leading citizens were lawyers; most of them were drawn from or else connected by marriage with old families like the Moores, the Barbours, the Keiths, the Rusts, the Picketts, and the Farrs. It seems strange in retrospect that so many lawyers could have lived so well in such a small community. But Fairfax is no longer small. Today it is an incorporated city and more people live within its limits than lived in the entire county forty years ago when we settled there.

Living at Pickens Hill offered us an opportunity to begin to participate in local affairs. I had not had that opportunity before and greatly enjoyed taking advantage of it. I became a member of Rotary and served as president of the County Chamber of Commerce. When a county community chest was organized, I was asked to become chairman of its first campaign for funds.

In due course I acquired not only a variety of local interests but also interests in adjoining states. Richard F. Cleveland, the Baltimore attorney who worked with me in organizing the National Policy Committee, was chairman of the board of St. John's College in Annapolis. In the mid-thirties that ancient and honorable institution (the third oldest college in the country) had fallen on evil days. Its president was Amos Woodcock, a brigadier general in the National Guard who had acquired some notoriety through his unusual exploits during maneuvers. According to the *New York Times*, the referee had declared him dead during one annual maneuver and captured during the one that followed. This versatile man assumed a role of unctuous piety when appearing before the board of the college, but the chairman of the board had been reliably informed that moral conditions in the dormitories left much to be desired. Further, under Woodcock's benevolent rule, the college had become practically bankrupt having accumulated a large debt and being entirely without endowment. It was obvious that the college would have to close down unless drastic remedies could be devised to insure a new lease on life.

At this juncture Cleveland asked me if I would join him on the board to see if together we could do anything to save the college. I agreed and it soon became obvious that the first thing we had to do was to fire the president. Since Woodcock would not resign, it fell to my lot to move in the board for the termination of his appointment on such and such a date, and there was unanimous concurrence. A rather gruesome aftermath of this was that when the general's quarters in the Bryce House, where he lived from time to time, were cleaned out, it was discovered that he had installed an army cot in one of the most beautiful colonial rooms in America and that his furniture consisted of the cot and a pile of empty tin cans in the corner.

We had cleared our first hurdle, but much higher ones remained. The situation of the college seemed almost hopeless and we were at our wits' end during the winter of 1936–37. The following spring I happened to attend a conference on education at the Episcopal Theological Seminary in Alexandria and found that Stringfellow Barr was also there. I had known Barr at Oxford and learned that he and Scott Buchanan were then working with the Robert Hutchins Committee on Liberal Arts at the University of Chicago. This gave me an idea. Why should not he and Buchanan come to St. John's and try out their ideas there? Negotiations continued for several weeks. Barr wanted Hutchins to become president, but Hutchins was not interested. Further, he was opposed to Barr and Buchanan going to Annapolis. However, Cleveland and I persuaded our board to invite Barr to become president, with Buchanan as dean, giving them complete freedom to install the kind of four-year required liberal arts course in which they believed. We then went to Chicago with this invitation and in the end secured an acceptance in spite of Hutchins's opposition. Thus, in the autumn of 1937, the Great Books Program was launched at St. John's and the college was saved.

That same year, 1937, saw my entrance into Virginia politics. Ever since returning from Europe in 1930 I had been hoping that some day I would be able to go down into the arena and fight for some of the things that had come to mean so much to me and about which I had talked so much while working for the World's Student

Christian Federation. I had even discussed with Mr. Moore the desirability of my running against Howard Smith, who had succeeded him in the Congress, but he discouraged me on the ground that I had not yet lived in the district long enough. However, the Fairfax seat in the Virginia House of Delegates became vacant through death after the 1936 assembly session and in due course, with Judge Moore's encouragement, I announced for this seat in the Democratic primary of July, 1937. Up to that time nomination in the primary was usually tantamount to election. Further, only a few more than two thousand people voted and the expense of running for office was minimal. The *Richmond Times-Dispatch* of May 7 welcomed my announcement, headlining its leading editorial: "An Ideal Candidate."

The thought of representing Mr. Washington's county and of occupying the seat once occupied by Mr. George Mason thrilled me, and I was determined to win. It was the first time in my life I had ever campaigned, and I thoroughly enjoyed it. My candidacy attracted the support of a number of young men who subsequently entered politics themselves and over the years converted the county to a more progressive and liberal outlook. One of my first political lieutenants was a recent graduate of Georgetown University Law School, John A. K. Donovan, who eventually served as a state senator and cast one of the decisive votes against "massive resistance." Among others were Omer L. Hirst, now a state senator, and Edwin Lynch and John Webb who became delegates. Working with these I began to learn the art of political organization and the way to win elections. But the man from whom I learned most was Frank Gicker who was my agent in the McLean precinct. Though that was a conservative community, Frank always carried it for me. He made it a habit to arrive at the polling place (the Fire House) before the polls opened and to stay there until after the polls closed. I can see him now, standing on the bank before the entrance to the Fire House, with voting list in hand, checking off one by one all those who entered. By mid-afternoon he knew how many votes he needed and he had two cars standing by ready to bring to the polls those who had not yet voted and were sure to vote for me.

It happened that my opponent in the 1937 primary was not a particularly strong candidate. The worst he could say about me was that I was a "western man" (meaning that I had come from the Valley of Virginia 150 miles to the west) and that I had not attended the local schools as he had done. So I became "The Gentleman from Fairfax," receiving about 60 percent of the vote in the primary and with no opposition in the general election.

Until recently the General Assembly of Virginia met every two years for sixty days, beginning early in January of even years. At that time the house (unlike the senate) was still a place where exciting debates took place occasionally on fundamental questions of government policy and procedures. Further, I have seen the course of debate in the house change the opinions of its members as the force of fact and the appeal to reason tipped the scales in their minds one way or the other. Nothing is so satisfying as to make a speech which does just that. The art of public speaking (taught me by my father) is one of the few skills I possess, and the practice of it used to be my greatest pleasure.

James H. Price was governor of Virginia at that time. He was generally in sympathy with Federal New Deal legislation and in due course he and I became aware that we were associates in a common cause. When I arrived in Richmond, I put up at Rueger's Hotel because it was near the Capitol, was not expensive, and was not as noisy as the Richmond where most of the delegates stayed. The drawback was that I was rather isolated from the other members, but by the end of my second term this came to be somewhat of an advantage. In January, 1938, I was received by everyone with the greatest friendliness and courtesy. The lines had not yet been sharply drawn among members of the assembly between those who favored and those who violently opposed the New Deal, and Price was still an honored, if somewhat independent, member of the Byrd Organization. The speaker of the house was Ashton Dovell of Williamsburg. Judged by competence, technique, appearance, and deportment, he was undoubtedly one of the most impressive speakers the Virginia house has had in this century. Further, he possessed the self-assurance and sense of authority which one instinctively associated with royal governors before the Revolution. I respected him very much.

It is the custom of the general assembly to hold a special session in the restored Capitol at Williamsburg for one day during its regular biennial session. The procedure is that after the invocation and announcements, a formal resolution is presented organizing the meeting and a junior member of the house who has been designated in advance by the speaker seconds this resolution with a brief speech. The speaker had asked me to be the seconder at the 1938 special session, and, on February 12, in the restored hall of the House of Burgesses I spoke as follows:

Mr. Speaker and Gentlemen of the House:

To come to this place is to enter into communion with the spirits of the past. It requires but little imagination to sense the presence of those giant-like figures who have gone before us in this House, beside whom we seem dwarfed indeed. . . .

As I reflect this morning on the list of representatives from Fairfax County one name especially comes to mind, the name of Mr. George Mason of Gunston Hall; Mason the Constitutionalist (perhaps the greatest Constitutionalist America has yet produced), and the inspired author of our immortal Declaration of Rights which was presented and adopted in this very village in the late spring and early summer of 1776. I like to think of that Declaration as the Magna Carta of the Democratic Party in this State.

Perhaps the high point of my speech was when I said:

I particularly like to recall that in enumerating the natural rights of every citizen Mr. Mason added to "life, liberty and the pursuit of happiness" the *"means* of acquiring and possessing property," the clear implication being that where those "means" do not exist, it is the business of government to create them.

There, gentlemen, is a touch-stone for our economic policy—a goal for our statesmanship. It is a goal which is perhaps further from being realized now than 162 years ago, but it is a goal toward which we must strive.

Without quite realizing it at the time, I had thrown down the gauge of battle to the Byrd Organization and had defined the issues of the contest. However, since the distinction between supporters and opponents of the "Organization" was still quite vague, I found it possible to do a number of things in 1938 that were not at all possible in the session of 1940. It was obvious that the governor's measures needed more support if they were to be approved by the assembly, and so I organized a series of weekly dinners attended by fifteen or twenty of the most influential members of the house where legislative proposals could be examined and where views could be freely exchanged. Among those who came were several Organization stalwarts, including Blackburn Moore who eventually emerged as Byrd's most powerful and faithful lieutenant and who served longer as speaker than anyone else had ever done. His term covered the whole period through the heyday to the decline and fall of the Byrd Organization.

The second most decisive moment in my life occurred toward the end of the 1938 session. Harry Carter Stuart was a senator from Russell County in Southwest Virginia. He was a relative of that great cavalry officer, J. E. B. Stuart, and nephew of a former governor. Senator Stuart was one of the largest land owners in Virginia and lived in baronial style in a pre-Civil War columned mansion. One day he invited me to a small cocktail party in his suite at the Jefferson Hotel which included several very charming Richmond ladies. During the course of the party he called me out into the hallway for a private word. It seemed that he had a personal message from Senator Byrd for me. The message said in effect that the senator had been impressed by what I had been doing in the house, considered me a coming man, and felt that I could have a successful career leading to the highest offices in Virginia politics if I joined him. He said Senator Byrd invited me to do so. I knew instinctively and without reflection what I had to say in reply. I asked Harry Stuart to present my compliments to the senator and tell him that I deeply appreciated his invitation but that I felt I could serve Virginia better in other ways. This incident settled for all time my relations with Harry Byrd. It was probably the only refusal he had ever received to such an invitation. Being the kind of man he was, he could not understand my reasons for declining, nor would he forget or forgive.

A delightful incident of that winter was my meeting the venerable Henry T. Wickham, senator from Caroline County and president pro tem of the senate. Seventy years before, he had been a student at Washington and Lee during the presidency of Robert E. Lee. He was one of the most authentic and impressive pre-Civil War types I had ever seen, truly Olympian in appearance, and I approached him with some awe. When I introduced myself, he misunderstood my middle name, thinking I said "Pickett." In spite of my putting him right, his mind started spinning in the direction of his first assumption. "Do you know where George Pickett was during that charge of his at Gettysburg?" he asked. Since I hadn't the slightest notion, Senator Wickham observed disdainfully, "Hiding behind a hay stack." It occurred to me that after all a general had to have a post of command somewhere, but bitter reminiscences would not permit the old man to stop.

In order to shift our conversation to more pleasant matters, I told Senator Wickham that my mother was Flora McElwee from Lexington and suggested that he might have known the family while he was a student there. "Are you a nephew of Annie McElwee?" he asked. When I assured him that that was indeed the case, he launched into a charming story about Miss Annie's cat to whom he had composed an ode in Greek. It seemed that he had been deeply devoted to Annie who could not have been more than fifteen at the time, and the recollections of her over all those years warmed his heart and mellowed his mind.

Governor Price was sufficiently pleased with my performance during that session to put me on his Advisory Legislative Council and also to appoint me to the board of William and Mary College.

The following August I was invited to become a sponsor of and to attend a Southern Conference for Human Welfare to be held in Birmingham, Alabama, November 20–23, 1938. This conference was organized by a group which was dissatisfied with the moderate and rational approach of our Southern Policy Committee and which included members who were in sympathy with the far left. It seemed important for me to keep track of these new developments in the South and so I accepted, at the same time writing Brooks Hays, on September 13, that "we do not want the Southern Policy Committee to become organizationally involved in an enterprise of this kind." The facade of the temporary committee calling the conference could not have been more respectable, with such sponsors listed on the letterhead as Luther Patrick, Sam Roper and Lister Hill of Alabama, and Brooks Hays of Arkansas. During the autumn, the governor of Alabama, Bibb Graves, sent invitations to the other southern governors to attend. When Governor Price received his invitation, he asked me to go in his stead as the official representative of the Commonwealth of Virginia and gave me a commission to this effect dated November 17, 1938. Upon arriving in Birmingham I found that a thousand delegates had assembled from every part of the South. Among them were such distinguished citizens as Governor Graves of Alabama, Governor-elect Burnett Maybank of South Carolina, Senator Bankhead of Alabama, Barry Bingham of Kentucky, John Temple Graves the columnist, and Justice Hugo Black. Finally Mrs. Franklin D. Roosevelt had come down from Washington to provide the conference with the highest possible patronage. It seemed that the organizers had attached importance to my presence because I was informed that I had been appointed chairman of the Resolutions Committee and a member of both the Organization Committee and the Awards Committee.

However, before the end of the first day serious doubts began to disturb me. It became obvious at once that the people who were really pulling the strings were not those who appeared in public. Further, I noticed in the audience a man named Burke, husband of Alice Burke of Richmond. I did not know her, but she had once been pointed out to me in the lobby of the House of Delegates as secretary of the Communist party in Virginia. Other persons also appeared whose presence increased my sense of disquiet. Consequently I declined to serve as chairman of the Resolutions Committee and left Birmingham a day and a half before the end of the conference prior to the addresses of Mrs. Roosevelt and Hugo Black. After my departure I was elected one of the permanent vice-presidents of the continuing organization. When I heard of this, I immediately wired my refusal to accept a vice-presidency, but in spite of that my name was listed as such in the Conference Report, along with the names of Luther Patrick, Brooks Hays, Claude Pepper, Tarleton Collier, Barry Bingham, Burnett Maybank, and others. On November 25, I wrote Brooks Hays:

I am unwilling to collaborate with members of the Communist Party in establishing a public agency whose membership is to include both Communists and non-Communists. I will defend to the limit the right of free speech for the Communists, but I will not occupy jointly with them positions of responsibility in the same organization. My reasons are obvious. I know that their talk about the Bill of Rights is the sheerest hypocrisy and that the moment they secured control the rights which I want for them would be instantly denied me.

The organization of the Southern Conference for Human Welfare was an unmitigated disaster for the South. It was eventually taken over by left wingers, it accomplished nothing of any value during its years of existence, and it effectively sabotaged the work of the Southern Policy Committee. Further, association with it, however tenuous and transitory as mine was, dogged me as well as many other southerners through the McCarthy era.

Frank Graham unwisely accepted the chairmanship of the continuing organization, and this played a part in his 1950 defeat for nomination to the U.S. Senate, after which he took a post with the United Nations and moved to New York, to the great loss of North Carolina and the whole South.

In my case thirteen years elapsed before my day and a half's presence at Birmingham caused me serious trouble. While I was working for the State Department in 1951, I became aware that the F.B.I. was giving me the most thorough going over it had ever done, and I ascertained that interest centered on the Birmingham Conference.

Since it was known that I was going to run against Harry Byrd for the Senate in 1952, it was obvious that someone was fishing for material to use against me. So I phoned the White House and asked them to make an appointment for me with Edgar Hoover. A deputy saw me and I gave him a complete dossier with copies of my Commission from the Commonwealth of Virginia and of the correspondence describing my precipitate departure from the conference and my rejection of any connection with the continuing organization. I begged him to add these documents to my file for future reference. His acid comment was "you certainly are lucky to have saved these!" My bitter reaction was "how many citizens as innocent as I would not have saved their papers."

I have long felt that the files of the F.B.I., filled with mountains of trash as they are, could, in the wrong hands, destroy this Republic.

As a member of the Governor's Advisory Legislative Council since 1938, I had been assigned the task of preparing legislation to establish a merit system for employees of the state government. It was a pleasant assignment. The council had appointed a Committee on Personnel Administration to work with me whose membership included Virginius Dabney of the *Times-Dispatch*, Rowland Egger of the University of Virginia, Warner Moss of William and Mary, and several other able individuals. We spent nearly two years preparing our report of which we were rather proud, since experts in the field regarded the merit system which we recommended as the best proposed for adoption by any state up to that time.

Similarly, other members of the council were preparing a wide variety of measures at the governor's request for introduction at the 1940 session of the general assembly. Among these were abolition of the medieval fee system for sheriffs; changes in the penal system, including establishment of probation and parole; a substantial increase in teachers' salaries with provision for their retirement, and a number of other forward looking proposals. Taken as a whole, Governor Price's program was the most progressive that had been prepared by any governor in this century. It is true that Harry Flood Byrd had been one of Virginia's best governors during 1926–1930, but he was concerned primarily with the structure of government and with establishing a modern road system to get the farmers out of the mud. He had done just that and the farmers never forgot their debt of gratitude to him. Governor Byrd also had been responsible for the enactment of an antilynching law in Virginia—

the only one enacted by any southern state. But apart from that he showed no interest in human welfare—in education or in social legislation.

In the summer of 1939, I had no opposition in the Democratic primary, but danger signals flashed in the general election. Richard Farr, a respected Republican lawyer at the Court House, had conducted a quiet campaign and came within a couple of hundred votes of defeating me. The showing he made convinced him that next time he had a good chance of winning.

As the 1940 session of the assembly approached, one would have supposed that it would have been thoroughly constructive and that as a result of its work, Virginia would begin to move forward along the path of progress. We had a good governor and the measures to implement his recommendations had all been drafted. I had learned the ropes in the first session and was prepared to exert myself to the limit in the second. Instead of accomplishment, however, nothing awaited the governor's program but frustration and defeat.

The tragedy of Virginia, and even of the South, during 1940–60, resulted from the fact that shortly after the inauguration of Franklin Roosevelt in 1933, Harry Byrd as the junior senator from Virginia who had originally supported Mr. Roosevelt for the nomination, turned against the president and over the years since had become more and more intransigent and vindictive in his opposition. Governor Price, on the other hand, as a moderate, was generally in favor of the New Deal. Senator Byrd profoundly resented this challenge to his supremacy in the Commonwealth and word went down to his lieutenants in the legislature that all of the governor's principal proposals were to be torpedoed and sunk without trace so that he would not get credit for anything. This was actually done and Price died shortly after completing his term, surely of a broken heart.

The bitter irony was that in January, 1942, when Colgate Darden became the Organization's new governor, he had ready made for him a complete package of reform legislation prepared by Price's lieutenants two years earlier. He wisely reintroduced these measures; they were all passed and his administration naturally got full credit for our labors.

But to return to the session of the House of Delegates in 1940; my experience with the Merit System Bill illustrated the cynical ruthlessness with which all of Price's proposals were defeated. The governor's supporters in the house numbered 35 or 40. Byrd controlled

55 or 60 delegates. The speaker had been promised high rewards if he presided efficiently over the executions. He did so, but he was never rewarded and died a disappointed man. Merit had nothing whatever to do with the way the majority voted. It was politics in its rawest, most naked, and most brutal form. When House Bill 111 to establish a system of personnel administration for the Commonwealth (called the Merit System) came up on the calendar for final vote on March 5, the speaker allowed five minutes in all for consideration and discussion of an intricate measure that had required two years to prepare. I decided to go down with flag flying and band playing, so I took the center aisle and used up three minutes in explaining the bill before asking for questions. There were none. I resumed my seat. The vote was called for, and the speaker quietly reached for the red button to show "the boys" how to vote. There were 47 Nays and 35 Yeas. I was touched two years later when I was no longer in the house but working for OSS to receive a letter from Bernard Miller of Culpeper saying that everyone missed me so and that he had been asked to introduce the Merit System Bill that year so that it would still be known as the Miller Bill!

In spite of the general mood of destructiveness that had settled over the assembly, I enjoyed a number of personal triumphs. In the course of debates in the house I made a speech one day on a subject which I have quite forgotten. When I sat down I noticed that the speaker, Ashton Dovell, was scribbling something on a scrap of paper which he handed to a page and directed him to me. That scrap of paper is before me as I write. It reads: "Well, you were closer to Madison just now than any member has been during the session—Speaker." Few compliments that I have ever received thrilled me as much as this one did.

But my greatest triumph had to do with the discharge of the Committee on Roads from further consideration of a resolution entitled "Citizens Road League of Virginia." This resolution had authorized an inquiry into the sources of revenue of a so-called "citizens" league whose representatives were extremely busy lobbying on behalf of legislation favorable to road construction firms. Some of us who resented the subterfuge of the league's name decided to have a little fun unmasking it. Our resolution had been bottled up in the all-powerful Roads Committee which was considered untouchable, and we could not pry it out. So one day, with righteous indignation, I took the floor and made the speech of my life requesting that the committee be discharged. The house agreed 59 to 28. It was quite a moment for me, as I was told by one of the clerks of the house that that committee had not been discharged before in the memory of anyone around the capitol. I loved those Virginians. If "the word" had not come down, reason and right were almost sure to win. We inquired into the affairs of the league, published the names of the road construction firms which were supporting it, together with the amounts of their donations, and so rendered the league wholly innocuous for that season, at any rate.

The accomplishment of the 1940 session which I look back upon with the greatest satisfaction, however, was killing the Heller Bill. This bill, named for the senator from Botetourt County who introduced it, provided that the custodians of all public buildings in Virginia should deny the use of those buildings to any person who might advocate the overthrow of the government of the United States by force. The measure was in the spirit of Joe McCarthy a decade before he came on the scene. It breezed through the senate without a dissenting vote. When it came over to the house, I enjoyed having a field day with it, pointing out its many absurdities, asking whether "custodian" could be confused with "janitor," and reminding the members of the house that under the terms of the bill neither Robert E. Lee nor Stonewall Jackson would be allowed to speak in a single Virginia courthouse. I finished by moving that the bill be sent back to committee and the house agreed. But toward the end of the session its sponsors brought it out of committee again after hearings had been held.

David K. E. Bruce was magnificent during those hearings. At that time he was a Virginian and was serving as delegate from Charlotte County. David did not enjoy public speaking and I can see him now standing before the committee with pale face holding in his hands, which were shaking just a bit, a volume containing some of Mr. Jefferson's letters. He called the attention of the committee to the letter which Jefferson had written to a Mr. Smith and with deep feeling read a sentence which said that from time to time the tree of liberty would have to be fertilized by the blood of patriots. In spite of our efforts the bill passed the house on the final day of the session. However, that was not the last word. David and I went to the governor and persuaded him to veto it.

There were, of course, many other measures in which I was interested. I worked particularly hard on plans for the reorganization of county government but achieved no success except in the case of permissive legislation for Fairfax. Two incidents occurred during that session which seemed rather trivial at the time but which were actually portents of impending political doom. My Republican opponent from Fairfax appeared with a group of farmers to protest against a bill intended to clean up Bang's disease in Virginia's dairy herds. This disease was widespread among the herds of northern Virginia and milk from these herds could produce undulant fever in human beings; however, the life of a consumer seemed for the moment less important to some of these dairymen than the lives of their cows. The other incident was that I committed the unpardonable offense of voting out loud against a resolution to support Virginia's senators in Washington in their opposition to a federal anti-lynching bill. And I was heard to do so.

I had another experience that winter, unrelated to the assembly, which at the time did not seem to have any particular bearing on my political fortunes. Subsequently, it cast a very long shadow indeed. There had been a dispute (primarily about wages) between the printing pressmen's union and the publishers of the two Richmond papers. After long and futile negotiations, both sides had agreed to arbitration and I was asked to hear the evidence and make the decision. The proceedings were held in Richmond and occupied all the time I had left over from the assembly. After endless hours of hearings, it was obvious that the pressmen should receive a pay raise. To determine what they should receive I asked for wage scales for pressmen doing comparable work in five or six of the largest southern cities, adjusted those wages to the government's cost of living index so that the wages would be comparable, and then figured the average wage. I discovered that if the Richmond pressmen received the average wage paid in the South for the same kind of work, they would get half of what they were asking for. My decision was that they were to receive this average wage, and I considered that eminently fair. The pressmen were pleased, but John Dana Wise, general manager of the *Times-Dispatch*, told me later that he regarded it as the worst decision ever made by an arbiter in any labor dispute in the South. His objection was that I had set a precedent for "rational" decisions. The following September, the Richmond newspapers merged.

When the Democratic primary of August, 1941, approached, Charles Pickett, an attorney at Fairfax Court House, announced his intention to oppose me. He was a stronger candidate than my opponent had been in the 1937 primary, but I defeated him without much difficulty. However, shortly after the primary I began to realize that I would be in serious trouble in the November general election since the County Democratic Committee sat on its hands and refused to rally to my support. Some of the citizens of Fairfax were legitimately concerned with the fact that I spent little more than weekends in the county, since my office was in New York. Further, the community as a whole was very conservative and our Congressman, Howard Smith, was popular with many Democrats. He instinctively disliked and mistrusted me and sensed a direct threat to himself in my ascent of the political ladder. From Smith's point of view the sooner I was bumped off the better, though I had gone up to the Court House and announced for him when the White House unwisely attempted to purge him in 1938. Moreover, I was wide open to attack on two counts. I was a notorious "war hawk" as far as Nazi Germany was concerned, and this troubled pacifically minded citizens. But my cardinal sin was that I wanted to eradicate Bang's disease in the herds of milk cows in Fairfax County. Richard Farr had opposed me in the general election of 1939 and Richard Farr was opposing me now. It was he who had brought the delegation of farmers to protest against the Bang's eradication measure which I was supporting in the House. Feeling among many farmers ran high and Farr exploited that to the limit.

However, the whole family, including Andrew aged nine and Robert aged seven, campaigned hard that autumn and the above factors would not alone have caused my defeat if it had not been for other and more sinister developments. There was a weekly paper called the *Herndon News and Observer* published in Manassas but distributed in the rural southern half of Fairfax County. In the late summer a boxed editorial began to appear each week on its front page, making vague and mysterious allusions to undefined suspicious events occurring in the county due to the presence of outsiders. In due course the editorial pointed a finger directly at Helen who was an ardent believer in the New England town meeting type of community procedure. In place of one boxed column on the front page there were two columns printed side by side. One of the columns was an extract from a statement pleading for citizens in local communities to meet and discuss issues prior to the enactment of legislation. This statement was associated in people's minds with work Helen was then doing for the National Policy Committee, but the extract was printed without attribution. The other column, adjoining the first one, and both enclosed in the same box, was an extract from a Communist directive urging workers to assemble in their factories and discuss issues. The intent of the paper was clear. It was obvious that the author of the first column was a "fellow traveler!" In other editorials it was even suggested that my connection with the National Policy Committee and the Council on Foreign Relations indicated subversive interests—with the latter because it was financed by Rockefeller and Carnegie funds!

But much worse was to come. Helen was then working for M. L. Wilson, undersecretary of agriculture. However, there was another Helen Miller working at the same time in the Department of Labor. Her name was Helen Schnitzler Miller and she came from Ohio. My wife was Helen Hill Miller and she had come from Illinois. One day in midautumn Helen Schnitzer Miller was fired from the Department of Labor for being a Communist. I had never heard of her until that moment. When this event was reported on the local radio, the announcer said that "Helen Miller had been fired from government for being a Communist." That was a true statement, and I could not sue for libel. A "Helen Miller" had been fired for being a Communist but it was not my Helen. However, the damage had been done, and the rumor was spread all over the county. I am sure that Richard Farr had no hand in any of this. He was an honorable man. But the evening before election day my neighbor Ronald Blake came up to confirm what I already knew—that the farmers were puzzled and troubled about the rumors in regard to Helen and that I probably faced defeat on the morrow. Farr won by the narrow margin of some 180 votes.

I could take defeat, but what I could not take were the methods used to defeat me. The utter horror of what had happened invaded my mind and haunts me to this day. Until that moment I had not believed it was possible that in Virginia, the home of gentlemen, with its tradition of courtesy and fair play, there were creatures so low and despicable that they would plot to defeat a man running for public office by the invention and dissemination of infamous canards about his wife. What made it worse was that I had asked a northern girl to be my wife and to live with me in Virginia. That my fellow Virginians should have treated her thus was to me the ultimate outrage and indignity. As it turned out, I was never able to discover who masterminded those editorials and radio announcements. I knew that no local man could have invented such material without the help of a resourceful office in Washington. Was Charles Pickett the go-between? Did Howard Smith's staff furnish advice and copy? These were the questions in my mind. But Pearl Harbor prevented me from ever finding the answers.

The aftermath of that autumn's campaign was macabre. Richard Farr dropped dead forty-five minutes before he was to take his seat in the House of Delegates, and three other people who, while less innocent, were merely agents of the real villains, all died within a year—the publisher of the weekly paper in which the editorials had appeared, the editor of that paper, and a woman who had spread rumors. Their enjoyment of the sweets of victory had been brief. As far as I was concerned, I was certain of one thing and that was that if I survived the war, there would be a day of reckoning with the Byrd Organization.

The Virginia press had rallied to my support magnificently. Before the election the *Richmond Times-Dispatch* said in an editorial: "A preposterous and dishonest campaign of innuendo conducted from behind ambuscades, and consisting mainly of insupportable insinuations, is being carried on against one of the most brilliant and useful members of the Virginia General Assembly. This un-American and un-Virginian fight is being made in Fairfax County against FRANCIS P. MILLER."

After the election the same paper said that the result in Fairfax County was "the climax of a campaign of dishonest innuendo and malicious misrepresentation unequaled in Virginia's recent political history," and continued: "It is passing strange that Mr. Miller failed to poll the full Democratic vote in this county of the Eighth Congressional District, whose party leader and Representative in Congress, Howard W. Smith of Alexandria, was openly supported for renomination by Mr. Miller in the primary of 1938, when challenged for his seat by William E. Dodd, Jr."

The *Roanoke Times* said that "the only explanation seemed to be that Mr. Miller was unmercifully knifed at the polls by members of his own party."

The *Norfolk Virginian-Pilot* said:

The witch hunters conducted against Mr. Miller a campaign of misrepresentation which culminated in the artful suggestion that he was linked with "subversive" agencies—as fantastic an accusation against this thorough American and thorough Virginian as has ever managed to find acceptance by Virginia voters in their right senses. The entire campaign was conducted by innuendo—by sly accusations which pointed at the selected target without ever calling it by name and thus laying itself open to an action for libel. The political vendetta that accomplished his defeat touched a new low in mendacity and meanness.

The *Richmond News Leader*, which was still edited in those days by Dr. Douglas Freeman, said: "Francis Pickens Miller, who has been narrowly defeated after a most vicious campaign, is one of the best-trained, most genuinely independent men in Virginia public life. He has been a most useful influence in the House. Even when we have thought him wrong, on occasion, we have felt that he put his adversaries on their mettle. Virginia needed him and needs more like him, and must lament the circumstances that led voters of Fairfax to reject him."

The *Petersburg Progress-Index* said: "All that we know about Mrs. Miller is that she is the author of a recent and notable biography of George Mason of Gunston Hall, published by the Harvard University Press, a book which bears evidence throughout of her devotion to the Bill of Rights and to the government of the United States. If Fairfax and its section of Virginia have came to regard such doings as subversive, then it is a good thing for old George that he is in his grave."

During 1938–41 I enjoyed serving on the board of William and Mary College to which the governor appointed me. The president of the college then was John Stewart Bryan, one of the finest gentlemen of Virginia. At the same time Mr. Bryan was also owner and publisher of the *Richmond News Leader*. Upon joining the board I found that the rector, Gordon Bohanon of Petersburg, and several other members were growing a bit restive at not having a genuinely full-time president. While Mr. Bryan was in Richmond tending to his business affairs, an underling named Charles Duke was left in charge of the college. This was most unsatisfactory since Duke was a business manager type with no understanding of higher education and its problems. What was to be done? How could we secure a full-time president without giving such offense to Mr. Bryan that he would turn against the college? It was an extremely delicate matter and had to be handled with great care. Finally we devised a plan. We would discuss our dilemma with Mr. Bryan and propose that he become chancellor with the understanding, if he agreed to this, that we would then find a younger man to be the executive for the college as president. This proposal seemed to appeal to him; actually we received the impression that he would be very happy to be relieved of administrative responsibilities. So a committee of three (of which I was one) was appointed to find his successor, and when after months of search we came up with a man, Mr. Bryan said that he could not have been more pleased since the individual we were recommending was his choice too. So we ordered for the chancellor a cap and gown from London, similar to those worn by the Bishop of London when he was titular head of William and Mary before the Revolution, and we felt rather proud of ourselves for having handled the affair so well.

While president of the college, Mr. Bryan lived in the beautiful Wren residence on the campus and served the best luncheons in Virginia—oysters on Smithfield ham with vintage wines. On the day the board completed its task we were invited to lunch with him. As we entered the dining room of the Wren house, Mr. Bryan said to me, "Come here, Francis Pickens, and sit on my right." When we had all taken our places, he continued, "I want to propose a toast to Francis Pickens, the only man I know who could run a stiletto through my heart and turn it with such finesse that as I expired I would look up into his face with affection and gratitude!" What a toast! I smiled wanly but did not respond as there was nothing to say. However, years later when Mr. Bryan's son, Tennant, turned the full fury of the *News Leader* upon me, I recalled that toast and reflected that there might have been more to it than appeared at the time. After Colgate Darden became governor, he reappointed me to the William and Mary board and long afterwards remarked with that rare sardonic humor which I so much enjoyed that it had been the costliest political appointment he had ever made.

During those first years of political struggle the one sure light that illumined my world, which no gloom or darkness could obscure was our home at Pickens Hill. We had frequent political visitors and no one was more welcome than Colonel LeRoy Hodges, the state comptroller, when he occasionally came up from Richmond, with or without the governor. He had become my closest friend and was a fascinating combination of conflicting characteristics. On the one hand he was literally an old-fashioned authentic Virginia Cavalier, while on the other he was a radical social reformer even when executive director of the State Chamber of Commerce. LeRoy actually believed that Virginia society could be transformed so that all her citizens would have a chance to enjoy life, liberty, and the pursuit of happiness, and his faith sustained mine.

Because of the kind of person Helen was, because of the kind of home we had at Pickens Hill, and because we were within easy driving distance of Washington, during 1933–42 we welcomed an endless stream of New Dealers. Shortly after Roosevelt's first inaugural, Rex Tugwell brought Henry Wallace out to see us. Wallace liked us and our place so well that he became a fairly frequent visitor and a good friend.

He was as nearly apolitical as it was possible for a cabinet member to be. As a consequence I had been much concerned about the need for mobilizing more congressional support for his agricultural programs. It happened that an old comrade of the Fifth Field Artillery in World War I, Emmet O'Neal, was now congressman from Louisville, Kentucky, so I invited Mr. Wallace and Emmet out for dinner one evening, hoping that as a result of their getting to know each other, Emmet might be willing to help in the House. After a good meal we went into the library where a cheery fire was blazing. Henry arranged himself on the sofa in front of the fire and I began to explain briefly what I had hoped would be the topic of our evening's conversation. By the time I had finished Henry had fallen fast asleep and when he woke up an hour or so later, he said, "Well, I guess I had better be going home." The next day I phoned O'Neal and apologized profusely to him but it was obvious from O'Neal's reaction that the secretary of agriculture had not taken advantage of the evening to increase his strength in the House.

But as far as plants were concerned, Henry Wallace was not only a genius, he was also a profound and wise philosopher. He came to New York once while I was working for the council to have dinner and talk with a group of scientists. I was invited to join the party. After dinner one of the scientists asked "What were the essential characteristics that a scientist must have when he is attempting to crossbreed different strains of plants." Quick as a flash Henry shot back: "Sympathy for the plant!" I loved him for that and bitterly regretted that I had to break with him in 1948 when he made the tragic mistake of allowing himself to become a candidate of the extreme left.

Our visitors likewise included many people whom I had met on my travels around the world. Joe Oldham and his wife came hoping to interest me in assuming responsibility for doing in the United States the kind of work he had been doing in England—an effort to involve the intelligensia and promising young public figures in a serious consideration of the Christian faith. J. H. Hofmeyr came from South Africa; Visser 't Hooft and Jetty from Geneva; the von

Thaddens from their castle Trieglaff in Pomerania; T. Z. Koo with his magic flute from China; and Saito, the head of the Y.M.C.A. in Japan.

Saito was no relation to the Saito who was Japanese ambassador in Washington during 1934–38, but once when the Y.M.C.A. Saito was visiting me, he expressed the hope that I would cultivate the acquaintance of the ambassador. Our relations with Japan were becoming more and more difficult, and it occurred to me that contact with him might prove useful. In any event, it could do no harm. So I invited Ambassador Saito to come out to Fairfax to have dinner with Helen and me and assured him that I was inviting no other guests so that we might have a completely free and uninhibited conversation. He accepted and arrived in full evening dress in a large black limousine. He was also quite drunk. I helped him in and we eventually made it to the table. But during the meal his liquor got the best of him and I had to assist him to the washroom to vomit. He felt better after that and began to talk with terrifying indiscretion. During the course of the evening he actually informed me who were his pipelines into the Department of State. I reported this the following morning but have not yet recovered from the shock of realizing that the peace of the world was in the hands of such men. Ironically enough, when in early 1939 Saito returned to New York from Europe where he was then stationed and was asked by newsmen what was the purpose of his visit, he replied according to the *New York Times* that it was to drink good whiskey with good Americans. After all, there was a touch of honesty about him.

Some months before the Ambassador Saito dinner I had had another caller as a result of the initiative of an intimate Japanese friend from Tokyo. My friend was on a visit to Washington and requested permission to bring an acquaintance of his out to our home to see us—a Miss Shia who was working in the Japanese section of the Library of Congress. When Miss Shia arrived, she turned out to be a very mousy little person, so quiet and shy that she might have been an old maid school teacher in a small country village. She said little or nothing and Helen and I decided not to see her again. Years later when I was an intelligence officer in Europe, I learned that mousy little Miss Shia had been one of the top Japanese spies in the United States. She had used her position in the Library of Congress to establish all too intimate relations with a number of Americans and had a direct channel into the Department of State. The most intriguing aspect of this lady's operations was that she transmitted to Tokyo the information thus obtained in beautiful acrostic verse. It was fortunate for Miss Shia that she had been assigned to work in the United States. Instead of shooting spies, we normally take very good care of them. After Pearl Harbor she was sent with other Japanese suspects to a mountain resort to wait in comfort until she could be exchanged.

But of all the people who visited us at Pickens Hill the one I remember most vividly was Denise Clarouin. I have seen many beautiful women in my time; Denise was one of the two or three most beautiful. She came after the conquest of France but before Pearl Harbor. She was a leader in the French underground and had come to this country with an introduction to Helen to secure funds for their operations. When I think of her I think of the best of France—I also think of the worst in human nature because eventually she was betrayed to the Gestapo by her own French lover, and died an unspeakably horrible death en route from Ravensbruck to Auschwitz.

XIV ✐ Crusade in Virginia

When I returned from Berlin in the summer of 1946, Helen and I realized once more that a chapter in our lives had definitely ended and that the new chapter which was about to begin was unknown. In a sense I had to start all over again. A member of the board of the Carnegie Endowment for International Peace asked me if I would accept its presidency but I preferred to remain in the South. Subsequently, the board, of which John Foster Dulles was chairman, chose Alger Hiss for that position. For similar reasons I declined two college presidencies. I knew well enough that life in Virginia would be hard and lonely but I also knew that the struggle for a more democratic regime was something I would have to undertake. Fairfax was not central enough to be a good base from which to engage in state-wide politics, and one day Helen said, "Why not move to Charlottesville?" The idea appealed to me, so we drove to Charlottesville. Just after the war there were few or no houses for sale but, by an incredible chance, the very day of our visit one of the most beautiful residences near the Farmington Country Club came on the market and we snapped it up for occupancy the following spring. In June, 1947, we moved down. Emma and Worther Smith went with us, and we took along not only Robert's pony but our favorite cow, much to the amusement of our new neighbors.

Upon separation from the service the previous autumn, I found myself for the first time in my life financially independent. Uncle

Harvey's widow had recently died and some one-eighth of his estate had come to me through mother, who generously passed it on as she already had an income of her own. This meant that I could not only decide what I wanted to do but that I could invest capital in doing it. What I wanted to do was to get back into Virginia politics as rapidly as possible. However, I had been out of the state for five years during the most crucial period of my career. Politics being what it is, a comeback after such a long interval would not be easy; I was now fifty-one and there was no time to lose. A far greater handicap was the fact that during my absence the political climate in Virginia had changed. The supporters of Governor Price had either retired from the scene or rejoined the Byrd Organization. Further, my two closest political friends were dead—Governor Price himself and Colonel LeRoy Hodges. The only person of any state-wide political experience who was still opposing the Organization was Martin A. Hutchinson, a Richmond attorney, who hailed from southwest Virginia and who ran against Byrd for the Senate in 1946. I had not yet met Robert Whitehead.

On the wall of St. Patrick's Cathedral in Dublin, Ireland, is a tablet above the tomb of Dean Swift. Part of the inscription says in Latin: "Here lies the body of Jonathan Swift whose fierce indignation can no longer lacerate his heart. Go, traveler, and imitate if you can, one who strove with all his strength to champion liberty." As I looked out on the Virginia scene after World War II, my heart too was lacerated with fierce indignation. In part, this was a result of my experiences during the autumn of 1941. In part, it was the result of my fuller understanding of why Virginia had become the kind of society she then was. Our Commonwealth had had the most glorious history prior to 1830 of any one of the original English colonies. The House of Burgesses from which our general assembly was derived had been established in 1619 and had served as the training ground for the statesmen of subsequent generations. To mention Wythe, Mason, Washington, Jefferson, Patrick Henry, Edmund Randolph, Marshall, Madison, and Monroe is sufficient illustration of the intellectual brilliance and political genius which characterized Virginia society toward the close of its second century. Later there was the incomparable Robert E. Lee who in the midst of universal disaster became the symbol of the courage, tolerance, patriotism, and faith which sustained those who followed him—the ideal of the perfect gentleman.

That was the history of the Virginia I loved. It was the contrast

between the promise of the early years and the actualities of 1947
that lacerated my heart and filled me with fierce indignation. In
1860, some 70 percent of the voting population of Virginia voted for
president. By 1904, the percentage had fallen to 27, due to the im-
position of the poll tax in 1902. When I checked on the number who
were voting after World War II, I discovered that we had the lowest percentage of white adults voting of any English-speaking community in the entire world. In 1945, when about three million people
lived in Virginia, only 138,788 citizens had voted for governor in the
only election that then mattered—the Democratic primary. This
meant that less than five people out of every one hundred inhabitants (5 percent of the population) had sufficient interest in government to want to have a voice in selecting their rulers—the state
officials and members of the general assembly. Further, at that time
we had one of the poorest public school systems in the Union. The
reason was plain. Though Virginia was the second wealthiest state
in the South in the proportion of income to the number of school
children, she invested in education a smaller proportion of her state
and local revenue than any other southern state. It was obvious
that Virginia had not fulfilled her great promise of continuing to be
the leader of progressive forces in America. Something was radically
wrong. What had gone wrong? According to the historian Toynbee,
Virginians had consoled themselves after the War between the
States by fixing their gaze upon the glories of the past rather than
upon the opportunities of the future. In his view this had resulted in
ossification of the body politic. Whatever the correct diagnosis, the
mass of Virginians in 1947 were more or less content with things
as they were. The people had been conditioned by the ruling families to political docility and impotence.

Two incidents illustrate the political climate of that time. Prior
to the Second World War when I was a member of the House of
Delegates and being courted by the Virginia establishment, I was
invited one Sunday to dinner at the home of one of the richest men
in Richmond who was a principal benefactor of the Byrd Machine.
A lady was present who was a large landowner. Someone began to
bait me gently for favoring the abolition of the poll tax as a pre-
requisite to voting. I remarked that it seemed odd to me that if the
Virginians who had come here in the seventeenth century had remained in England, their descendants would now all be voting there,
whereas the majority of the descendants of those English settlers

who had sought freedom in the New World, three hundred years after the arrival of their ancestors in Virginia, were still denied the right to vote here. The landowning lady with large holdings in Goochland County then said with emphasis, "But I do not want my white tenants to vote." Her theory apparently was that the right to vote went with the land and since the land was hers she alone should vote.

The second incident happened in the summer of 1947. We were having our new home near Charlottesville painted. One of the painters was a white man named Mowbray. That is a Norman name, and his ancestors may very well have crossed to England with William the Conqueror in the eleventh century and then to Virginia in the seventeenth. While he was painting in the hallway one day, I said, "Mr. Mowbray, have you qualified to vote?" He looked up at me incredulously and replied, "Colonel, you know I don't belong to the folks who vote." Here was a man of Norman descent, telling me in Virginia in the year of grace 1947 that he did not *belong* to the people who voted. I was outraged that any Virginian should feel like that; but what outraged me even more was that so many Virginians accepted without question the mores of a society that produced this sense of alienation from the body politic and this acquiescence in alienation as if it were normal—as if it were a feature of the natural order.

As far as the past half century was concerned, I knew who was responsible for converting Virginia into the kind of society where these conditions prevailed. It was the Byrd Organization. That was the enemy and that was what I had to fight. The leadership of the Byrd Organization was in those days a self-perpetuating oligarchy. The nucleus of the oligarchy consisted of the senator himself, the chairman of the compensation board, the speaker of the house, Sidney S. Kellam (the boss of Virginia Beach) and four or five congressmen and state officials. These gentlemen were accustomed to see each other frequently at the Commonwealth Club in Richmond and it was in their conversations there that the future of the party and of the Commonwealth was most frequently determined. In the 1940s these men usually knew two or three terms in advance what the sequence of governors would be.

The character of the Byrd Organization is so essential to my story that it is necessary to describe it in some detail, since there never has been any other political machine like it in the United States. In order to insure that my description may be as accurate as possible, I am going to quote from a memorandum which I subsequently prepared for Adlai Stevenson.

Byrd and his closest friends and advisors are Tories in the 18th century meaning of the word. Their political philosophy is not so much a rational system, as a set of feelings and emotions related to their traditional status in the community:

(1) They believe that the best government is the government which governs least.

(2) They think of the function of government as having to do primarily with money rather than men.

(3) They believe that a small group of persons in any society are the only ones qualified to provide good government, and they recognize themselves as belonging to this group in Virginia.

(4) They profoundly mistrust the mass of the people and will do everything in their power to prevent the establishment of government "of the people, by the people, and for the people."

The power of the Virginia "organization" is due to the fact that it is a part of the structure of State government. The "organization" maintains itself in office through (1) the poll tax,* and (2) pressure it can bring to bear on city and county elected officials through regulating their salaries and expense allowances. The poll tax restricts the suffrage to a manageable electorate, while the city and county officials are relied upon to pass the word along to those who have the right to vote. Pressure on local officials is applied through the State Compensation Board, consisting of three people—the Chairman, who is appointed by the Governor; the State Tax Commissioner, who is appointed by the governor, ex-officio; and the Auditor of Public Accounts (elected by the General Assembly), ex-officio. This Board possesses statutory authority to set the salaries and expense allowances of county and city elected officials within brackets established by the Legislature. When the "organization" finds itself in a tough fight, the Compensation Board offers inducements or applies pressures depending upon which are needed. It takes a stout-hearted and courageous county official indeed to resist. The Board's influence is quiet, effective, legal and cheap—because paid for out of the State's treasury.

The age of the "organization" gives it added prestige. It came into being in December 1893 when Tom Martin, a railway lawyer, unexpectedly defeated Fitzhugh Lee for the United States Senate. Martin was alleged to

---

* This tax was only $1.50 per annum, but no one could vote who had not paid it for three consecutive years prior to a given election. Further it had to be paid six months before the election, that is, before candidates had announced or issues were known. Finally, the tax was entirely voluntary. The would-be voter had to take the initiative to pay it, and there was a constitutional provision preventing the sheriff from taking a lien on property in an effort to collect.

have won the election by buying the votes of enough members of the Democratic caucus of the Virginia Assembly.* The "organization" has not been defeated more than once or twice in a state-wide election since 1893.

The Constitutional Convention of 1901–2 resurrected the poll tax and put it into the State Constitution, thus providing the "organization" with the tool it needed to destroy the Republican Party and create a one-party state. As a result of the poll tax, and especially because of the way it was administered, the Republican vote in Presidential elections in Virginia declined from 135,000 in 1896 to 48,000 in 1904. Since poor white people were eliminated as well as Negroes, the Democratic vote was also cut from 155,000 to 87,000 between the same years. . . .

In view of the fact that an effective state-wide Republican organization had long since ceased to exist, and in view of the fact that the Republicans had no primary of their own, they had over the years developed the habit of entering the Democratic primary since it was the only place where they could affect the outcome of a state-wide election. Consequently, the 139,000 who voted in the 1945 primary probably included 30,000–40,000 Republicans and 100,000 Democrats.

This was the situation in 1947 when I began to consider what to do. There was to be a state-wide election in Virginia in 1949 and the first step obviously was to run up a banner to which citizens who shared my views could repair. I secured Martin Hutchinson's co-operation and in the spring of 1947 we organized a little Committee for Democracy in Virginia whose purpose was to work for "a wider and more general participation on the part of the people of Virginia in the processes of government" through abolition of the poll tax and other measures.

We were, of course, eager to secure the sympathetic understanding of the press for our modest enterprise, but I had discovered shortly after returning from Berlin that the attitude of the press towards me had changed during my years of absence in war service. In 1941, it could not have been more appreciative. Now it was indifferent to say the least. One of the first things I had done after getting out of the army was to go down to Richmond to spend an evening with Virginius Dabney, editor of the *Times-Dispatch*, to renew our prewar friendship and get caught up on state affairs. It was Dabney who had written the editorial about me entitled "The

---

* In those days U.S. Senators were elected by State legislatures. I was once given the names, by an old gentleman at Blackstone, of the twelve members of the caucus who were alleged to have received $1,000 apiece to change their votes from Lee to Martin.

Ideal Candidate" in 1937, and it was he who had acquired a national reputation as a southern liberal. Further, he was regarded as an intellectual leader by the young of the South.

In the course of our conversation he startled me by saying in his quiet, bland way that while I had been absent his views had changed and that he had "gone conservative." At the time, the possibility of any man suddenly changing his basic outlook on life seemed so incongruous to me that I did not take his remarks too seriously. So I laughed and replied, "V., you won't stay conservative very long while I am around." Later it became apparent that he meant exactly what he said and that I no longer had his editorial support. This was one of the hardest blows I was to receive.

It was not too difficult to understand why Dabney had to change his views if he were to remain with the *Times-Dispatch*. Fifteen years before, an incident had occurred which illustrated the extent to which Harry Flood Byrd expected the Richmond papers to kowtow to his wishes. During 1934–36, Mark Ethridge was president and publisher of the *Richmond Times-Dispatch*. At that time Colonel Samuel LeRoy Slover of Norfolk owned a controlling interest in the paper. Byrd had opposed the AAA New Deal program of the Department of Agriculture and Ethridge thought it would be interesting to find out how the farmers of Virginia felt about that program, so the *Times-Dispatch* took a poll which showed that approximately 80 percent of the farmers who replied favored it. The results of the poll were published and this annoyed Byrd so much that he asked Slover to fire Ethridge. Instead, Slover asked Ethridge to have breakfast with him at the Hotel Jefferson to discuss the matter, and arranged for Byrd to join them in the course of their conversation. When Byrd appeared, he expressed his indignation to Ethridge so strongly that the latter, outraged by his direct assault on the freedom of the press, responded with comparable warmth. That ended the consultation. Slover stood by Ethridge and refused to fire him, but in the course of time the latter found the atmosphere in which he had to work too stifling, and left Virginia for Kentucky to the irreparable loss of our Commonwealth. Byrd had won, and since then I cannot recall an instance when the Richmond papers have done anything that would have greatly offended him. Naturally if Dabney were to continue to be a Richmond editor he would have to adapt himself to the Byrd policy line.

The odds against me were heavy, but whatever the odds I knew what I had to do and proceeded to re-establish my contacts throughout the state as quickly as possible. In the course of doing this I met Robert Whitehead of Nelson County and was greatly impressed by him. He had become a member of the House of Delegates in 1942 and had already established a state-wide reputation. As far as speaking was concerned, Robert at times reminded me of what Patrick Henry must have been like in his prime. He was far and away the ablest debater in the house and in due course he also became a master of state finance. Further, he was completely independent in his thinking. To visit him in his little white law office on the courthouse green at Lovingston where his father and his grandfather had practiced law before him was to re-enter the world of Thomas Jefferson.

One weekend in the early spring of 1948, Robert Whitehead and I were both present at a retreat for laymen organized by the Episcopal Church. I had heard that he was thinking of running for governor the following year and would have supported him had he done so. However, time was passing and it was important for me to know his intentions. At the end of the retreat I had already entered my car and was getting ready to leave when he came up to speak through the window. I asked him what his plans were. In reply he asked me my age. I told him 52. He then said, "Francis, you are older than I am. It is your turn now, and I will run next time." That settled it, and we formed an alliance that lasted until his death. By such chance conversations the course of men's lives is determined! We both agreed that before we made public our definitive decision we should wait until we knew who would be the candidate of the Byrd Organization, though it already appeared almost certain that State Senator John S. Battle of Charlottesville had been given the nod.

John Battle had served with me on the Governor's Advisory Council and I both liked and respected him. He was an impressive looking old-fashioned southern gentleman with courtly manners who had the reputation of being somewhat easygoing. Though he was completely loyal to Senator Byrd, he had not been closely identified with the plot to destroy Governor Price. I did not know in what direction his interests had been moving since 1941 but I thought of him as a man who might make a forward-looking governor. If he were willing to commit himself explicitly to doing some of the things that had to be done, Whitehead and I probably ought to support him. So I drafted a brief memorandum outlining a moderate program of progress for the state which represented the minimum I was willing to accept and then asked John to come out to my house at Farmington one afternoon to have a look at it. He read it carefully and then said, "Francis, you know that I cannot commit myself to that." "That means," I replied, "that I will probably have to enter the race too."

Battle announced in early June, fourteen months before the primary; Horace Edwards, the mayor of Richmond, a Byrd Machine stalwart who was also chairman of the Democratic State Central Committee, shortly followed suit. I never discovered the true explanation of this unheard-of phenomenon—two Byrd lieutenants splitting the Organization vote and thus opening the door to the possibility of some outsider winning. But I presume that Edwards was piqued because he had misunderstood the signals and thought he had had the nod. At any rate it looked like a situation that was made to order for me, so I announced toward the end of June.

In spite of the split in the Organization, the odds against me in June, 1948, were still formidable. I had no political organization, no patrons, no funds except my own, and no politically experienced confederates except Whitehead and Hutchinson. I did not even know the names or locations of some of Virginia's hundred counties. But I did know that elections were won by good organization more than by anything else. So I set out to apply the lessons in political organization that I had learned in Fairfax, to raise as much money as I could, and to explain to the people why I was running. It was a colossal task, but one which I hugely enjoyed. In the course of the thirteen months prior to the primary I drove myself 40,000 miles around the state, organizing and speaking in every county, city, and town and revisiting some of them many times. By the end of the campaign a fairly good state-wide organization was functioning, and since it was the pre-T.V. age, the fifty thousand dollars that my friends raised, in addition to twenty-five thousand that I put in myself, enabled us to do a moderately effective job. Our greatest weakness was that we had so few political professionals on our campaign team. Able amateurs on fire with a cause can do a lot, but the best of them are not quite equal to the kind of adversary we were opposing.

My speeches dealt with the pressing needs of the state and with the concrete issues we faced—such as increasing teachers' salaries very substantially, getting rid of pollution in our streams, conserving our forests, abolishing the poll tax as a means of limiting the number of people who vote, etc. In discussing the small size of the

electorate I frequently remarked that for nearly fifty years the political scene in Virginia had resembled a ball park in which no real
game was being played. One team came out on the field from time
to time and batted out flies, but long ago the spectators had become
bored and gone home. My intention was to stage a contest which
would fill the bleachers again. But my main theme was that the
purpose of my campaign was to "set Virginia free."

In 1619, Edwin Sandys had been secretary of the Virginia Company in London when the colony's first liberal charter was granted,
establishing representative government through a House of Burgesses. He had said previously that it was his ambition to found "a
free state" in the New World. I liked the phrase and I felt that after
three hundred years it was only proper that someone should resume
the task that Sandys had set for himself but which had never been
completed. My major speech on this theme was given over Radio
Station WRNL in Richmond on February 10, 1949, and the best
way to convey a sense of what the whole campaign was about is to
quote from that speech. After listing various concrete issues I said:

> But not one of these concrete issues, important as it may be, is really
> the main issue of this campaign.
>
> The main issue is: are we or are we not going to have a free society in
> Virginia? Unless we can settle this issue, no other issue can be settled
> satisfactorily. Unless we settle this issue, we cannot hope to solve any
> one of our major problems. These problems exist because the Common-
> wealth of Virginia has not been functioning politically as a free society. In
> a free society, men who recognized these emerging problems would have
> stepped forward and secured remedial action long before the problems
> became acute.
>
> Virginia has not been functioning normally as a free society because
> of the political clique that has controlled the Commonwealth during the
> past half century. This clique is composed of backward-looking men who
> have little imagination and small faith in the future of this Republic. They
> do not concern themselves with the problems of a free society. Their main
> concern is to keep themselves in power. They have not wanted to main-
> tain in Virginia the political conditions required for the survival and
> growth of a free society.
>
> One man has to all intents and purposes continued to govern the State
> for nineteen years *after* ceasing to occupy the Governor's chair. Senator
> Harry Byrd has run Virginia for nineteen years *after* the people ceased to
> hold him responsible for that office. He has run it through his overseers
> as if he were an absentee landlord. The question is not whether he has run

it well or ill. The question is that he has run it without the people's expressed consent. I propose to free the administration of Virginia from
private controls, and restore the government to the people.

The chief overseer of this absentee landlord has been Mr. E. R. Combs,
Chairman of the Compensation Board. Mr. Combs is also clerk of the
Senate. The people of Virginia pay him for his services in these two posts
salaries totaling ten thousand five hundred and fifty dollars, an amount
larger than the salary of the Governor of Virginia. The majority of Virginians have never heard Mr. Combs' name. Yet for years, he has been
the most powerful political figure in our midst. He is the operating boss
of the Byrd machine.

The Byrd machine has long been a subject of discussion among Virginians. Some deny its existence. Others refer to it as a "nice clean machine" and remind us that political organization is necessary. Obviously
political organization is a necessary device for making the people's will
effective in public policy. But, we know the difference between good and
bad organization. . . ."

Despite the myths that had grown up around it, I went on to
charge that the machine which Mr. Combs headed was as "ruthless
and powerful as any in the United States." I said,

Its lever of control is the Compensation Board, of which he is Chairman.
This Board sets the pay for local officials within limits authorized by the
Assembly. When local officials appear before Chairman Combs and his
Board seeking adjustment of their pay, it probably never occurs to him
to distinguish between his function as a servant of the Commonwealth
and his function as operating boss of the machine. In his person the organization of the machine and the structure of the State Government have
been fused.

One result of this fusion of government and machine is that the government, which should serve all the people of Virginia impartially, is acces-
sible in a special sense to those who know the right people or who have
an inside track. When a county or city elects officials who do not have the
State machine's approval those officials not infrequently find the doors
of the State Government closed to their legitimate requests for better State
services or for fair consideration of local interests.

Machine control has given us what we have all come to know as "the
invisible government of Virginia." In this form of government, decisions
are reached by men who do not hold elective office and have no direct
responsibility to the people of the State as a whole. The seat of that invisible government is in Mr. Combs' office. I propose to abolish this invisible government.

The persons elected to office by Virginia counties and cities are exceptionally able and public-spirited officials. They are politically re-

Cartoon by Fred O. Seibel on gubernatorial campaign,
February 12, 1949
Photographed by Lowell A. Kenyon, Chevy Chase, Maryland
Courtesy of the Richmond Times-Dispatch

sponsible to the people who elected them. Local officials who are aware of this responsibility resent having to kowtow to a political potentate in Richmond to secure necessary adjustments of their salaries. The people of every county and city resent it because they know that this pernicious practice has done more than anything else to destroy local government, which is the foundation of our liberties. As long as this practice continues, county and city officials are not free men. I propose to set them free.

Due to the type of leadership the controlling clique has provided, Virginia's influence among the States has fallen to its lowest point since the Republic was founded. Under its present management, Virginia carries little weight in the councils of the Democratic Party or of the nation, and is no longer a source of political leadership for western civilization. We must restore Virginia to the position of political prestige in the nation and in the world which she merits by reason of her great traditions and the present capacities of her people.

We know that the foundations of this Commonwealth were laid by men inspired by the dream of a free society. We know what price those men were willing to pay to realize their dream. Because of the price they paid, we know that it is our responsibility to carry forward the work which they began.

My administration will be dedicated to establishing in Virginia political conditions which will make it possible for a free society to develop and flourish. Every Virginian worthy of the name wants that to happen.

New leadership is required for the Democratic Party in Virginia and for the State Government, because the present leadership has demonstrated over a period of many years that it has neither the wish nor the capacity to build a free society. These men are incapable of building a free society because deep in their hearts they do not believe in a free society. They have no real faith in the future of our way of life or of this Republic. They profoundly distrust the judgment of the people. For them the show is over and the curtain is being rung down. They are time-servers—waiting for the sands to run out—half-heartedly fighting a rear guard action for a cause that has lost its meaning.

This is why they must go.

We know that the show is not over and that the curtain is not being rung down. We know that our way of life has meaning and that its meaning is related to the future history of mankind.

The purpose of this campaign is to revive our faith in a free society in order that we Virginians may play a worthy part in the days that lie ahead—a worthy part in our Commonwealth, in this Republic, and throughout the western world.

I appeal to all who share this purpose to join me in this enterprise.

As an overseas veteran of two world wars, I appeal to veterans who fought for freedom overseas to enter this fight for the exercise of political liberties at home.

I appeal to civic-minded citizens and agencies that want good government on both local and state levels.

I appeal to all Virginians who are aware that the only final answer to the menace of Communism is for us to demonstrate by deeds the superiority of our way of life and of our form of government.

Among the various concrete policy issues raised during the campaign I regarded the plight of our public school system as the most important. My proposal was to use the millions that had accumulated in the state treasury as a result of Virginia's pay-as-you-go policy to raise the level of teachers' salaries. This was the essential first step. The pay of teachers was so low that the best ones were leaving the state and this outflow of talent had to be stopped. New buildings could come later.

At first there were five gubernatorial candidates—Remmie Arnold of Petersburg and Nick Prillaman of Martinsville in addition to Battle, Edwards, and myself. Towards the end, Prillaman withdrew in my favor. Throughout the campaign we made many joint appearances at which the candidates spoke in turn. And as time passed, I began to twit John Battle on his apparent lack of interest in education. During the course of the winter when my turn came in our joint appearances, I made it a practice to say something like this: "Folks, you know we are a group of entertainers touring the state and each member of our troupe provides a different act on the program. One member [I meant Battle] carries with him a key to the Inner Sanctum. He is the only one of us who can go in there. If he were to get that key out and enter the Inner Sanctum, he could tell us how many millions of dollars have been hidden there that could be used for our schools. And that is what I am asking him to do right now."

After I had repeated this on several occasions, it began to get under John's skin, so much so that at times I thought I could hear him groaning slightly as I challenged him to go and have a look. Further, the sympathy of our audiences was shifting to me. Finally, during the second week of April, he announced one evening at a meeting where I was not present that he had found $57,000,000.00 in the state's surplus funds which could be used for building new schools! Shortly after that both of us spoke at the annual convention of social workers in Roanoke, and I congratulated Battle upon the amount he had found but insisted that it was not enough. I told him I knew there were millions more in the Inner Sanctum and urged him to go back and check again. For the first and only time in the campaign this jibe made John so angry that he lost his head, grabbed the mike, and tried to reply as the meeting broke up in confusion. However, two weeks later he announced, as I recall it, that he had found an additional eighteen million. After the campaign was over, Colgate Darden remarked to me one day, "Thank God, Pickens, that campaign ended when it did. If it had continued two more weeks, John would have promised a hundred million for public school buildings and I would not have gotten a cent for the University of Virginia."

After Battle became governor the surplus money he had discovered was labeled the "Battle Fund" and was dedicated to the construction of many new school buildings throughout the state. I commented at the time that though these buildings could not have been erected without the "Battle Fund" they were in reality "Miller Memorials" since they would not have been erected at all if I had not run for governor in 1949.

I had many intriguing and some fascinating experiences during that campaign but the one which my memory relishes most had to do with Bill Minton, chief of the United Mine Workers in Southwest Virginia. The congressman from that area was John Flannagan who had always received the support of the U.M.W. and who expected them to follow his lead. There were some indications that Flannagan intended to declare for Edwards and I determined to call on Minton, whom I did not know, at the first opportunity. His office was in Norton and, without an introduction of any kind, I simply walked in one day and told his secretary, Ruth Gunter, I would like to see him. She looked up at me and asked, "Aren't you Mr. Willie McElwee's nephew?" Surprised, I replied that indeed I was. "Well," she explained, "he lived in my grandmother's boarding house when he organized a bank in Big Stone Gap in the early 1890s." She went at once into Minton's office and when she came out said: "Go right in." The chief of the Mine Workers and I had a friendly chat in the course of which he asked me where I was born. I replied "Middlesboro" (that is just across the state line in Kentucky). "I was born there too," he said, with more than ordinary warmth. I did not ask him where he stood in the campaign; I just made his acquaintance, but, though I was not aware of it at the time, it was decisive for Bill Minton that both of us had been hatched in the same nest.

Shortly after this, in Bristol, I heard that Flannagan was going up to the Wise Court House to announce his choice for governor, so I phoned Minton to ask if he knew what that choice was. In reply he asked me to cancel an engagement I had had in Abingdon two days later and instead to come over to see him at one o'clock. There was not a word about why he wanted me. My manager for the Ninth District, an undertaker named Gene McConnell, went with me and as we entered Minton's office we found him seated at his desk with a large Bible open in front of him and a dozen of his district leaders standing around the wall. As he looked up he said, "I've just been reading to the boys out of the Good Book."

After introductions all around Minton explained that we were going to have a little meeting of seventy-five or so in the Union hall at Dorchester some two miles distant and that we had better be going. There was no further explanation, so as we rode along I inquired, "Do you want me to speak?" He nodded, but I persisted, "What about?" "Give them the works," he said. When we reached the hall, instead of the seventy-five he had promised there were at least five hundred miners assembled from every part of the area. They were sitting in the aisles, on the window sills, and had overflowed onto the stage. We elbowed our way to the platform and a meeting began unlike any that I had ever seen before or would ever see again. It lasted for two hours. First Minton spoke. He told the miners at length about the way of salvation described in the Bible; then he shifted to politics and explained that word had come down from Washington for them to support Edwards, but that he had replied, "We know what our interests are down here, and don't need advice from anybody." Finally he said, "I told you who was going to save you in the next world," and then turning and pointing at me, he exclaimed, "And here is the man who is going to save us in this. Get up and speak." I have never been so flabbergasted in my life, but I did the best I could. Then Minton spoke a second time, and I followed him once more. In the end I had the miners on their feet, yelling that they were going to make me governor of Virginia. When it was all over, I asked Gene McConnell what we had been through; he replied, "A hard-shell Baptist revival." I had never been in one before, and I have never been in once since, but the miners were mine for life. In 1952, when I was running against Harry Byrd for the Senate, I was told that I won in Wise County by the largest majority any state candidate had ever received. After all, Bill Minton and I were both born in the same place. That was enough; for he never asked me how I stood on Taft-Hartley or any other policy issue.

There was a second incident in Norton I love to recall. The moun-

Cartoon by Fred O. Seibel on gubernatorial campaign, July 14, 1949
Courtesy of the Richmond Times-Dispatch

tain people thereabout are very laconic. One day I was campaigning up and down Main Street when I came across one of the most authentic types I had ever seen—tall, lean, weathered, with an eye that went naturally with a squirrel rifle. I asked him to vote for me. There was no reply. However, he was interested enough to go up to Wise County Court House that evening to hear me speak. Back in Norton after the meeting he saw me coming out of a snack eating place and approached as a man does when there is something important on his mind. He said, "Mister, I liked what you said up at the Court House. Tell me, how can I git out of Russia without having to leave Virginia?" That was one of the most profound remarks I had heard during the campaign. My reply, of course, was "Vote for me."

He had compressed into twelve words the unarticulated feelings of thousands of Virginians who in those days vaguely sensed that they lived in an oppressive political society. They did not understand why, but they knew very well that, in many localities, if a poor man sharply deviated from the Byrd policy line and openly joined political rebels against the Organization he ran the risk of incurring economic reprisals in one form or another. It might be that no credit would be given, it might be that a bank loan would be called, or it might be that he would suddenly find himself out of a job. I knew of instances when this actually happened to my supporters. This fact gave pause to all but the most stouthearted. Whatever the discontent of the poor, it did not make much difference, however, as far as my campaign was concerned, because most of them were not qualified to vote, and so could not express their discontent at the polls.

Around the first of June, 1949, I had Battle beaten by some 25,000. I knew it and he knew it. The story of how that margin of victory was converted within two months into a 23,729 margin of defeat is a story of the Byrd Machine at the summit of its power, conducting an operation which for the sheer brilliance of its tactics has few equals in American politics. Leaving aside ethical considerations and the question of how unscrupulous this or that move may have been, it was a classic of its kind. Without taking any votes away from me, the vote for John Battle was increased by 50,000 or by about 50 percent of his June 1 total. This is how it was done:

1) By Compensation Board pressure on the county officers.

Harrison P. Spotswood had been a colleague of mine in the House of Delegates. He was now the commissioner of revenue of Orange County. I knew that he inclined toward Edwards, but I never put him on the spot, and whenever I visited Orange Courthouse he would take me along Main Street and introduce me to people. Word of this got down to Richmond. One day I went into the lobby of the Hotel Richmond and found Harrison seated in one of the massive chairs which adorn such lobbies. He did not rise as I approached but remained where he was with his face wearing the kind of woebegone expression that a man would have if he had lost his dearest friend. Looking down at him I asked, "Harrison, have you been over there?"

at the same time jerking my thumb in the direction of the Capitol where the office of the compensation board is located. "Yeah," he replied. "Did they ask you," I continued, "whether you have been a good boy?" "They sure did, Pickens," his doleful voice confessed. "I am sorry," I said and walked away never to see him again. Several weeks after this, the Orange paper announced that the salary of the commissioner of revenue had been raised $500.00 a year, and from then on Spotswood was for Battle.

Similar pressure was applied in other counties. In one, an elected official who had announced publicly that he was supporting me was sent for by the district judge who expressed concern for his growing family in view of the rising cost of living and added that he was going to see if he could get him a raise from the compensation board. The implication was clear. The official thought it over and then informed my local manager that he would have to shift to Battle; and so it went.

2) By Senator Byrd himself labeling me as the candidate of the CIO.

For years Byrd had used the CIO as his whipping boy and as the sinister scarecrow with which to frighten simple-minded citizens. Like Bilbo in Mississippi he chose as his opponent in any race the person or institution most likely to antagonize Virginians. The CIO in those days filled that role perfectly. Actually, the CIO at that time was a completely negligible political force in Virginia, for it could not deliver more than seven or eight thousand votes. But after Martin Hutchinson had unwisely made a personal attack on Harry Byrd, the senator in reply went down to Harrisonburg and pinned the CIO label on me, thus creating the maximum hostility to me among conservatives and insuring the maximum vote for Battle among people who feared that organization. After the campaign was over, a very substantial resident of Staunton said to me one day, "Colonel, I liked you very much and wanted to vote for you, but I could not stand the thought of the Commonwealth's being run by the CIO."

3) By arousing race prejudice.

I had had in mind appointing Luther Jackson of Virginia State College, an eminent Negro educator and a very fine man, to the State Board of Education. In the question period at the end of a meeting in northern Virginia, a person, who later was identified as a "fellow traveler," asked, "Will you appoint Negroes to state boards?" I replied, "I will make appointments on the basis of merit—not of race." This answer provided ammunition for large ads supporting Battle and opposing me in county papers across the South Side. An advertisement in the *Pittsylvania Star* of June 24, 1949, read: "We oppose Francis Pickens Miller because

(1) Miller stated in Arlington Virginia, Friday, May 20th (We quote the *Arlington Sun*): 'That a change is inevitable in Virginia.' Miller said further, 'Personnel should be appointed to various boards and commissions in the State government on the basis of qualifications and not race.'

(2) *Red-Blooded Virginians* are not willing to accept a man for Governor of this grand old Commonwealth who advocates any such practice. . . ."

4) By producing a letter from Petrillo supporting me.

Petrillo was chief of the AFL Musicians Union with headquarters in New York. He was a petty tyrant, was dubbed "czar" of the musicians, and I had as little use for his methods as did Harry Byrd. Further, I knew that the Richmond agent of that union was working for John Battle. It never occurred to me to ask for Petrillo's support, and if it had been offered, I would have rejected it. Consequently my surprise was great one evening at a labor rally in Richmond to have a man come up and hand me a letter to read. It was undated and unsigned but it was on Petrillo's letterhead and was addressed to the Virginia members of the American Federation of Musicians. Whoever drafted that letter was a skilled craftsman. The key paragraph said:

The State of Virginia will hold its Democratic Primary on August 2nd to select a Democratic candidate for Governor. It is most important that you lend your support to Francis Pickens Miller, a liberal and progressive anti-machine candidate. It is in the interests of yourself, the organization to which you belong, and all the workers of Virginia—organized and unorganized—that every effort be made to elect Francis Pickens Miller.

It was obvious that there was mischief in the air, and I did not have to wait long to discover its extent. A night or two later I was driving through the Northern Neck with my radio on when John Battle came on the air. He had an announcement of the greatest importance to make. He said that Virginia was once more threatened by a northern invasion, and with unaccustomed passion in his voice he read Petrillo's letter. Then in the style of a true demagogue he called on all right-thinking Virginians to line up on the banks of the Potomac and defend the Commonwealth once more from these sinister and subversive forces that were threatening to invade us from the North. It was so unlike John that I could not believe my ears. But the deed was done, and full-page ads in many of the county papers carried the news of the letter to every part of the state with due stress upon the kind of man I must be to receive support of that nature after having publicly repudiated outside interference. I knew that none of my lieutenants had asked for such a letter, and I also knew that I could trust Jack Smith, head of the State AFL, when he denied all knowledge. It took me two years to find out who had contacted Petrillo. The man responsible was a labor leader outside of Virginia and I have always assumed that what he did was to comply with a request from Petrillo's agent in Richmond who was working for John Battle. Only someone who wished to do me the maximum amount of harm could have composed that epistle. It was worth at least 10,000 votes for the Byrd Organization.

5) By securing large financial assistance from Pennsylvania Republicans.

Toward the end of the campaign Battle's war chest had been seriously depleted by the cost of radio and newspaper advertisements though contributions had been pouring in from all over the country. Some months later I was reliably informed that Tom Blanton, chairman of the State Democratic Committee and treasurer of Battle's campaign, had gone to see one of the Pews in Pennsylvania and after explaining Byrd's predicament had secured the amount required. The irony of the situation has always appealed to me. Here was a northerner, a Pennsylvanian, a Presbyterian, and a Republican, providing massive assistance to defeat a Virginia Presbyterian Democrat in a Democratic primary in the South. It was clear that loyalty to party or church was quite secondary compared to the appeal of self-interest.

6) By bringing pressure on Horace Edward's supporters to shift to Battle.

Edwards probably had 60,000–70,000 votes around the first of June and Sidney Kellam, Battle's campaign manager, was aware that a substantial portion of Edwards's support came from people who normally belonged to the Byrd Organization. So he mounted a massive state-wide telephone campaign. This effort was so persuasive that ten or fifteen thousand votes were shifted, leaving Edwards with less than 48,000 on election day.

7) But the *coup de grâce* was given by persuading Republicans to enter the Democratic primary.

On August 2, 1949, for the first time, Republicans were holding a state-wide primary, on the same day as Democrats, to choose their nominees for state offices. But Byrd was equal to the occasion. He went to Henry Wise, the elder statesman of the Republican party, and told him that he needed 50,000 votes to save Virginia from the subversive forces that I represented. Wise agreed to deliver them provided Byrd used his influence to persuade the Virginia delegates to the Republican National Convention to support Robert Taft for the presidency. Byrd promised to do so, and a few days later there was a front-page story in the *Richmond Times-Dispatch* and other Virginia dailies that Henry Wise was urging all Republicans to leave their own primary and enter the Democratic primary, since only in this way could the sinister forces be defeated that were threatening the Commonwealth.

In his statement, printed July 14, 1949, in the *Times-Dispatch* Henry Wise told his fellow Republicans:

> More is at issue than a party label. . . . Resenting outside interference and the threat of dictatorship, I feel that it is the duty of every citizen of this Commonwealth, regardless of past party affiliations, to join in the effort to repel this unholy invasion by aliens into our domestic affairs, and that by an overwhelming vote for John S. Battle we serve notice upon all such meddlers that we will forever rest our foot upon the tyrant's neck.

Prior to this the Republicans had been made aware through Byrd's charge that I was the CIO candidate, and also, through the Petrillo letter, of what frightening consequences would ensue if I were elected, and so they were only too eager to save Virginia from such a dreadful fate.

Immediately after Wise's appeal, the attorney general (Lindsay Almond) ruled that it was perfectly legal for Republicans to vote in Democratic primaries. Then John Battle publicly invited them to do so. The result was that 316,612 Virginians voted in the Democratic primary of August 2, 1949—74,000 more than had ever voted for a Democratic candidate for president of the United States. Where did the additional voters come from? Since only 8,888 Republicans voted in their own state-wide primary on that day, it is obvious that most of the 74,000 were Republicans. As far as Democratic votes were concerned, I won the nomination for governor. But it was denied to me by this massive invasion from the other party. The Republican leader, Senator Ted Dalton, confirmed this in an article in the *Washington Post* for September 3, 1950. He wrote:

> Strange as it may seem, the Republican Party in Virginia, although dead

on its feet, last year was the deciding factor in the election of John S. Battle (Democrat) as Governor. It happened in the primary campaign in which Battle, the organization candidate, was pressed in a three-cornered race.

Republicans everywhere in the State, and particularly in the western part where we have considerable strength, deserted our own first gubernatorial primary and flocked to the Democratic primary to support Battle —presumably because the GOP of Virginia is generally more favorable to the Democratic organization here than to the anti-organization group. The Byrd organization may deny that it owes its political neck in the State government to the Republicans (Senator Harry F. Byrd, the political maestro of Virginia, feels that the Republicans did not help), but the county and precinct workers know otherwise.

Subsequently, in a speech on the floor of the Virginia state senate on February 12, 1952, as quoted in the *Richmond Times-Dispatch*, Senator Dalton said that he had a "little gratuitous advice" to give to the state Democratic "organization":

We of the minority party have cooperated and helped you—when you were *in extremis* in the gubernatorial primary of 1949, thousands and thousands of us rallied and saved your necks by electing the fine gentleman who now sits upstairs (in the Governor's chair). We're not asking for a payoff. All we want is a fair and square deal. . . . If you keep turning us down our people will say we've got to look elsewhere for friends.

Thus Senator Dalton publicly recognized what for years had been common knowledge, namely that Virginia was being ruled by a coalition of the Byrd party and the Republican party.

Several years later there was a sardonic footnote to this story. Old Henry Wise told my friend, Marion Caskie, that though Byrd had asked for 50,000 Republicans to come into the Democratic primary, they had actually sent in 60,000. But, said Wise rather bitterly, "Byrd did not keep his part of the agreement."

On April 16, 1965, sixteen years after that campaign, The *Richmond News Leader* said editorially: "Virginia Republicans time after time have proved to be Mr. Byrd's best friends. How do you think we licked Francis Pickens Miller?"

On July 31, 1948, I had made the following estimate of what the vote would be a year later:

Miller	110,000
Battle	100,000
Edwards	65,000
	275,000

Cartoon by Fred O. Seibel on gubernatorial campaign, July 31, 1949
Photographed by Lowell A. Kenyon, Chevy Chase, Maryland
Courtesy of the Richmond Times-Dispatch

My son Andrew wrote this estimate down with the date, and the card on which he wrote lies before me. That is about what the vote would have been if only Democrats had voted in the primary. But because of the wholesale Republican invasion of the primary and a massive last minute shift of vote from Edwards to Battle, both engineered by Byrd's lieutenants, the vote on August 2, 1949, turned out to be:

Miller	111,697
Battle	135,426
Edwards	47,435
Arnold	22,054 (entered race later)
	316,612

In retrospect it seemed surprising that I had done as well as I had considering the fact that I was not supported by a single daily paper except the *Waynesboro News-Virginian*, whose publisher, Louis Spilman, became my state-wide campaign manager. The *Norfolk Virginian-Pilot* did not support me but it treated my candidacy with a certain benevolence. It was a different story with the press in Roanoke, Lynchburg, and Richmond. The families that owned those papers, the Fishburns, the Glasses, and the Bryans, were hard-core members of the Virginia establishment and resented the threat to their way of life that my candidacy posed. Of all these papers the most vehement editorial attacks during the last two months of the campaign came from the *Richmond News-Leader*. The editor of that paper had been Douglas Freeman, the distinguished biographer of Robert E. Lee. In an unhurried conversation at his office one day early in 1948, Dr. Freeman had encouraged me to run and expressed the hope that I would attack the "invisible government of Virginia." He never attacked me while he continued to be editor. This restraint was more than Tennant Bryan (son of John Stewart Bryan), now publisher of the paper, and John Dana Wise, who had become general manager of both Richmond newspapers, were willing to accept.

Jack Wise had come to Richmond from South Carolina. He was the purest pre-Civil War type southerner I have ever met. The years between 1830 and 1850 were his spiritual home in time. Once in 1948, when I was trying to fathom his philosophy of government, I mentioned the problem of pollution in the James River. I pointed out that it had become so bad that fish could no longer live in that part of the river that flowed by Albemarle County, and I was about to add that it was perfectly obvious that government was the only agency capable of taking remedial action; but before I had time to make this point Wise brought his fist down on the desk and declared, "I would rather see the James remain an open sewer than have government do anything about it." That was the philosophy I was challenging, so it was natural that Wise should want to do everything in his power to defeat me. The realization of his objective was facilitated by Dr. Freeman's retirement and by the appointment of James J. Kilpatrick of Oklahoma, one of the paper's news reporters, as editor of the *News Leader.*

Kilpatrick was made to order for the job Wise and Bryan assigned to him. He had a sharp and ingenious mind, and when circumstances required, he could use a vitriolic pen. The *News Leader* took to the warpath immediately and attacked me relentlessly. Nor did my defeat diminish the paper's attacks. It is customary among civilized people to refrain from kicking a man when he is down, but Kilpatrick had no compunction on that score. In fact he seemed rather to relish doing it. On August 5, 1949, three days after the primary, he wrote a contemptuously derisive editorial entitled, "Mr. Miller, Full Time," the thesis of which was that "the gubernatorial campaign now appears to have had one unexpected, but praiseworthy, result: It has given Francis Pickens Miller a job" (that is, organizing the Democratic forces in Virginia). The editor described me as a man whose occupation was a mystery and who seldom had had any genuine employment. One of my friends wrote to Tennant Bryan and strongly protested against the tone of this editorial, but Bryan replied that it was published with his consent and he subscribed to the point of view it expressed.

Some years later Kilpatrick and I were speaking on the same program at Longwood College in Farmville. Meanwhile he had become the champion of "massive resistance" to the laws of the land and the father of the resurrected doctrine of "interposition." True to form, when he rose to speak, he broke the rules of the meeting, which he had accepted in advance, and launched into a personal attack upon me. After his talk one of the leading citizens of Farmville, who would not have agreed with my political views, came up to me to apologize for Kilpatrick's behavior. "You know, Colonel," he said, "that man is not a Virginian and he is not a gentleman." As far as I was concerned, that about summed it up.

Tennant Bryan had two hatchet men on his Richmond papers. One was Kilpatrick; the other was a German-born journalist whose real name was Kurt V. Hoffman but who as a columnist for the editorial page of the *Times-Dispatch* wrote under the charming

Virginia name of Ross Valentine. Prior to the outbreak of World
War II he had worked for some German-language papers in New
York that appeared to have Nazi sympathies. During the war he had
found it pleasant to reside in a small Vermont village and for a short
time after the war he wrote editorials for a Republican paper in
Bennington. He expressed himself with a show of erudition and with
the faint suggestion that Nordic views about race were not entirely
repugnant to him. He was made to order for Jack Wise's strategy of
keeping things exactly as they were in Virginia. Kurt Hoffman's
references to me became increasingly vicious until one day he gave
me the great advantage of libeling me. Bryan sent an intermediary to
inquire what satisfaction I wanted. I sent back word that all I required was for Valentine's whole column on a certain day to be
devoted to an apology with the copy to be submitted to me in advance for correction. On January 8, 1953, the *Times-Dispatch* published on the editorial page the agreed column in which Valentine,
recalling what he had said earlier, wrote:

I wish to apologize for the implication of "intellectual dishonesty" and
the phrase "the Kansas City level."
The first of these, while intended to absolve Colonel Miller from moral
dishonesty, can nevertheless, be interpreted as a reflection on his intellectual integrity.
The second, intended as a synonym for "whistle stop tactics" could be
interpreted as covering a multitude of sins. I had no intention whatever to
accuse the colonel of reprehensible tactics.
I, therefore, completely retract both. This column attempts to be fair
without fear or favor. I regret the use of such generalizing language in
the heat of a political struggle.

After that, Kurt Hoffman was more careful in what he said
about me.

Jack Wise was a tragic figure in Virginia during his last years.
He, like Edmund Ruffin a century before, consecrated his life to the
task of preventing long overdue change. And as the world of the
past that he was trying to preserve began to disintegrate around
him, like Ruffin after the collapse of the Confederacy, he took his
own life. He had great capacity and it was a pity he could not have
lived to serve a better cause.

It is not surprising that it was difficult for me to secure the support
of the leading daily papers. As far as Richmond, Lynchburg, and
Roanoke were concerned, one family in each city owned both morning and afternoon papers. There was no competition and hence a

complete monopoly of the press. People could read only the editorial opinions that one man or one family in their respective communities wanted them to read. Jack Wise, in addressing a meeting of editors, put the matter quite simply: "Apart from letters to the editor, of course, let's tolerate no other opinion on our editorial page than what we hold to be the right opinion—our own." Further, the selection of news and headlines was influenced by the same philosophy. No wonder many Virginians acquired a cockeyed view of the world about them. If citizens were to become better informed, it seemed to me to be essential that they should have a choice between papers representing different points of view. Consequently I tried for several years to interest various people in launching another paper in Richmond to break the monopoly there. But that enterprise would have required an initial six or seven million dollars, and with national advertising already sewed up, the risk was too great to attract investment. It is an ironic fact that two hundred years after the newly adopted Constitution guaranteed "freedom of the press" to all Americans, that freedom is now enjoyed and can only be enjoyed by one man or one family in most medium-sized American cities.

Whatever one may think of the owners and publishers of some of Virginia's metropolitan newspapers, many of the reporters working for these papers were unmatched for their integrity and competence. There is no finer body of journalists anywhere.

The structure of organization in the 1948–49 campaign was extremely simple because of the paucity of persons and the scarcity of funds. By spring it was obvious that we had to have a campaign manager. Louis Spilman, publisher of the *Waynesboro News-Virginian*, had made a tour through the state and phoned me that he thought I was winning. Around May 1, he agreed to take charge of the campaign. He brought with him complete devotion to the cause, indefatigable energy, and rare contacts with the press in every part of the state. From then on I knew that my schedule of speaking engagements was in good hands. At about the same time, L. Harvey Poe of Richmond became my finance chairman and applied himself to what turned out to be an ultra-difficult assignment and a thankless task.

The most pleasant recollection I have of that campaign is the support I received from Virginia women. The chairman of the committee that rallied them to my cause was Meta Glass, half-sister of the former U.S. Senator Carter Glass and the retired president of Sweet Briar College. There was no greater lady in Virginia. And the di-

rector of the committee was Etta Belle Northington of Fredericks-
burg. Under their leadership a group of women organized by Elizabeth Willis carried Richmond, and other similar groups helped make
possible victories in Northern Virginia and the Hampton Roads area.

Further, nothing cheered me more in the spring of 1949 than the
realization that youth was responding to my appeal. It had been
many years since young people in Virginia had been interested in
politics. What I was trying to say and do evoked hopes and expec-
tations that apparently had been waiting for just such a moment to
express themselves. The campaign became for some an emotional
crusade and they went to work with inspired enthusiasm to bring
Virginia back again into the mainstream of national life. My deepest
regret in retrospect is that I was not able to provide them with the
thrilling taste of victory, since defeat is especially bitter for the
young. But their deep moral commitment promised the eventual
triumph of the cause in which they believed.

Altogether I had a fascinating assortment of people working for
me—in fact, they had such diverse backgrounds and interests that
I never felt it would be wise to bring them all together in one place.
For instance, the best organizer in my campaign was Thomas Jefferson Sheehan, an Irish bricklayer, who was a segregationist at heart
but because of his devotion to me never let his race views come between us. Then there was Oliver Hill, the eminent Negro lawyer
who carried the Prince Edward school desegregation case to the Supreme Court. Among others were Senator Robinette of Lee County
—the only member of the state senate who supported me—a most
courtly gentleman who in a cutaway coat addressed the mountain
people of his district in elegant Shakespearean language; and Virgil
Goode, Commonwealth's Attorney of Franklin County, whom I like
to think of as the last authentic frontiersman, wearing a coonskin
cap with a long squirrel rifle in his hands. Virgil wrested control of
Franklin County from the Byrd Machine and maintained its independence through the years. Then there was James Ashby, clerk of
the court in Stafford County, a Virginia gentleman of the old school
who understood what I was trying to do and gave me his generous
support. Toward the end of the campaign he organized a crab feast
for me at Marlboro, his home on the banks of the Potomac, and it
was the one purely idyllic political afternoon I have ever known.

Finally there was Robert Whitehead, the finest associate that any
man running for public office ever had. He fought for me so hard
that once, after a radio speech in Richmond, he passed out from sheer

exhaustion as his wife was driving him home to Lovingston, and she did not know whether he was dead or alive until she reached their doctor. One of the people to whom I owed most in that campaign was a student in the Law School of the University of Virginia. He came from Boston and his name was Deering Danielson. Deering invested more than twelve thousand dollars in my political activities and though he had intended to settle in Charlottesville, he was so disappointed by my defeat that he decided to leave the state. Similarly, my managers in Norfolk and Danville, as well as a number of other supporters, found that it would be easier for them to make a living if they left Virginia where they would be beyond the reach of the Byrd Machine. I am still haunted by remembering how many people had their lives blighted in one way or another because I could not win.

As usual Helen was my mainstay throughout the ordeal of the final weeks. When my headquarters office broke under the strain and practically ceased to function, she left her work in Washington and took charge, aided enthusiastically by Andrew and Robert. In victory and defeat I rely on her.

On the day of the primary Helen again experienced the ruthless discrimination of the Byrd Machine. As we went into Mr. Shaver's store at Ivy, a few miles west of Farmington, to cast our ballots, the judge said to her: "Mrs. Miller, you can't vote. Your name is not on the list." In those days, judges of election were supplied with lists of voters who had paid their poll taxes, and sure enough, Helen's was not there. But the law also provided that if a citizen produced his poll tax receipts for each of the three preceding years, he must be allowed to vote regardless of whether his name was, or was not, on the list. So Helen asked me for the car keys and started for the door with the judge calling after her, "Suppose you can't find them?" Helen shot back: "I take very good care of my things." In ten minutes she had driven the three miles home and returned with her receipts. She voted, but someone had left off her name and to have that kind of thing happen to Helen again opened old wounds.

Another thing that really hurt me during that 1948–49 campaign was the punch line that John Battle used in his closing speeches. In referring to me he said, "You know, it is an evil bird that fouls its own nest." This was so out of keeping with John as I had known him that I could not explain it except on the ground that the boys in the Organization, sensing defeat, had pressured him into adopting a tough line. But the smart remains to this day. After the campaign was over, I mentioned to Pete Perry, one of Battle's managers, my surprise that he would have stooped to that level, and Pete replied, "But you were criticizing Virginia." "I was not criticizing Virginia," I retorted, "I was criticizing the Byrd Organization because of what it had done to Virginia." "But Byrd *is* Virginia," Pete shot back as he moved away. That was the mentality of faithful Byrd lieutenants only twenty years ago.

The hardest personal blow I had to take that summer was the death of my mother. She had had a glorious life of more than 87 years and had exerted a greater influence upon my character and outlook than anyone else. As an old-fashioned southern lady she had disapproved of women voting, but that spring Robert Hutcheson had taken her down to the Court House where she registered, paid her back poll taxes, and qualified to vote. However, she never had a chance to drop her ballot for me into the box, and I have never forgiven myself for not being with her more at the end. Coming, as her death did, at the peak of the campaign, it was difficult to carry on during the ensuing weeks as if nothing had happened, but there was no alternative and I was confident that she would have wished me to continue to fight as hard as I could.

XV ✑ Another Challenge to the Machine

It was clear to me in the autumn of 1949 that, regardless of the consequences, I had to continue on the path upon which I had embarked and that meant challenging Byrd himself for the U.S. Senate in 1952. We had built a fairly good organization during 1948–49 and it was essential to keep it in being. The presidential campaign in the autumn of 1948 had also served our organizational interests well. Martin Hutchinson, Robert Whitehead, and others had formed a Straight Democratic Ticket Committee and since Byrd as usual was doing nothing for the national party this committee helped carry the state for Truman. After August, 1949, my aim was to maintain contacts and keep the lines of communication open through correspondence and occasional meetings.

Senator Byrd had become so alienated from President Truman that during the rest of 1949 and all of 1950 I served as a sort of observation post for the White House. Truman had frozen all appointments in Virginia because of Byrd's attitude and I had the delightful experience of persuading the White House to confirm the appointment of the postmaster in Berryville (Byrd's home town) since I did not see why that good man should be made to suffer because he was a neighbor of the senator.

Toward the end of 1950, because of President Truman's interest in me, I was assigned to the intelligence division of the Department of State and worked there until February, 1952, when the time had come for me to prepare for my next campaign. I knew that once again Senator Byrd would defeat me in the Democratic primary with Republican votes, but it seemed my destiny to pave the way for the future through defeat. In any event I was convinced that contesting elections was the best way to educate the people politically, and since the gauge of battle had already been thrown down, I was not one to side step a fight in a good cause. I had thrown down the gauge when speaking to a political club in Richmond in December, 1950. In the course of that talk I had said: "I know of nothing more contemptible than for the rich and powerful, who also consider themselves well-born, to kick working men about as Harry Byrd has done in order to secure and maintain political control." Having said that, I knew I had a fight on my hands.

Byrd's attitude toward day laborers had been made abundantly clear during the Great Depression by the wages he paid in his orchards, and by the excessively long hours his men worked.

Another incident illustrates Byrd's feeling toward "the lower classes." Once when I was in Raleigh, North Carolina, for a speaking engagement, my friend McNeill Poteat, minister of the Pullen Memorial Baptist Church, told me that for many years he had been saving a story for me. It seems that when Max Gardner was governor of North Carolina in the early thirties he invited the recently appointed U.S. senator from Virginia, Harry Flood Byrd, to come down for a dinner with a select group of his political friends, among whom Poteat had been included, according to southern custom, to bless the occasion. As general conversation began after dinner, Gardner said to Byrd: "Senator, I wish you would explain to these gentlemen your Virginia plan for transferring the burden of taxation from the rich to the poor." In response, Byrd with complete seriousness explained how it was done. McNeill Poteat's comment to me was that never in his life had he been so nauseated by the discourse of an eminent politician. Twenty years ago it was still true in Virginia that a mule belonging to a poor farmer was taxed at a higher rate than the same mule would have been taxed had it belonged to a corporation. But in those days the poor farmer had no way of protesting, since the poll tax had deprived him of his vote.

In the spring of 1952, an amusing incident occurred. Virginia law forbade the block payment of poll taxes. At Berryville a group of Trappist monks had recently established a retreat house. A friend of mine in government service, who was a devout Catholic, felt the need of spending a quiet week end in meditation at this place of re-treat. One of the monks had been appointed to the office of receiving guests, and in that capacity was allowed to talk. Before leaving, my friend, hoping to interest the brotherhood in my candidacy, re-marked to the guestmaster that he trusted the monks were becoming familiar with political developments in Virginia. "Yes indeed," the Father is reported to have replied, "and Senator Byrd has not only given us young trees for our apple orchard but has also paid all our poll taxes."

The senator delayed his announcement until just before the dead-line for filing, and I filed immediately. This campaign, even more than the first, had to be conducted on the tiniest shoestring. Every-one knew that I could not win, and no one likes to back a sure loser. Less than a thousand dollars came into my office as contributions from fellow Virginians. Hence I had to pay for most of the campaign expenses myself. Of all my friends, only two were insistent that I should run. One was Trudye Fowler (wife of Henry H. Fowler, sub-sequently secretary of the treasury under President Johnson). The other was Bolling Lambeth of Bedford. I regarded Lambeth as a very able attorney and he agreed to become my campaign manager. We opened a small headquarters office in Richmond with a free-lance news reporter named Adams in charge, ably assisted by my elder son, Andrew, who was then nineteen years old and who began to acquire his political expertise through that experience. Robert, who was seventeen, drove me all over the state and was a constant source of encouragement. The fact that this campaign lasted only one-quarter the length of the first was about the only thing in its favor.

I challenged Byrd to meet me in public debate, but he refused to do so and consistently refrained in all his speeches from discuss-ing substantive issues that confronted the state and the nation. When addressing meetings of rural people, his punch line frequently was, "You know the schools of Virginia were not good enough for Miller. He went to Oxford." This always drew a big laugh and proved to be a telling political argument. Byrd repeated his cheap sally again and again though he was a member of the board of Washington and Lee where I had graduated and, of course, knew that I had been a student there.

Toward the end of the campaign, billboards appeared in various parts of the state which said "Vote American—Return Harry F. Byrd to the United States Senate—Maintain your Democratic form of

Government." Literature was also being distributed using the same language. This was too much for me. Hence, on the Fourth of July, I went on the air over a state-wide network and said:

These advertisements and slogans are unmistakably clear. They say that those who vote on July 15 for Harry Byrd will vote American. They suggest, with equal clarity, that those who vote for Miller on July 15 are not quite as American as those who vote for Byrd, and may even be un-American.

Thus, Harry Byrd has raised the question of Americanism in its sharpest form, and I propose to discuss it. I am old-fashioned enough to have a sense of honor. By his appeal, "Vote American," Harry Byrd has impugned my honor and questioned my patriotism. No man on earth can do that without having to give an account of himself. I ask you, therefore, Harry Byrd, to advance to the bar of Virginia public opinion and listen to what I have to say—and answer the questions I am about to ask.

First of all, I should explain, since you don't seem to be aware of it, that I know a good bit about America and about what it means to be an American. My people played an active part in founding this Republic. The most precious possession which I have is a sword given by the Continental Congress to my frontiersman ancestor, Colonel Andrew Pickens of South Carolina, for having whipped the Tories and Redcoats during our Revolutionary War. Incidentally, though all of my ancestors fought on the American side in the Revolution, your direct ancestor, William Byrd, III, of "Westover," wrote on July 30, 1775, to General Sir Jeffrey Amherst, of the British army, that he had refused to command Virginia troops opposed to the King, that he was ready to serve His Majesty, and that he would be glad of an opportunity to convince Virginians of their error and bring them back to loyalty and duty. The fight I am making now is a continuation of the fight that my ancestors made in 1776 for the rights of man against the Tories.

This brings us to our own time. Senator, will you be kind enough to answer the following questions?

(1) Harry Byrd, did you appear in the uniform of your country during World War I? Were you ever on the field of battle beside men who were dying for freedom and for their way of life? If you were not, what kind of an American are you to raise the question of Americanism in relation to a man who has volunteered in two world wars, who has seen five years of active military service overseas, and who, in the first world war, was a combat soldier in the Old First Division of the Regular Army?

(2) Ten years after the first world war, you, Harry Byrd, were Governor of Virginia. One of the most evil men of our time was Benito Mussolini, of Italy. He did as much as any one of three or four other men to destroy democracy in Europe and to plunge the world into a holocaust of bloodshed. Yet, on December 9, 1927, in a public speech in Richmond, you re-

ferred to Mussolini "as one of the few great supreme leaders the world has ever produced." What kind of an American were you, Harry Byrd, to express that opinion about one of the human monsters of our time?

(3) On November 7, 1941, one month before Pearl Harbor, you, Harry Byrd, voted with the Republican minority of the Senate against allowing American merchant ships to arm. You will recall that, at that time, Hitler's submarines were sinking defenseless merchantmen on the high seas. What kind of an American were you to vote against giving American seamen a fair chance to defend themselves in the open seas against Hitler's submarines?

(4) On June 8, 1942, you voted against increasing the base pay of servicemen from twenty-one dollars a month to fifty a month, though we were already at war. Harry Byrd, what kind of an American were you when you cast that vote?

(5) In the post-war period, the survival of America and the American way of life depended upon keeping the Communists out of Western Europe. As of today, this has been achieved through the Marshall Plan and the rearmament of Europe which that plan made possible. The Communists fought this plan more violently than they have fought any other American move since World War II, because they knew that, if the Marshall Plan succeeded, Western Europe would become allied with America and not with Russia. Harry Byrd, what kind of an American were you on March 13, 1948, when you voted with "Pass-the-biscuits" Pappy O'Daniel, of Texas, and Henry Wallace's running mate, Glenn Taylor, of Idaho, against the Marshall Plan?

(6) After World War I, a man named Edward A. Rumely was convicted of trading with the enemy and served his time for this offense. Later Rumely became executive secretary of one of the extremist organizations called the Committee for Constitutional Government, Inc. Part 5 of the hearings of the House Select Committee on Lobbying Activities is devoted to the hearings on the Committee for Constitutional Government, Inc., which were held June 27-29 and August 25, 1950. Page 99 of this document reproduces a list of payments in connection with the sending of franked material. This document reports (Order No. 4205, March 10, 1950) payment by Homer Dodge, the Committee's Washington representative, of $775.90 for 70,000 copies of certain material, with the notation, "Senator Byrd franked package." Harry Byrd, what kind of an American were you to lend your frank to a man who had been convicted of trading with the enemy in war time? That wasn't good economy, was it? When your frank is used, the American taxpayer pays for the cost of postal delivery. In this instance, you had the American taxpayer pay for the postage on propaganda distributed by a man who had traded with the enemy in time of war.

In the past, you, Harry Byrd, have had a monopoly on many things in Virginia. You even have a monopoly on the official state bird—the redbird, which you use for your own private purposes. You use it, as you often use things that belong to the people of Virginia, as if it were your personal property. But there is one thing in Virginia that is not your private property. There is one thing on which you do not have a monopoly, and that is patriotism. Among my supporters, there are thousands of Virginia fathers and mothers who have lost their sons or relatives on the field of honor. Your appeal, "Vote American," is an insult to them and to the memories of their heroic dead.

Harry Byrd, you stand before the bar of **Virginia public** opinion. Please answer this question: What kind of an American are you to imply, in light of the above record, that those who vote for you are better Americans than those who vote for me?

Your arrogance, Senator, has overreached itself.

Every right-thinking Virginian realizes that the cloak of Americanism in which you have wrapped yourself, is out of place. It is in keeping with your pretence of being a Democrat, with your very recent pretence of being a New Dealer, and with all the other phony pretences which you have used during the course of this campaign.

Up until the time of this speech I had confined my attacks to Byrd's voting record. The *Washington Evening Star* of August 26, 1951, had reported the senator as having said during a speech at his annual orchard picnic, "If I were asked today to name the New Deal measures that I favor, I would not name a single one." I knew that his voting record was negative but I did not realize how negative it had been until I began to examine it. When I did so I discovered that he had voted with the majority of the Republican senators more frequently than Senator Robert Taft himself, who had become by that time "Mr. Republican." So I went to town on his having voted against most of the measures that many Virginians had come to regard as essential to their way of life—Social Security, minimum wage, agricultural adjustment, soil conservation programs, etc. Over a long period of years the Richmond newspapers had practiced the policy of not publishing Byrd's complete voting record. Consequently, as I began to make the record public, many people were astonished and to some my statements seemed so improbable that they accused me of lying. Even the *Richmond Times-Dispatch* began to wonder if I was telling the truth; in hopes that I was not, the managing editor assigned to one of his best reporters the job of going to Washington to check on the official voting records and then to prepare a story for the Sunday issue before the primary, showing in the form of a chart (1) how I had said Byrd voted on 32 key measures since 1935, (2) how he had said he voted, and (3) how the

Congressional Record showed he voted. When the story was turned in, it showed that my statements about Byrd's votes were true, but it also showed that on three occasions the votes as listed in the Congressional Record indicated that Byrd had voted differently from the way he had told Virginians that he had voted. The managing editor was so flabbergasted by discovering that the facts as reported seemed to reflect on Byrd that he ordered the suppression of the story even though it had been his own idea and he had assigned it. Consequently, the people of Virginia were never informed that my charges were correct. But I sympathized with the managing editor. He really was on a hot spot. He knew the "king could do no wrong" and who was he to tell the people otherwise. So he saved his skin, but the reporter who had been ordered to write the story left the *Times-Dispatch* in disgust as soon as he could in order to join another southern paper which he thought had more reputable standards. Several other reporters also departed.

Even though I had known that defeat was inevitable, the evening of the primary election day was one of the most trying of my life, and because of that I shall never forget the thoughtfulness and consideration of my dear friends Beecher and Frances Stallard who invited Helen and me and our sons to have supper with them. Their affectionate sentiments did much to lessen the impact of the impending blow. Beecher had been defeated for the state senate a year before by a fraudulent racist trick and he well understood what I was going through.

On that July 15, 1952, more than 345,000 Virginians voted in the Democratic primary. Byrd received 216,438 and I received 128,869. In analyzing the vote it appeared that some 80,000–90,000 regular Republicans had again entered the Democratic primary and this meant that I had about split even with the senator as far as the votes of Democrats were concerned. The only consolation I got out of the returns was the knowledge that I had received 17,000 more votes against Byrd than I had received against Battle. And I also knew that I had kept the liberal banner flying in Virginia.

My assumption that there had been a massive Republican invasion of the Democratic primary was confirmed at the Democratic National Convention later that summer when Congressman Bill Tuck of Halifax, Virginia, told Edgar Brown, Democratic national committeeman from South Carolina, that Harry Byrd had made a deal with the Republicans to throw the state to Eisenhower if they offered no opposition to his candidacy for re-election to the Senate in the November general election. Byrd was unopposed that autumn.

The story of the part many Virginia Democrats played in the presidential campaign of 1952 is one of the sorriest chapters in the history of our state party. For years the Virginia party had employed the technique of sitting on its hands during presidential election campaigns and then claiming all of the perquisites of loyal party members after a Democrat had become president. This time it was to be different. The Byrd Machine leaders were not to sit on their hands—they were to betray Adlai Stevenson and the national party.

The Democratic National Convention meeting in Chicago that summer adopted a loyalty pledge. It was weak enough; it merely required delegates to insure that the names of the candidates chosen by the convention would be listed on the presidential ballot in their respective states as Democrats. Nothing could have been more innocuous. But the Virginians present were feeling their oats and refused to sign. The question before the convention was whether a state delegation which abjured even so slight an attachment to the national party as the proposed pledge should be seated.

When the convention was polled on this matter, the vote of Illinois was decisive. In the delegation meeting, an initial decision to vote against seating was reversed at the insistence of Jake Harvey; when the result was made known, other states eager to go along with the Stevenson forces fell into line. Sam Rayburn gave John Battle the rostrum: Battle, in an impassioned speech, said, "We expect to go along with your nominee—I am grateful to you for your action of this afternoon. I shall never betray your trust."

Upon his return to Richmond, Battle was welcomed like a conquering hero; during the early autumn he made a speech on behalf of the national ticket, and, on September 20, introduced Stevenson at a rally in Richmond. But, on October 17, Byrd dissociated himself from the Democratic national ticket and platform in a much publicized state-wide radio speech. From then on, Battle adopted a policy of masterful inactivity. As a result of Byrd's speech, the state went for Eisenhower by 80,000 votes.

I have always heard it said that the wounds of a friend are the hardest to bear, and I had a vivid experience of the truth of that saying in my relations with Adlai Stevenson. Knowing that the Byrd Machine would cut his throat, I asked his permission to organize support for him in Virginia as we had done for Truman in 1948. I was personally eager to work for him publicly because I admired him and his political philosophy extravagantly. It is possible that he would not have made a great president, but during the 1952 campaign he embodied political excellence as it had never been embodied before during my lifetime by a candidate for the presidency.

However, when I requested permission to organize on his behalf, Stevenson turned me down. This was the deepest political wound I ever received. While governor of Illinois, he had become a friend of John Battle at governors' conferences and preferred to trust his fortunes in Virginia to John, assuming that the vote of Illinois to seat Virginia in the convention would assure him the support of the Byrd Organization. In 1956, though his candidacy had been sold down the river by the senator and his lieutenants in 1952, he again refused to allow me to organize for him, having learned nothing from his former experience. He would not even let me finance an office to promote "Volunteers for Stevenson." This time no one organized for him and he lost Virginia by nearly 118,000. I saw him only occasionally after that, but just two weeks before he died we had a friendly chat and he urged me to come to visit him in New York.

Stevenson's greatest contribution to our national life was his appeal to the conscience of the American people and to their idealism. And even though defeated for the presidency, he did more for the national Democratic party than most elected presidents have done. During the years 1952–60, under his guidance, the national party became a reality. It concerned itself with major issues of policy through an advisory council which formulated the lines along which it suggested the party should move forward. But even more important were the procedures introduced by Steve Mitchell, whom Stevenson appointed national chairman in 1952. In my opinion, Mitchell was the best chairman the party had between 1940 and 1968. While dealing correctly with the regular state organizations, he was determined to keep lines of communication open with men like myself and with the Democrats for whom we spoke. As a consequence, I worked very closely with him as long as he was chairman. Among the practical results of our collaboration was a dinner in Washington attended by some twenty Democratic leaders from every part of Virginia which led to Virginia's raising its full quota of financial support for the national committee for the first time in many years. One of the most amusing aspects of this dinner was that, due to Byrd's policy of insulating his lieutenants from the national party, some of the most influential Virginians present had never met a national chairman before. The dinner had an ironic aftermath. I gave $2,000 to set a standard for the others, but my name never appeared on a list of contributors. Fred Switzer, the Virginia national committeeman, explained to me afterwards that he had allocated my contribution to each of the ten Virginia districts ($200 to each) in order to help them raise their respective quotas, and he knew I would not mind!

Another practical result of my collaboration with Steve Mitchell was the promotion in Virginia of individual sustaining memberships in the national party. This was a new type of fund-raising support which Steve had introduced, and it proved to be extremely fruitful. By paying $10 a year a Democrat could become a sustaining member of the national party and acquire a sense of direct participation which he could never acquire if his contacts were limited to his state party. My office in Charlottesville became the agency for securing sustaining members and in the course of several years many hundreds were signed up in every part of the state.

The year 1953 was a hard one for me. In the spring of 1948, as I said earlier, Robert Whitehead and I had made an agreement that if I ran in 1949 he would run four years later. As 1953 approached, Robert said that he could not afford to run unless a specific sum were deposited in a bank before he announced. As I recall it, he mentioned the figure of $48,000. Whatever the figure was, his friends raised it and waited for his announcement. But in the end he decided he would not run and I shall never forget my sense of despair mingled with a touch of bitterness as he told Helen and me goodbye one day after a political consultation with a group of friends at our house. He said, "Francis, I don't care to be a sacrificial lamb!"

The Byrd Machine candidate against whom he would have run was Tom Stanley, who was not an effective campaigner. I had kept my part of the agreement and Robert had been truly magnificent in giving me unlimited support of every kind—speaking, organizing, and above all in giving me the benefit of his wisdom and advice. I was sure then and I am sure now that he could have beaten Stanley. Why did he shy at the post? I never could understand it, and I have never discovered the reason.

After Whitehead bowed out, I made one more attempt to secure effective opposition to Stanley in the primary. I asked Senator Harry Carter Stuart of Russell County in the Ninth District to come to lunch at my home in Charlottesville. During our conversation I told him that he could become governor, as his uncle had, if he would run. It was obvious that his entry would split the Organization vote and the total of what he took from the Organization and what my friends could mobilize for him would be more than enough to win. We had a long and friendly talk. He seemed impressed and when he left for Richmond, I was hopeful. The next morning he told the press he was going to support Stanley.

The Stuart fiasco made it clear that the only political role left for me in Virginia was to work for the national party and to keep in being as much as I could of the organization I had built during 1948–52 against the day when younger men could take over and carry the movement forward. Among the many moves I made, none gave me more satisfaction than bringing Neil Staebler from Michigan to Virginia on two separate occasions. He was chairman of the Democratic Central Committee in his state and I had been drawn to him because of his philosophy of "participative" politics. I have never met a man who embodied more completely the spirit which ideally should characterize all democratic politicians. Further, I was thrilled by the fact that a northern leader of the party was sufficiently interested in our problems in the South to come down at his own expense to talk to us about them. He would have made an excellent chairman of the Democratic National Committee if he had been appointed after the Kennedy victory, and that is what should have happened in January, 1961.

When the spring of 1960 arrived, the results of the West Virginia primary made it clear that John F. Kennedy would become the Democratic nominee at the national convention. I had previously preferred Hubert Humphrey, who possessed many of the qualities I had always associated with Theodore Roosevelt. However, Kennedy money and charm had eliminated Hubert, so I took steps to create as much enthusiasm as I could for Jack. I organized a luncheon at the Farmington Country Club for more than two hundred of my friends from every part of the state. Robert Whitehead, State Senator Edward Haddock of Richmond, Graham Morrison, former U.S. assistant attorney general, and Armistead Boothe of Alexandria had agreed to speak and their names had appeared in the press. Early on the morning of the day when the luncheon was to be held, the phone rang and Boothe's smooth voice reported that Charlie Fenwick (an Organization state senator from Northern Virginia) had seen him the night before and urged him not to attend. He added that he had agreed and was not coming. Fenwick was a kind of double agent for the Byrd Machine and through the years discouraged all attempts to do anything for the national party outside of the Organization on the ground that it would "rock the boat," even though he knew very well that the Organization was not going to do anything.

Helen and I attended the Los Angeles convention that summer where it became apparent that Bill Battle, John Battle's younger son, was to be Kennedy's man in Virginia. He and Kennedy had known each other during the war in the Pacific. Their relationship meant that I was destined never to be entrusted with organizing the forces of democracy in my own state, and ironically enough it was always a Battle whose presence prevented me from doing so. However, I knew that at that time the name "Battle" did not strike a responsive chord among labor union members and in the Negro community, since in past years it had been synonymous with leadership of the Byrd Organization. Bill Battle understood this too and he was not unresponsive to the suggestion that my friends should organize another "Straight Democratic Ticket Committee" to get out the liberal, labor, and Negro vote. I secured Ray Niblack of Charlottesville to act as executive director of the committee with a modest budget of around $30,000. Our two-pronged attack commended itself to Senator Jackson, then national Democratic chairman; the two efforts were launched simultaneously and excellent co-ordination was maintained between them throughout the campaign. At the request of Kennedy's national headquarters I also organized a Virginia Committee on Religious Freedom, which I was told later was the best of its kind in the country.

As a result of all these efforts, the Republican margin of almost 120,000 in 1956 was reduced to 40,000 in 1960. This was a great tribute to Bill Battle, Ray Niblack, and those who worked with them.

The campaign ended with an ironic denouement for Helen. She had been asked to be one of five or six nationally known newspaper women to brief Mrs. Kennedy from time to time during the course of the autumn in preparation for radio and television appearances. She had enjoyed doing this and when she was leaving after the final briefing session, Mrs. Kennedy thanked her for all the help she had given and added, "Jack is so pleased when women are willing to work for him, because they do not expect to receive recognition!"

My own brush-off from the Kennedys took place the following February, and my hopes for the Democratic party, which Steve Mitchell had raised, were extinguished at the same time. For years I had always known and been in touch with the chairman of the Democratic National Committee, whoever he might be. So when

Kennedy appointed John Bailey, rather than Neil Staebler, to succeed Jackson, I made an appointment with Bailey. After explaining the Virginia situation briefly, I pointed out the desirability of my continuing to have with him the same kind of relationship that I had had with Steve Mitchell. Finally he broke in and said, "Colonel, I don't know how to operate except to deal with the people who are in control." Out of politeness I continued to chat for a few moments, even though I had gotten his message loud and clear. But he quickly cut me short by repeating his guiding rule in politics, so I arose, wished him good luck and left. I have not been back in the chairman's office since.

As of 1968 the national Democratic party was at its lowest ebb since Raskob was chairman in the twenties. This was due in part to Lyndon Johnson's failure to understand either the meaning or the function of a political party in a democracy, but the disintegration began before Johnson became president. It began under the Kennedys who were responsible for appointing John Bailey. The latter must be held chiefly accountable for the party's subsequent plight. He had been trained by politicians who only dealt with those in control, and consequently ignored the "coming men" who were not yet in control. He forgot that if a party is not to become moribund, the chairman must also keep the lines of communication open to these "coming men." The inevitable logic of Bailey's policy was the disaster at the 1968 Democratic National Convention at Chicago.

During the years of my struggle for democracy in Virginia I was often sustained in defeat by that sentence from John's Gospel: "Except a grain of wheat fall into the ground and die it abideth by itself alone, but if it die, it bringeth forth much fruit." As I survey the Virginia scene now, the fruit of my campaigns seems plentiful, and some of it seems rather good.

XVI ✑ Nonpolitical Life
in Virginia, 1947-1960

For fourteen years we lived in our second Pickens Hill near the Farmington Country Club, Charlottesville. Helen commuted each week to Washington and I, when not engaged in politics, participated in diverse activities—some civic and some religious, some local, some South-wide, and some world-wide.

After we settled at Farmington in June, 1947, our dearest friend in France, Pastor Pierre Maury, a minister of the Reformed Church of France, flew over to see us for ten days or so. I had invited him to come to baptize our boys who for a variety of reasons had never been baptized. Reinhold Niebuhr assured me later that it was a great heresy to suppose that it made any difference who performed the rite of baptism. Of course it made no difference in the validity of the rite. However, Pierre had meant so much to us when we lived in Geneva and attended his church in Ferney-Voltaire that the idea of having our boys baptized by him appealed to us, all the more so as both Helen and I have Huguenot ancestors.

In December, my old friend Colonel Roulier (now known as Rémy) came to visit us. As were were seated in the library around the fire, he stood up and said to me, "Colonel, stand to attention." I did so, and he began to read a citation from the French Republic. I was thrilled. He was presenting me with the medal of the Legion of Honor which he pinned on me and we embraced. It was an exquisitely French occasion arranged for the benefit of Helen and our boys. The official public presentation was made later in New York.

While Rémy was in Charlottesville, he showed Helen a short manuscript reporting a conversation he had had with de Gaulle in 1942, entitled *de Gaulle—A Man Little Understood*, which he hoped she would help him get published in America. It was so excessively laudatory that Helen was sure no publisher would be interested and consequently Rémy left the manuscript with me for safekeeping. It had been edited by de Gaulle himself in 1947 and interlineations or corrections in his own handwriting adorned many pages, including one based on a wartime interview which read as follows: "Look, Rémy! At that time France needed two strings to her bow. She needed the string de Gaulle. She also needed the string Petain. But on condition that both of them would be at her service. . . ."

Early in June, 1950, Rémy wrote an article for a French newspaper quoting de Gaulle as having said this. The general at that time did not want the French people to know that he had made such a statement. Consequently, he was evasive and told the press he had liked Rémy too much to call in question the accuracy of his statement which was the same thing as saying that Rémy's report of the conversation was false. This was more than Rémy could take so he wrote me immediately, asking for a photostatic copy of the quote; Helen had one made in a few hours and dispatched it to Paris by overnight air mail. On June 22, French papers carried reproductions of the photostat that turned the tables and made the general appear to have been the one who was cavalier with truth. When devotion of the kind Rémy had for de Gaulle is brutally repudiated, the breach can never be healed and time is required for readjustment. Rémy spent much of the next decade in Portugal.

Shortly after moving to Charlottesville, I was asked to become a member of the board of Mary Baldwin College in Staunton. Since that was where my mother was educated in the 1870s and the books she had used there had become my text books when she prepared me for entering Washington and Lee University, I felt that I too was a product of Mary Baldwin, and during fifteen years I enjoyed the nostalgic experience of attending board meetings.

As an elder in the First Presbyterian Church of Charlottesville I was also active in the denomination in which I had been brought up, the Presbyterian Church (U.S.), which meant the *Southern* Presbyterian Church. I was sent by our presbytery as a commissioner to three of our general assemblies and in 1953 had the very great honor of being elected moderator of the Synod of Virginia, one of the ministers remarking with a wry smile that though I could not be governor of Virginia, they were going to give me the highest post in the church.

It seemed to some of us that the hour had arrived to raise seriously the question of our reuniting with the Northern Presbyterian Church. A commission had been at work for several years and had recommended reunion. Our constitution required that this recommendation be referred to the presbyteries for their consideration, with the affirmative vote of three-quarters of the presbyteries necessary for adoption. The task of securing adoption was obviously formidable, but we were convinced that it should be undertaken. The case for reunion seemed to us to be unanswerable. Our separation had come about as a result of the War between the States, and there were no differences between us as far as Confession of Faith and Book of Church Order were concerned. It was imperative to bring our church out into the mainstream of the great ecumenic movement that was beginning to flow with increasing power through the churches of all lands.

So, in the summer of 1954, Frank Price collected a committee and we set to work. I was asked to act as executive secretary with an office in Charlottesville. We estimated that for $25,000 we could do a reasonably good job over the next nine months during which the presbyteries would be voting; our treasurer, a Texan, promised to raise $10,000 in Texas if we would raise $15,000 in the rest of the church. My plan of organization was a simple one. It was to find a man in each of the hundred presbyteries who would be an active agent for reunion, to supply him with persuasive arguments and literature, and to arrange for speakers whenever they were requested. We were encouraged by the initial response. I traveled as much as I could and spoke at every opportunity.

But the attack of the opposition gained momentum as their appeal became more irrational and as the blows of some of their speakers hit lower. Two of the most ardent opponents of reunion were conservative southern businessmen who were active laymen. Both men were theologically unlettered; they were also ignorant of the intellectual, spiritual, and moral forces at work in the contemporary world. One had been born in Michigan, brought up a Methodist, migrated to Florida where he acquired wealth through real estate, and somewhere along the way had shifted from one church to another. Though he was now a Presbyterian elder, he showed no signs of understanding the polity of our church, but talked as if he thought we had a congregational system of church government similar to the Southern Baptists. This man spent most of the time during which the presbyteries were voting crusading in every part of the South for the *status quo*, and subtly injecting just the right amount of racial poison to evoke maximum prejudice. The Supreme Court had rendered its first decision on schools the previous spring and it was an opportune time to appeal to the lower side of our natures. But he reserved what he thought was his knockout blow for Dr. John Mackay, who had been my dear friend for forty years and who is one of the truly great Christian leaders of our time. Dr. Mackay was at that time president of Princeton Seminary and had recently served as moderator of the Northern Presbyterian Church. While moderator he had addressed a letter to the churches of that denomination, discussing what the Christian attitude toward communism ought to be and describing the effective Christian way to oppose communism. This was during the heyday of McCarthyism and many good people were confused about what to think and how to act. The *New York Times* said in a leading editorial that Dr. Mackay's letter was the finest statement that had yet appeared on the subject.

I had two public debates with this elder: in New Orleans and in Houston. Toward the end of his speech in New Orleans I could not believe my ears when I heard him say that the *New York Times* had recently published an editorial implying that John Mackay was sympathetic to the Communist line. This was his clincher. How could we reunite with a church which had such a man as moderator! I had not seen the editorial and long ago learned not to reply to a charge in public debate unless I had the facts in my hands.

A day or two later I flew to New York, got a copy of the editorial, and flew back to Houston. At the end of his talk there this man repeated what he had said in New Orleans. I asked the congregation's permission to read the editorial, and as I did so people began to titter. It was apparent that a false statement had been made. Instead of retracting or apologizing he came to me afterwards and said, "Colonel, if that wasn't in the *New York Times*, it certainly was in the *Herald Tribune*." I must confess I was at a loss to know how to handle a man of this type in the sanctuary of a church, though his performance was as foul a blow as anything I had encountered in twenty years of politics.

False witness had been borne against one of Protestantism's most respected and trusted leaders. But the sequence was a little different from the story of Peter and Ananias. In that story Peter said to Ananias, "Thou hast not lied unto men but unto God" and Ananias fell down dead. But in this story it was as if the church had announced as its finding: "You are a pretty good fellow and besides you are a man of property and a liberal contributor, so we would not think of bringing you before a church court. Not only do we intend to forget this unfortunate episode, but we have in mind appointing you to a church board." The Southern Presbyterian Church had become "permissive" like the society about it, and when all discipline disappears, corruption of the body politic becomes inevitable whether the body be a church or a nation.

The other antiunion man was even less theologically literate and equally unscrupulous. At Dr. Jackson's church in Columbia, South Carolina, he told the congregation in my presence that an F.B.I. report indicated that John MacKay was associated with Communist front organizations. If it had been a political meeting, I would have shot back "any man who makes such a statement is a liar or a thief, since contents of F.B.I. reports cannot come to the knowledge of private citizens unless they have been stolen." But in a church sanctuary the best I could do was to pay an emotional tribute to Mackay as a man and as a Christian statesman which proved to be wholly incapable of undoing the damage that had already been done.

In my experience, the Big Lie, if given sufficient circulation, always wins the first round. It takes truth some time to catch up with it. This is what happened in our debate on church reunion. We secured the support of half of the presbyteries but that was not nearly good enough, since the support of three-quarters was required. The cause of our defeat was epitomized in a telephone conversation I had with a man who was working for reunion in one of the Deep South presbyteries. He had told me that he thought he could carry his presbytery. Since this seemed to me highly improbable, I was not surprised when we lost, though only by six or seven votes. Wishing to congratulate him on the job he had done but at the same time to twit him a bit on the phone, I said, "Bob, I thought you told me you were going to carry that presbytery." "Colonel," he replied, "you never saw anything like the political campaign the opposition put on down here. They sent cars out into the backwoods and brought in elders we had never seen before from churches that we thought had been closed down years ago." "What in the world," I asked in feigned amazement, "could have caused them to work so hard?" "You know perfectly well," Bob said. I admitted that I might, but insisted on his giving me his explanation. He did not want to do it over the phone and stalled for a long time. When I wouldn't take silence for an answer any longer, he finally blurted out, "Niggers and damn Yankees." "Do you mean to tell me," I asked, "that a great Christian church is making an historic decision on that basis?" "You know it is," he shot back, and hung up. And I knew that he was right.

I have had several bad periods in my life. The period after the spring of 1955 was one of the two worst. In 1949 and 1952, a majority of Virginians had indicated that they did not want me to help bring the Commonwealth back into the mainstream of American life. Now my own church had refused to follow my lead. The methods used to defeat reunion had nauseated me and alienated me. For some years afterwards I felt that I was without a church except in the larger sense of my membership by faith in the Church Universal. I had been elected in 1954 to the Central Committee of the World Council of Churches. Service in that body helped to renew my faith and served as my main contact with reality.

It came about through the thoughtfulness of W. A. Visser 't Hooft, who made me a member of a small commission of the World Council of Churches to recommend a theme for the meeting of the assembly of the World Council to be held in Evanston, Illinois, in 1954. This commission met in Geneva in the summers of 1951, 1952, and 1953. I attended the first two sessions. Some of the greatest figures in the Protestant world were there, including Barth, Brunner, and Niebuhr. At one of the meetings I was thoroughly amazed by Barth's attitude toward both Niebuhr and Brunner. He treated them and their views from time to time with impartial contempt. As Brunner and I were shaving in the washroom the next morning, I asked him why Barth had that attitude toward him. He explained that it went way back to their student days when Barth was a member of a student corps (equivalent to an American fraternity) and he was not. The corps members treated students who were not members just as Barth was treating him now. I reflected that great theologians were as much in need of the grace of God as any other poor sinners! But I was not going to let the matter rest there, for Barth had also lost his temper with Niebuhr the day before and had been rather discourteous. So during the course of the day I met Barth by chance and told him that many of us regretted his attitude. He said he was sorry that he had lost his temper. I replied that it wasn't his anger to which we took exception, it was his acting in such a childish way. I suppose it was the first time in his life that the great man had been told that he was acting in a childish way—and I must say he took it magnificently. The year following he came up behind me while we were at a meal, put his hands on my shoulders, and asked: "Colonel, have I been behaving better this time?" I loved him for that.

In the spring of 1954, when the World Council assembly met at Evanston, every section of the human race was represented and every important non-Roman church except the Southern Baptists. It was a thrilling experience to observe such diversity struggling to express its unity.

The Central Committee, to which I was elected, was roughly the equivalent of the Roman Catholic College of Cardinals for the non-Roman Christian world. There were 100 members and the term of office was until the next meeting of the assembly—in this case six years. Three American laymen were proposed. One of the others was my friend Charles Taft of Cincinnati. Members were not chosen as representatives of particular denominations, but an attempt was made to include every important segment of the church's total life with some measure of equity.

The Central Committee met annually and I attended meetings at Davos, Switzerland, in 1955, at Galyateto, Hungary, in 1956, at New Haven, Connecticut, in 1957, at Nyborg Strand, Denmark, in 1958, on the island of Rhodes, in 1959, and at St. Andrews, Scotland, in 1960.

Transcending all other emotions I experienced while serving on the committee was the sense of awesome wonder as I watched the work of God go on year after year, creating through all too frail and fallible men one of the greatest movements in history—the ecumenic movement, pioneer of the Church Universal of my hopes and dreams.

The one great drawback to my service on the Central Committee was my relation with my own Southern Presbyterian Church. The other members of the Central Committee, while not representing their particular denominations, usually had influence in those denominations as members of the establishment or ranking officers in the ecclesiastical hierarchy. I was not a member of the establishment in my church and I had little or no influence with the organizational hierarchy. Further, I was now *persona non grata* with a large section of the denomination because of my activities on behalf of church reunion.

At the Central Committee's 1956 meeting in a former resort hotel on top of a mountain near Galyateto, some fifty miles northeast of

Budapest, Hungary, Bishop Ting, head of the Episcopal church in China, was among the delegates. I had met him when he was a student in America and so I arranged to talk with him. It was the first time I had conversed with a completely brainwashed Chinese and it was a shocking experience. He took the line that Frank Price and all our other missionaries in China had been nothing but American spies. I told him he knew that was not so, but he would not budge. Later when he spoke to the whole committee, he stressed the "freedom" of Christians in China. After that speech Franklin Fry, the chairman of the Central Committee, remarked to me, "I've heard double talk before, but this is the first time I ever heard triple talk." Through hearing Ting I acquired some intimation of the irrational mass madness that now seems to infect the whole Chinese people. Here was a so-called Christian bishop ministering wholeheartedly not to the work of reconciliation but to the dissemination of the Big Lie.

During the course of our meeting at Galyateto we were taken for an outing to see one of the government farms and to have a picnic. The farm, as judged by our standards, was pathetic. The picnic, on the contrary, was a thing to be remembered. It was a perfect summer day. The scene was a vast vineyard in the midst of which tables had been set with rural delicacies and local wine. Into the midst of this Arcadian atmosphere intruded a government speaker. He was the minister of agriculture. As he droned on and on about Communist achievements, I grew bored and spying Charlie Taft seated in the shade of an apple tree apart from the company, I started off to join him. On my way I passed a table of three young Hungarians and stopped to ask if they spoke English. One replied that indeed he did; his family lived in New Jersey. He was an electrician from Budapest (useful for bugging the hotel), and he invited me to join them for a glass of wine. As I sat down, the imp of Satan, often at work in me, prompted me to say, "I'm going to propose a toast—Here's to Freedom." The effect was electric. The three boys jumped onto the table, raised their glasses and shouted in Hungarian, "To Freedom," with the Communist cabinet member speaking only a hundred feet away. For a moment I thought the counterrevolution had already started. But nothing happened. The boys sat down quietly, the minister of agriculture continued to drone statistics and the incident appeared to have passed unnoticed. But it gave me an inkling of the passion for freedom beneath the surface which was to break out in open national revolt a few weeks later.

The 1957 meeting of the Central Committee in New Haven was memorable for me because of a conversation I had with Billy Graham who had been invited out for a day from New York where he was conducting one of his campaigns. I knew that he was to be one of the principal speakers at a convention of some 10,000 Southern Presbyterian men to be held later in the year at Miami, and I had also been reading in the papers some of the splendid things he had been preaching in New York about race relations. So I said to him, "Dr. Graham, I hope you will say the same thing in Miami about race relations that you have been saying in New York." "Do you really mean that?" he asked in a surprised way. I replied that I did, and he made no further comment.

I also happened to be on the program of the Miami conference and I looked forward to hearing what Graham would say. He spoke for an hour and a half without once mentioning race relations in the South. Two or three times he came right up to it, and each time quickly turned away and ran as fast as he could in the opposite direction like a scared rabbit. LeRoy Collins was then Governor of Florida. When his turn came to speak, he laid it on the line like an Old Testament prophet. One of the delegates returning on the train to Virginia remarked, "Well, Billy had his chance, but LeRoy took it."

I have often reflected on the tragedy of Billy Graham, the most popular Protestant speaker in the English-speaking world, and yet without the courage to speak out at a time when speaking out was mandatory for Christian leaders. If he had spoken out that year at Miami and in subsequent years throughout the South, what he said would have had more influence with the Southern Baptists, to whom he belongs, than what anyone else could have said, and would have helped immeasurably to create an atmosphere favorable to compliance with the law of the land. Instead, he always said what he thought his audiences wanted to hear, and as a result he never pricked their consciences or issued a call for repentance and reconciliation in regard to the greatest moral problem of our day. The Christian gospel cannot be preached at a time like this without giving offense to many. I never heard of Graham giving offense to anybody. On the contrary, he is idolized by the rank and file of Southern Protestants and courted by successive presidents. This could not have happened if he had ever spoken in the White House as a true Christian prophet would be compelled to speak. On the contrary, he speaks as if he were the perfect Hollywood version of what a popular Protestant preacher is supposed to be like, and as such he has given to millions an erroneous picture of the Christian faith and of the Christian church.

The 1959 Central Committee meeting at Rhodes was memorable for Helen as well as for me. After completing a piece for *Esquire* in Austria while I attended meetings, she went to mainland Greece and to Crete and Mykonos. She fell in love with the land and its people and decided to write the book that she would like to have had before she came but which did not exist. She has now published five books on Greece; we go back whenever we can, and I am writing this chapter in a balcony on the island of Cos, looking out over the Aegean toward Halicarnassus—one of the most beautiful vistas in the wide world.

At St. Andrews, Scotland, where the Central Committee met in 1960, I made a plea for recognition by the churches of the implications for mankind of the ominously growing gulf between the standards of living in the North Atlantic area and the standards of living in Southern Asia, Africa, and South America. Nothing could have pleased me more than to have had Dr. Fisher, the lovable Archbishop of Canterbury, trot up to the podium as he had a way of doing and say, "I agree with what Mr. Miller has said."

As I look back on the six meetings of the Central Committee of the World Council of Churches I attended, the thing that gives me the most pleasure is the memory of Visser 't Hooft at work as general secretary. During the third of a century since we had first met, he had become an extremely skillful operator and had grown tremendously in every way. I doubt if there was another person in the Protestant world who could have done as well as he did in guiding the World Council of Churches during its first twenty years. He was a master builder. And it was fortunate for Christendom that during the most critical period in the inception of the dialogue between the Roman and non-Roman worlds the two key men were Dutch theologians who had known each other well for many years—Msgr. (now Cardinal) J. G. M. Willebrands, executive under Cardinal Bea of the Secretariat for Promoting Christian Unity in Rome and W. A. Visser 't Hooft in Geneva.

While serving on the Central Committee of the World Council of Churches, it was very gratifying to be asked by the Virginia Council of Churches to become its president for 1957 and 1958, and I thoroughly enjoyed being associated with its executive secretary, the Reverend Myron Miller. Because of my presidency of the Virginia

Council, I was a delegate to the Triennial General Assembly of the National Council of Churches which met in St. Louis, December 1–6, 1957. Martin Luther King and I had been invited to speak, one after the other, at the same hour on the program. He was then only twenty-eight years old, but I was deeply impressed by the richness and largeness of his vocabulary, by the artistic structure of his speech as a whole, by the quality of his voice, and by the use he made of it. I know of no man in my time who could use Shakespearean and Biblical English as effectively as King did. The theme of my remarks was that while much civil rights legislation was required, the function of the church was primarily to provide reconciliation between the races, remarking that "though two persons could easily get divorced in a law court, that was not the place where people normally became reconciled with each other." This sentiment was not received with any marked enthusiasm by my audience, though I believe its truth is even more applicable today than it was then.

During the years 1952–60 I spoke often in various parts of the South. More invitations came from North Carolina than from Virginia, which seemed to reflect the fact that in general North Carolinians liked my brand of politics. Indeed, a leading North Carolina paper, unlike Virginia dailies, gave me warm editorial support during my campaigns!

At least one of these speeches is worth recalling. When Kerr Scott was governor of North Carolina, the Presbyterian Synod of that state asked me to address it at its meeting in the chapel of Queens College, Charlotte. It was during the period when Joe McCarthy was befouling the life of the nation and I decided to speak on the menace of the Big Lie. The governor was a commissioner and was seated directly before me during my address. As I warmed to my subject, his face grew darker and he appeared to be very angry at something. I had supposed he would agree with my remarks, but I began to wonder. When I had finished, the synod recessed for five minutes to give the elders time for a smoke in the lobby. As I emerged from the sanctuary, the governor was standing in the middle of the lobby and I went up to pay my respects. There followed a scene so extraordinary that words cannot convey the drama of it. The governor indeed had agreed with me. When I presented myself he almost yelled, "Miller, they are all liars," and as he uttered these words he began to whirl rapidly around, waving his arms as if he were a windmill, and repeating again and again, "all liars." The "all" were the wealthy

Presbyterian elders (manufacturers and bankers) who were his bitter political opponents and who were standing about him in the lobby. These were the same men who had driven Frank Graham from public life, and my words had struck such a responsive cord in Kerr Scott that he had suddenly blown his top.

We trooped back into the church to resume the session. The next item on the docket was an address by the governor. And when the elderly moderator announced in a sweet brotherly voice that it gave him great pleasure to present the first citizen of the state, the governor, the whole synod rose to pay its respects. But Kerr Scott had been bereft of his speech. He was still so angry that he did not trust himself to say anything and he never rose from his seat to go to the platform or to respond in any way. He just sat there with arms folded and face dark with fury. Finally, after a long and embarrassing silence, the synod proceeded to the next item on the docket. I thought to myself that it was inconceivable that such a drama could occur in Virginia, and there followed the further thought, "How I would love to campaign in North Carolina!"

Our friends Elizabeth and Ernest Ives invited us to visit them at Southern Pines, North Carolina, in the spring of 1957. While we were there, they suggested that we call on General and Mrs. George Marshall, and the prospect of seeing the general again pleased me beyond words. During our conversation I recalled his visit to SHAEF when he chatted with me in the garden of the Trianon Palace Hotel and told him how very much his noticing me had meant to my morale. While trying to recall on which of his trips to Europe this had happened, he began to talk about the trip undertaken for the purpose of persuading the British to abandon the "soft underbelly" plan, with which Churchill seemed obsessed, of taking allied forces out of Italy and sending them up the Adriatic to land at a spot where roads led over the Alps into Austria. The meeting with the British was to take place in a chateau in the south of France, managed by American troops. General Marshall arrived on the morning of the appointed day and since he anticipated that the conference which was to begin after lunch would be very difficult, he felt that it would improve his spirits if he had a haircut. The captain in charge assured the general that he had a couple of GI's, two brothers, who were excellent barbers. When they arrived, it was obvious from their accent that they had been born in southern Europe. The General asked them where, and they named a village over the pass on the very road the British were proposing that our troops should use to reach Austria. An interrogation began immediately with General Marshall asking every conceivable question about the nature of the terrain, the gradient of the ascending road, the narrowness of the pass, and its defensibility against troops coming from the sea. The process of haircutting was strung out until the general had drained the barbers dry. No intelligence briefing in the Pentagon could have served Marshall's purpose half so well. He felt greatly refreshed.

The meeting lasted three hours or more and was rugged. Finally the British were convinced that it would be unwise to attempt an invasion over that terrain. After the meeting broke up, Mountbatten* came up to Marshall in the corridor and said: "George, where on earth did you acquire such intimate knowledge of that pass and of the conditions our troops would encounter as they attacked up that road?" To which General Marshall replied, "Louis, I wouldn't tell you for two million dollars." Serendipity had intervened on his behalf and by such trivial threads hangs the fate of armies and of nations.

In the summer of 1958, Helen was in France and went to see the "Son et Lumière" program at Les Invalides in Paris. She was entranced by this new art form. It had been invented by Paul Robert-Houdin of Blois, grandson of the great French illusionist. The technique of "Son et Lumière" is a very different thing from the narration of historical events, however good the script and however polished the narrator. Through the use of sound effects as well as voice and music synchronized with imaginative variations in lighting, the audience feels itself involved as participants in the events described. It is a delicate medium which requires finesse in its production. When good, it is the most perfect way to present the story and explain the meaning of historical monuments and buildings.

In view of Helen's enthusiasm, I got in touch with Rémy, who had written the script for the Les Invalides program, and he arranged with Robert-Houdin for me to go to Blois and see the program there while returning from a meeting in Geneva the following February. The show was put on especially for my benefit and Robert-Houdin, Rémy, and I were the only spectators.

I was so impressed that I was determined to introduce this new art form into the United States where it could be used with great effect at such sites as Independence Hall in Philadelphia, Mount Vernon, and

---

* I am reliably informed that it must have been Field Marshall Lord Alanbrooke and not Earl Mountbatten who attended this meeting, but as General Marshall told me the story, it was Mountbatten.

Williamsburg. Robert-Houdin and Rémy came over twice at my invitation and Helen and I took them around and introduced them to the appropriate people at prospective sites. On the second trip they brought a beautiful model of Independence Hall with an illumination system installed. There were preliminary negotiations in several places and finally Philadelphia was settled on as the logical place for the first American production. A company was formed and I invested ten thousand dollars as a token of good will but lost all control over production. The show opened in the summer of 1960 and Helen and I went up for the *première*. By the end of the show we were sick at heart. The author of the script, Archibald MacLeish, had not understood the art form and had completely failed to create the illusion of actual presence which constitutes the unique secret of its appeal. Instead he had written a narration in beautiful prose. We knew at once that the Independence Hall show would not succeed. The only good thing about it was David Amram's musical score. The show folded at the end of the second summer, and I lost every cent I had put into it. I still hope for the day when someone with more capital and greater finesse can produce another show in America under the personal direction of Paul Robert-Houdin which would insure its being a success.

In Charlottesville I was very fond of Colgate Darden, then president of the university, and always regretted that during those years his attachment to the Byrd Organization prevented us from developing as close a friendship as I should have liked. He has a marvelous dry wit that expresses itself on the most unexpected occasions. Once he stopped me on the lawn of the university and asked, "Pickens, do you know what they did to Mr. Jefferson after he died in 1826?" I replied that I had not heard. "Well," he said, "the undertaker intended to embalm his body, but he made an awful mistake. He embalmed his spirit instead, and it has not been seen around here since!" "That's quite true," I commented, "and it's your job and mine to disembalm it!" President Darden did a superb job of desegregating the university without any fanfare or publicity. When the Richmond papers became aware of what was going on, a reporter was sent up posthaste to interview the president. The reporter said, "Mr. Darden, we understand there are Negroes enrolled here. Have you any statement to make?" The president looked out of the window and said in a surprised tone of voice, "Why, I haven't noticed any on the lawn!" The whole state laughed, and that was the end of that.

Of all the civic activities in which I engaged in Charlottesville it
was the desegregation of our community which I look back upon
with most pride. Nothing is harder for a community than suddenly
to be confronted with the necessity of having to change overnight its
basic mores—its patterns of social and racial relationships that have
been followed for generations. In 1954, when the Supreme Court
threw out the doctrine of "separate but equal," we had been making
such progress in Virginia that I regretted the ruling could not have
come a few years later, thinking that natural evolution would find
us better prepared for it.

However, the decision had now been made and I knew that we
had to comply with it. Governor Stanley's first reaction was: This
is the law and we are law-abiding people. But he spoke before word
had come down to him from Senator Byrd in Washington. In 1955,
the Supreme Court began to apply its new doctrine to specific cases
and the whole scene changed. Byrd in a press interview on Saturday,
February 25, 1956, called for "massive resistance" to what had become the law of the land. He said: "If we can organize the Southern
States for massive resistance to this order I think that in time the
rest of the country will realize that racial integration is not going to
be accepted in the South."

No senator for a hundred years had rendered himself or the whole
South a greater disservice. At that time Byrd stood at the peak of
his career. Had he accepted the inevitable with sorrowful dignity
and devoted the rest of his life to creating an atmosphere in which
compliance would have been possible without surrendering more
than was absolutely necessary, he would have gone down in history
as the most respected of the South's ultraconservative statesmen.
Instead, in an evil hour he cried out for "massive resistance." Ever
since the time when Richmond had been capital of the Confederacy,
the Deep South had looked to Virginia for leadership in matters of
this kind. Virginia had now given the lead, and the other states of
the Old Confederacy took up the cry and followed with abandon.

To the ordinary man on the street "massive resistance" meant
massive resistance—in physical form if necessary. The riots that
followed federal court orders in Little Rock, New Orleans, and other
southern cities were the natural reaction of people to the call to resist. How else was it to be done? For the turmoil of those days no one
shared a greater responsibility than Senator Byrd.

The Virginia assembly, meeting in special session during August
and September, 1956, passed "massive resistance" legislation pro-

viding that schools under federal court orders to desegregate should
be closed. Lane High School and the Venable elementary school in
Charlottesville came under such an order and were closed by the
Commonwealth during the autumn of 1958. The crisis was upon us.
What were we to do? In due course a federal court would order the
schools opened but meanwhile some parents were sending their
children to makeshift classes held in churches and segregationists
were organizing permanent private "free schools." Could we save
the public school system?

I have often tried to understand the basic reason for my believing
so strongly that the Negro should be accepted as an American citizen with the privileges, duties, and responsibilities of such citizenship like any other person—Italian, Irishman, German, or Scot. It
is always very difficult to understand the deepest sources of one's
own will to act. As nearly as I can make out, in the matter of race
relations, my source is a profound conviction that it is the will of
God that the Negro should be so accepted. That was the basis of my
liberalism when we were confronted with our crisis in Charlottesville. And I found that the men I could rely on most had similar convictions. Once a professor from the university stopped me on Main
Street and asked, "Francis, why is it that the only voice of liberalism
that seems to be left in the South is the voice of some of the
churches?" He too was finding out that the rational liberals, the
literary liberals, and the sociological liberals do not make very good
shock troops on the day of battle. William Faulkner, who was then
living in Charlottesville, had even ridden off the field with the remark that under certain circumstances he would take his gun and
fight for Mississippi again.

As I reflected during the early autumn of 1958 on what might be
done, a simple strategy began to take shape in my mind. The city
was under order of the federal court sitting in Baltimore to report
its intentions by the first of February. That would probably be followed by a final order to desegregate at the beginning of the next
school year in September, 1959. The likelihood of a peaceful transition seemed remote. Gun shops were selling out, there had been
a meeting of a thousand segregationists at the Court House where
some wild speeches were made, and a professor of engineering at the
university was reported to have remarked that he would be on hand
to apply the torch to Lane High School when the first Negro students entered. It looked as if we might have a Little Rock on our
hands. Could the climate of the town be changed so that we could

have orderly and peaceful compliance? I thought it could be changed if a dozen or more of the city's most influential citizens were willing to work with me. So when it seemed that the right moment for action had arrived, I sat down at my desk one day, took a pad, and jotted down the names of fifteen individuals who, in my opinion, carried more weight than any other people in town—the leading insurance men, manufacturers, merchants, hotel managers, etc. Then I began to phone around, inviting each one to be my guest at a luncheon in the Monticello Hotel on December 22, 1958. In any American city the size of Charlottesville the normal thing would be for at least a third of the men like those on my list to be out of town on business, or if in town not in their offices, or at least too busy to answer the phone. But in this instance every one was in town, everyone was in his office, and everyone came on the phone. Only one was to be out of town on the day of the luncheon. Fourteen accepted, and fourteen came.

After the meal, I explained our purpose. It was to consider how we could change the climate of public opinion so that Charlottesville could comply with the federal court order without disturbance of any kind and the public schools could be saved. This was an appealing objective because several important industrial plants had already intimated that they would move away from the area unless the schools could be opened, and the merchants and bankers knew that serious civil disorders would be very bad for business. Everyone present agreed that we must undertake the task. Profiting by my 1940 Century Group experience, I recommended that we should not have a formal organization or plan public meetings or give statements to the press but should work quietly as individuals, seeing everyone in the community who counted in any way—and particularly up and down Main Street. Before the luncheon was over, we had begun a list of people to be seen and divided it up. Each person present took the names that he knew best and felt he could influence. So we went to work. A second luncheon was held on January 14 to report progress and make further plans. All those who attended the first luncheon returned and two others were added to our group—the leading banker and a professor from the law school.

It was an auspicious moment for an effort of this kind. The city had an excellent mayor, Tom Michie, later a federal judge, who was in sympathy with what we were trying to do. The local paper, *The Daily Progress*, though owned by one of the town's most conservative citizens, had an editor, Chester R. Babcock, who also understood and sympathized with our efforts. Equally in our favor was the fact that the city was fortunate in having as its attorney, John Battle, Jr., elder son of the man who defeated me for the governorship. The younger Battle represented the city in its dealings with the federal courts and he had both seen the handwriting on the wall and comprehended its significance.

Knox Turnbull made available the spacious basement room of his insurance building as a co-ordinating center. There an index of names was kept, reports were received on contacts made, strategy luncheons were held, and small meetings were convened. Just before the date on which the city's attorney was to appear before Judge Simon E. Soboloff of the federal court in Baltimore, it was decided to publish a statement as an advertisement in *The Daily Progress*, explaining what was at stake and urging calm and a readiness to comply with whatever the order might be. Hardy Dillard of the university law school accepted responsibility for drafting the statement.

I had long realized that my name was anathema to hard core members of the Byrd Organization, and I had been frequently reminded of this. Once when I was in Washington having lunch with Brooks Hays in the congressional dining room at the Capitol, Bill Tuck, member of Congress from Virginia's Fifth District, came over, put his arm affectionately around Hays and said, "Brooks, you know Pickens is poison in Virginia." I knew that was true as far as Tuck and his like were concerned, and I considered his studied insult a compliment. I would not have had it otherwise.

But I must confess that I was a little caught out one day when one of those with whom I had been working so closely called me on the phone to ask if I minded having my name left off the list of signers of the statement to be published as an advertisement, because some of the bankers would be embarrassed if my name appeared on the same list as theirs. Since I had conceived and organized the entire operation, I felt that was more than I should take. So I replied that indeed I did mind and that my name was to be on the list. The result was that two ads appeared in *The Daily Progress*— the one Dillard had drafted and another signed by bankers. The separate statement by the bankers actually accomplished more than if their names had appeared in the general list, so it was just as well that they were unwilling to have their names appear with mine. The reason one of the bankers would have been so embarrassed was that Senator Byrd kept his account in his bank. Ironically enough I kept my account there too, but Byrd's was, of course, much larger.

When January 29, 1959, came (the day John Battle, Jr., was to appear in the federal court in Baltimore) the climate of Charlottesville had changed so much that we looked forward with confidence to the reaction of our people. The court's reception of Battle's explanation of the city's intentions was more favorable than we had dared hope. Judge Sobeloff actually complimented Mr. Battle on the fact that Charlottesville was the first southern city voluntarily to present a plan of school desegregation acceptable to a federal court. He ordered the plan to be put into effect at the opening of the next school year in September, and when the news reached Charlottesville, there was scarcely a ripple on the surface of public opinion. Every time I think of this effort I like to think of Mr. Hamm who owned the principal furniture store on Main Street. He epitomized the best there was in the South. Quiet, dignified, tolerant, with a touch of human sympathy, a genuine understanding of the Negro's plight, and a profound respect for law, he carried great influence with his fellow merchants.

The payoff for our efforts came the following September. I was in Europe when the schools were desegregated, but on my return I immediately asked Tom Michie, the mayor, whether it had gone off peacefully. He explained that the police had been trained in riot duty and a force of them had been held in reserve on Vinegar Hill the day the schools opened but they were not needed. On his way to his office that morning he had driven down by Lane High School where one policeman was on duty to see what was going on. There had been only a minor incident. No crowd had gathered but a white working man had passed just as the Negro children were entering. This man had expressed his feelings to the world in general, "You ———— ———— SOBs," etc. The policeman approached, put his arm on him, and said, "You are under arrest for disturbing the peace." As he led the astonished man away, he told him, "I won't prefer charges if you promise to go home, sit on the porch, and cool off." The man promised and that was all that happened when the schools were desegregated in Charlottesville.

A few months after the desegregation episode, "sit-ins" came to Charlottesville. Negro youths, quite rightly, wanted to sit at the counters in drugstores and quick lunch places just like anyone else. The question was, would the "sit-ins," when service was refused, lead to picketing and the picketing lead to riots? I decided to see what could be done. The wisest plan seemed to be to get agreement among the Negroes to do nothing for a specified time (which was promised) while I consulted the managers of drugstores and counter restaurants. A young man who sympathized with my views, who was a member of my church and also manager of the branch of a national chain store, acted as my go-between with the merchants. In due course he got agreement with everyone in town who was involved that on a certain date barriers would come down if everybody else was willing to do the same thing. But just outside the town limits at a new shopping center the manager of the branch of another national chain store refused to co-operate. The irony was that he was a northerner preventing southerners from doing what they knew had to be done and what justice required. This was too much. I asked Helen in Washington to find out who was the manager of the national chain to which this particular store reported. With her usual alacrity she at once phoned me his name and address. It was a Friday and when I reached him on the long distance, I explained what was happening, told him that the period of time which the Negroes had allowed me had run out, and that they planned to begin picketing the following week. I added that his local man was the only holdout and that if trouble resulted from the picketing, I would call in the press and tell them who was to blame; but that I would give his man until Monday noon to decide what to do. He capitulated Monday morning.

The really ironic feature of those very difficult and trying days in Albemarle County was the fact that many of the most fanatical segregationists were northerners. If it had not been for them, the transition would have been much easier. It was a wealthy Pennsylvania Republican with steel interests who was said to be a backer of the Defenders (the Virginia equivalent of the White Citizens Councils of the Deep South). His name was Middleton, and he had bought a farm on which to raise show cattle across the road from Farmington. Thomas Jefferson would indeed turn in his grave if he knew that Middleton's son had become the representative of his own county in the Virginia House of Delegates by completely repudiating his views on the nature of man and the purposes of human society.

The end of "massive resistance" in Virginia was hilarious. Lindsay Almond was the new governor. He had always been a 100 percent Byrd Organization man and had served, when attorney general, as the Organization's hatchet man in relation to me. But Almond knew the score and he was clever enough to devise a cunning scheme to outwit Byrd. On January 20, 1959, Governor Almond made a state-wide radio speech announcing that he was calling the general assembly into special session the following week. The tone of the address was racist. Its substance was nauseatingly segregationist—he had just begun to fight, he would give his right arm, he would go to jail, etc., etc. Byrd was completely taken in and wired Almond next day predicting that his "notable" speech would further stiffen resistance not only in Virginia but throughout the South.

But when the assembly convened on January 28, Governor Almond surprised the state by introducing legislation ending "massive resistance" and introducing "freedom of choice." After a furious debate lasting nearly three months, the legislation was passed by one vote in the senate and five or six votes in the house. One senator had to be brought in on a stretcher to vote for the governor's proposal. Several of the young men who had fought for me in 1949 had gone into politics and were then senators; they were among those who cast the decisive votes to end "massive resistance." By the decision of Virginia's governor and assembly the Old Dominion on that day walked out on the Deep South. The spell had been broken and there was no longer a Solid South. The massive resisters had lost their leader and the tide had turned in favor of reason and moderation.

Colgate Darden gave me a true version of what took place. With his usual way of introducing a story, he asked me one day if I had heard what had happened to the "boys" (members of the assembly) from the South Side (the black belt) the day they went up to Richmond for that special session. I, of course, said I hadn't and Colgate went on, "Well, that morning when they put their liquor in the back of their cars and started off for the Capitol they were really in high spirits. They had won their fight—Lindsay was for them—and the world was bright. When they reached Richmond they expected to find the governor clad in the uniform of a Confederate general manning a machine gun nest outside the Capitol building with the Stars and Bars floating in the breeze above him. But they looked everywhere and to their dismay could not find him. Finally they trooped into the hall of the House of Delegates. When they had all got in, Lindsay appeared, slammed the doors, bolted and barred them, and scalped the legislators alive." It was the most colossal political double cross in the history of Virginia. But if Byrd had known what was coming, he could have blocked the move.

In the autumn of 1960, when Robert Kennedy was speaking in Richmond, Lindsay Almond, who was still governor, came up to me, put his arm around my shoulders, and said: "Pickens, you have been right all along." I chuckle still when I recall it.

XVII ✐ A Term in the State Department: Georgetown, 1961-1965

January 20, 1961, was a day that I like to remember as much as any other day in my entire life. It was a day when America became alive again, when people began to dream great dreams and when hope began to rise throughout the land like sap in spring. For a moment the form and style of life seemed more important than affluence or power. All of this was due to John F. Kennedy who in his inaugural address that day told us: "Ask not what your country can do for you—ask what you can do for your country." Helen and I had excellent seats in front of the rostrum on the east side of the Capitol and though the northwest wind was howling over foot-deep snow, with a temperature of 18°, we were quite content to sit there for several hours because our hearts were warm within. From the Capitol we moved to a box just across Pennsylvania Avenue from the White House to watch the new president and his staff lead the inaugural parade.

When May came I was appointed special assistant in the Bureau of Cultural and Educational Affairs in the Department of State. This appointment constituted neither recognition nor reward as these are understood on the American political scene, but I was deeply grateful to Chester Bowles for finding a niche where I might discover or invent some useful work that needed to be done. With our habitual good luck, within hours after I had accepted the appointment, Helen and I found and bought a lovely little house with a charming garden at 2810 P Street in Georgetown.

Before we moved from Charlottesville to Georgetown I had a unique experience. The Negro American Legion in Charlottesville arranged a program in their Baptist church for my Negro friends to tell me goodbye. I can think of no greater honor that can come to a white man in the South than that. Their gratitude made much that I had gone through seem a small price to pay and was evidence enough that my efforts had not been in vain.

During the four years I was in the department I served under four assistant secretaries. The first of them thought that a thing was done when he had said that he intended to do it; within a year his habit of substituting words for action caught up with him and he was given his walking papers. The second, Lucius D. Battle, whom I had known when he was with Colonial Williamsburg, was exactly the right man for the job at that particular moment and should have stayed longer, but after two years he preferred to go as ambassador to Egypt. Why he wanted to be assigned to that pathetic Nasser-ridden country I was never able to understand, but he had done so much to save Abu Simbel that he probably felt his effort on that monument's behalf would help smooth our relations. Shortly after Battle's arrival in Cairo our fine USIA library there was burned by an Arab mob—conclusive evidence that the word "appreciation" does not appear in the Egyptian dictionary.

When Battle left the bureau, Harry McPherson was appointed our assistant secretary. He was a cultivated, charming, and able young Texan who was made to order for the post. But he had previously worked for Lyndon Johnson, when the latter was majority leader in the Senate, and McPherson had just begun to find his way around in the Department of State when the president called him back to work at the White House. The fourth assistant secretary was a career officer waiting for foreign assignment. He realized that he did not have time to innovate and so just "carried on."

This kaleidoscopic turnover of secretaries in our top policy post made it next to impossible to initiate and carry through long-range plans and was one of two principal causes for the difficulty of getting anything done. One illustration will suffice. In the spring of 1963, Lucius Battle told me that he would like to see a foreign student center erected in Washington, and I was instructed to start action toward that end. Other great capitals had such centers and we had none. There was a tiny office on M Street, run by a group of devoted men and women who operated on a wholly insufficient budget, and this was the place to which foreign students were referred on arrival.

At that time there were some three thousand foreign students resident in Washington and the number was growing. Of the sixty thousand or more in universities across the country many thousands visited the nation's capital each year. There was urgent need for a building with rooms for transients, with a cafeteria, with large and small meeting rooms, and above all with an information office which could refer new arrivals to reputable rooming houses and help them in many other ways.

I began by interviewing the presidents of the universities located in Washington and found considerable interest among several of them; one in particular expressed great enthusiasm for the proposal —President Anderson of American University. As a result of Anderson's initiative, Father Bunn of Georgetown, whom the other presidents regarded as the convener of their informal group, invited Battle and me to meet the presidents at a dinner where we could explain what we had in mind. All came except the president of Howard and I never understood why he was not interested enough to send a representative as that institution stood to profit by such a center more than any other. After Battle presented our proposal, the presidents endorsed the general idea and decided to appoint a committee to study the matter and prepare recommendations for action, the intention being that if the presidents approved the final plan as submitted by the committee, we would help raise the necessary funds. This committee worked for a whole year and did a thorough job. It filed its final report containing specific plans for a center in the autumn of 1964. By that time Battle had gone to Egypt, McPherson, though intensely interested in the proposal, was in transit, while his successor displayed no interest in doing anything about it. The result was that not only was a most worthy project never realized, but an enormous amount of time was wasted by a great many people, and worst of all the university presidents were led down the garden path by a government that did not know its own mind. This experience was disillusioning for me. It must have been much more so for the presidents.

I discovered within a few weeks of my joining the State Department that the great obstacle to getting things done was the built-in inertia of many of the old line civil servants. As far as character and loyalty were concerned, there were no finer people anywhere. But they had seen many administrations come and go and there was an established routine of paper work with no sense of urgency. The drive to get things done usually came from outsiders like myself who were brought in for relatively short periods of time. Several illustrations will show the effect of this built-in inertia on the formulation and implementation of policy.

In the summer of 1961, President Kennedy sent a letter to the secretary of state instructing him to look into what the government should be doing for the more than 50,000 foreign students in this country who were not here on government programs, to insure that they benefited as much as possible from their stay. This was typical of the imaginative initiative that Kennedy was constantly taking. It gave us a magnificent opportunity to do something really significant for these students. What happened? The president's letter found its way to the desk of one of our very senior civil servants. He was a most likable individual with genuine ability, and I came to be fascinated in time by the consummate skill he had acquired over the years in slowing down and sabotaging fresh initiatives. I had never seen such exquisite artistry in action. With great reasonableness and good humor he always threw a little dust in the air; then suggested that we allow it to settle, hinting that the time was not yet ripe, or that we needed more data, or that a committee should be appointed to look into the matter. In the end nothing much happened. It was so now with the president's instruction. The civil servant took several weeks to prepare his staff paper in which he recommended the minimum action possible—the designation of one foreign service officer to follow-up and to co-ordinate with appropriate agencies any action that he might initiate himself or might stimulate in the private sector. The officer designated performed this function well for about a year. Two years later I doubt if anyone could have found a residual trace of the effects of President Kennedy's instruction.

Another illustration concerns the surprising fact that until 1965 the government of the United States had never announced an official policy of promoting the study of the English language in non-English-speaking countries around the world. A great deal of this was, of course, being done by diplomatic missions which had the imagination to see the value of such promotion. But where missions were uninterested the State Department could not say, "This is the policy of the United States Government; get on the ball," nor could we ask all missions to review and revise their plans in light of a specific declared policy.

Several individuals in AID and USIA had begun to work toward the preparation of a policy in 1957. All that was needed was a one-page statement declaring the policy of the United States to be so and so. Since the matter was relatively simple with no sinister political implications of any kind, one would have supposed that a statement could have been drawn up in a week, cleared in a month, and issued by the president shortly afterwards. Not so. Because USIA and AID had never been able to agree on the wording, seven years after work had been begun, it was still going on. Harry McPherson, then the assistant secretary, asked me to see what I could do to terminate this incredible performance. I regard it as one of my greatest achievements in the department that before I left in June, 1965, such a policy was approved by the secretary and subsequently issued by the president.

A more distressing illustration has to do with handling requests from foreign countries. In early June of 1961, our embassy in an important African country cabled a request from the chief of state of that country for us to find an American to serve as chancellor of his new university. The cable was referred by the message center to the appropriate office. It finally wound up on the desk of an elderly gentleman of unimpeachable character who was not feeling very well and was just going off on his vacation. When he returned he apparently did not bring back with him any sense of urgency and September came before I discovered to my horror that there had been such a cable and that nothing had ever been done about it. I went into action immediately, consulted the country's top Negro educators, and a list of suggested names was cabled out. But it was too late. The chancellorship had already been offered to a left-wing European. The head of state of that country subsequently turned almost wholly to the East. This particular incident may have had nothing to do with his reorientation, but it was at least one little bit of evidence indicating that we were not taking his requests for help very seriously.

I experienced several genuine failures in my efforts to make the operations of our bureau more effective. One had to do with "The Hill." Since I knew quite well a fair number of congressmen, it was felt that it might be useful if I maintained these personal contacts and informed them of what we were trying to do. Of course I was well aware of both the theory and practice of separation of powers and checks and balances, but I had never seen the theory applied so rigidly as it was in relation to our bureau. I soon discovered that the distance between the Department of State's building and the Capitol was in many respects further, as far as we were concerned, than the distance from Washington to Paris.

I also discovered that the dimensions of our programs all over the world were not determined by the secretary of state but by John J. Rooney, congressman from Brooklyn. He was chairman of the appropriations subcommittee that scrutinized our proposed budgets. There was no balance there—only a check. When the representatives of our bureau appeared before him, he usually treated them as if they were emissaries from an unfriendly foreign power. In a less imperfect system of government than ours it would seem normal for the responsible legislator to be on such terms with his opposite number in the executive branch that they could exchange information and consult from time to time in an effort to agree on what the national interest required. Not so with Rooney—to him "separation" meant complete separation. As I look back on the matter now, it seems both incredible and ludicrous that I should have had to employ such circuitous and indirect channels as I did to get important information into his hands. Instead of going up directly to his office and leaving papers with his assistant, I had literally to resort to a kind of undercover operation in order not to offend him. And it was this petty tyrant who set the limits, according to his own whim and fancy, of the State Department's cultural and educational activities around the world. The irony of it was that Rooney represented a constituency which, according to the Bureau of the Census, was one of the least privileged in the country as far as educational and cultural advantages were concerned. No wonder that the programs of the State Department in this field long ago began to bog down, for our branch of the executive was no longer coequal with the Congress—we had become the servant of a particular congressman.

In spite of Rooney's attitude, I continued to attempt to interest individual congressmen in what we were trying to do. I asked one of our most enthusiastic supporters in the House if he could collect a few of his fellow members from time to time for informal conversations in his office with the assistant secretary from our bureau. This was done, but I never felt that these meetings accomplished very much.

My greatest disappointment during my term of office at State resulted from my failure to insure an increase in our exchange programs within the North Atlantic community. At a time when our military ties within NATO were loosening and strains were developing, particularly with France, it had appeared to me axiomatic that our cultural ties with Western Europe ought to be strengthened in every possible way and that our transatlantic activities ought to be stepped up in both directions. In order to discover what the Europeans themselves thought about this, I assembled the cultural attaches from the Washington embassies of the Atlantic community nations and asked what they hoped might be done over and above what we were already doing. As a result several excellent proposals were put forward, but I could not secure either interest in or support for them in the department. Everyone knew that Rooney would veto additional programs and so during one of the most critical periods of our relations with Western Europe since World War II, appropriations for that area, instead of increasing as the national interest required, became smaller and smaller.

By no means all of my efforts were as disappointing as these. There were a number of accomplishments on which I look back with a measure of satisfaction. One of these had to do with bringing Portuguese-speaking African students here who would otherwise have gone to Prague or Moscow. John F. Kennedy differed in many respects from his predecessor. He not only read a great deal, but he actually saw important cables coming in from the field. One morning in June, 1961, a cable came to his desk, reporting that more than a hundred Portuguese-speaking African students had fled from Portugal because of police action there and had sought refuge in France and Switzerland. The president turned to Maxwell Taylor who was in his office and told him to see that someone got on the ball and made sure that these students were offered the opportunity of coming to the United States to complete their studies instead of going to Prague or Moscow. The memorandum about this came to my desk, and a colonel at the White House continued to phone me urgently to inquire what action had been taken. There is nothing I love more than an assignment of this kind. Completely ignoring bureaucratic channels, I went to work. My first step was to send a man to Europe to interview the students. Before he could fly to France some of the students who were near Paris disappeared during the night and turned up in Bonn where a plane was waiting to take them to Ghana en route to Prague. While they were still in the air between Bonn and Accra, without consulting anyone I phoned our embassy in Ghana and instructed an officer to interview upon their arrival all the students who were willing to talk, offering them full financial assistance if they wished to come to America. In the meantime, Lincoln

University, near Philadelphia, agreed to establish a special African center for any students who might accept our invitation. Five years later there were over a hundred Portuguese-speaking students at the Lincoln center and so many had "chosen freedom" that a second center had had to be opened at Rochester University, New York. I look back with great pride upon the operation which made this achievement possible, knowing that if the memo from the White House had gone to the desk of an old line civil servant who would have felt bound to operate through channels, no man would have been sent to Europe and no phone call made to Accra. Everything would have been done regularly, with proper clearance, and too late.

One of the tasks assigned me while I was in the department involved a trip to Southern Asia. A mess had developed in connection with the operation of a binational educational foundation because of certain charges made by a returned American teacher which had already reached the desk of a very prominent senator. I was asked to fly out at once to investigate. It took nearly a month to get to the root of the matter and in the end it did not reflect seriously on anyone except the returned American teacher. My reward for solving the case came from the young security officer at our embassy in that particular country. I needed one specific and essential piece of information to complete my investigation. Since getting it involved questioning nationals who did not understand English, I asked the security officer to get it for me. A few days later he reported his lack of success. Subsequently, I got the information on my own, and when I told him he said, "Colonel, I wish you would stay here and join my staff!"

In the spring of 1965, I became aware that it was time for me to sign off. Harry McPherson had left and his successor was not interested in making use of me. After Kennedy's death the atmosphere of excited anticipation which he had created began to be dissipated in our bureau. Business as usual once more became the order of the day, and this suited not only Congressman Rooney but also the old line civil servants. They could now relax without fear of being suddenly confronted with major innovations which disrupted their routine. As a result of this change in atmosphere, I lost interest in the activities of the bureau and though an officer in the personnel section of the department laughingly remarked, "Colonel, you can stay on until you are eighty if you want to," I had had enough and asked to be retired at seventy.

Dean Rusk's role as secretary of state was one of the things that

troubled me most during my four years in the department. I had
known him casually during World War II and had seen him once
or twice afterwards when he was serving in the State Department.
He and I had little in common and I never felt attracted to him. I am
sure this feeling was mutual.

During John F. Kennedy's campaign for the presidency in 1960
his attention was called to an article in the April, 1960, issue of
Foreign Affairs on the respective roles of the president and the secretary of state in regard to foreign policy. The thesis of the article
was that the president, under the Constitution, was responsible for
formulating foreign policy and the secretary for executing it. This
was exactly what Kennedy wanted to read. The article was by Dean
Rusk. Kennedy had never even met Rusk, but after his election he
sent for him and offered him the secretaryship. The arrangement
was fairly satisfactory as long as Kennedy lived because he and Mc-
George Bundy made foreign policy in the White House. Rusk was a
competent administrator and would have made a first rate undersecretary. His priceless asset as far as the White House was concerned was that he made the best appearances before congressional
committees of any secretary of state in my time.

When Lyndon Johnson became president, the role of the chief
executive in relation to foreign policy necessarily underwent a drastic change. Johnson had neither the understanding of the world
scene nor the capacity for sympathetic and imaginative response to
changing conditions possessed by his predecessor. He would have
been served best by a secretary of state who did possess these qualities and who could have presented him with alternative proposals
for the development of policy, recommending the one he thought
best. Performing such a function required a secretary concerned
with the substance of policy as well as with procedures, tactics, and
mechanics. In his *Foreign Affairs* article, however, Rusk had maintained that the primary responsibility of the secretary of state was
not for matters of substance but for procedural matters and he faithfully performed his duties according to this thesis.

There was one exception. The secretary did have an obsession
with substance as far as the China policy of the United States was
concerned. He had helped make it in 1949–50, and his paramount
interest during the sixties was in defending and maintaining that
identical policy, though it was no longer relevant. As a result, under
President Johnson, the tenure of Rusk became nothing less than a
disaster for the United States. The world position of this country,

which had reached its highest point toward the end of Truman's administration, fell to an all-time low by 1968. For lack of American vision the free world began to distintegrate and neither Johnson nor Rusk was capable of renewing its vision .

Under Johnson the State Department desperately needed as its secretary a man who would thoroughly shake it up, put the fear of God into the heart of the time-servers, and then get on top of foreign policy throughout the entire government. In this way the proper balance between civilian and military influence on the formulation of policy would have been insured and our prestige throughout the world would have begun to be restored. But this was not a task which Rusk was capable of undertaking.

The most vivid impression that lingers in my mind as I look back on those four years is the appalling amount of time wasted by many government officials in meetings and on the phone because they did not wish to assume responsibility themselves for making decisions. Fearful that their careers might be jeopardized by wrong decisions and not being sure of themselves, they preferred to fuzz the issue in meetings or in endless telephone conversations which often concluded with no one being fully responsible. Bureaucratic habits are to some extent unavoidable in operations of great size and complexity, but when all is said and done, they remain one of our government's principal weaknesses—and the cost is astronomical.

While working in the State Department I occasionally accepted nongovernmental speaking engagements. In the summer of 1962, I received a letter from Miss Hortense Woodson, secretary of the Edgefield Historical Society (who also worked in Senator Strom Thurmond's office at Aiken), inviting me to come down to Edgefield, South Carolina, on August 1, to speak at the unveiling of a historical marker at Francis W. Pickens's old law office. Francis Pickens was the relative for whom I am named. He was a man of great wealth for his time with a large plantation called Edgewood and many slaves. Just before the Civil War he had been our minister at the Court of the Czars in St. Petersburg. Prior to that he had been somewhat of a moderate in national affairs, as those things go in South Carolina, but when the storm gathered he returned to serve as chairman of the Secession Convention and then became his state's war governor. Edgefield was also the home of the author of the ordinance of secession—no more Confederate town exists in the entire South.

As one reads what follows, he must bear in mind that I am well-known in those parts for my liberal views, but that the South is a place of many paradoxes. Sometimes blood binds where political differences tend to sever.

I have never been more courteously received or treated. Arriving by the night train, I was met by Jim Sheppard, a former lieutenant governor who took me to his home for the morning. While I was there, the very conservative congressman from that district, the Honorable William Jennings Bryan Dorn, phoned from Washington to make sure I was being properly looked after. Then there was a luncheon with some twenty distant Pickens cousins, and at three o'clock we went over to the Baptist church for my address. It was a very hot August day and I expected a handful of people. Instead there was a good crowd and the leading citizens of Edgefield were on the platform—politicians and ministers. Governor Sheppard in introducing me read a telegram from Congressman Dorn referring to me as a great American. I could not believe my ears.

My speech had been prepared with care and I had chosen as my theme "South Carolina's most valuable contribution to the life of the nation—the concept of a gentleman." As I drew near the end, I referred to the very difficult adjustments which white southerners were making and would have to make in our relations with the Negro. In this connection, I pointed out, we needed above all else to remember how the greatest gentleman the South had produced viewed his personal relations with Negroes, and told a story I had heard as a child in Rockbridge County, Virginia. The story was that after the war, when General Lee came to Lexington, he was observed taking off his hat to Negroes while walking down Main Street. Someone asked him why he did it. "Because," replied the General, "I don't want them to be more courteous than I am."

"I give you that," I concluded, "as our motto for the days ahead." To my astonishment, the audience gave me an ovation.

After the unveiling of the marker a charming lady took me in her car to see some of the old homes. Earlier in the day, I had noted to my surprise that on several of these homes bright new "Stars and Stripes" were flying but nowhere did I see the "Stars and Bars" of the Confederacy. I turned to my companion and, pointing to the "Stars and Stripes," said with a perfectly straight face, "Excuse me, Ma'am, but I thought this was a sort of Confederate day. Why are you flying that flag?" "Why, Colonel," she replied, "we are flying that in *your* honor." I could have wept. It seemed that I had helped to bring them back into the Union after a hundred years. When I got back to Washington, I remarked to Helen, "There is not going to be any trouble at Clemson when they desegregate. These South Carolinians will take it in their stride."

In 1967, President Johnson appointed me to the American Revolution Bicentennial Commission created by Congress to prepare for the celebration of our nation's two hundredth birthday in 1976. I served until President Nixon displaced me.

I could not bear the thought of growing old in Thomas Jefferson's County of Albemarle, surrounded by Goldwater Republicans. So we sold our house in Charlottesville and built another lovely house on the Outer Banks of North Carolina near Kitty Hawk. We call it "Tamassee," which was the name of old General Andrew Pickens's home in the South Carolina mountains. It is a Cherokee word meaning "The Place of the Sunlight of God."

XVIII ✍ In Retrospect

During the 1960s, when making a speech at the University of Iowa, I was introduced by a chairman who had formerly served on the staff of the *Des Moines Register and Tribune* and had known me for twenty-five years. Presenting me, he said: "Here is a man who has always seen what had to be done where he was, and has done it."

When I was twenty-eight or so I made a decision, in response to some gratuitous advice urging me to "get on the ladder," without realizing at the time what the consequences would be. I decided not to plan an institutional career for myself but to do whatever I felt needed to be done at the time. This is not a good prescription for security, but it is a marvelous prescription for the good life. No one could have had a better life than I have had during this momentous period of human history. Though I have rarely appeared on the stage, I have had a hand in some of the most creative and dramatic movements of my time:

> Making more real the Church Universal
> Turning the tide in America against Hitler
> Liberating Europe from Nazi rule
> Reviving democracy in Virginia
> Securing justice for the Negro.

Two of my dreams are coming true faster than I had ever deemed possible—the movement of Christian churches toward reconciliation and rapprochement, and the revival of democracy in Virginia.

The development of the World Council of Churches as an expression of the ecumenic movement among Protestants and Orthodox has been more than matched by the "updating" of the Roman Church. If John XXIII's goals can continue to be realized, the Roman Church will resume its traditional leadership of Christendom and the Church Universal which will then emerge—including the Roman, Orthodox, and Protestant traditions—will constitute the best hope of mankind.

As far as Virginia is concerned, the transformation has been astounding. Twenty years ago, Mills Godwin was a dedicated and vigorous champion of the Byrd Organization, and a convinced exponent of its philosophy; after the Supreme Court decision on schools in 1954 few were stronger advocates of "massive resistance" than he. Yet as governor in 1966–69 he said the same things and advocated many of the same policies that I did in the campaign of 1948–49. The twenty-one year olds in the generation that voted for him for governor were in their cradles during my gubernatorial race; the eighteen year olds who become eligible to vote under the Supreme Court decision of 1970 were born the year I ran for senator. No greater satisfaction can come to a man who has been in public life than to see his former opponents forced by the tides of history to adopt and execute policies which he favored as good for the Commonwealth and which at that time they opposed. Virginia has entered the mainstream of history.

On the other hand, two of my principal dreams seem less and less likely to come true with each passing year. One of these was for the emergence of a North Atlantic community with institutions gradually coming into being to express its common life. Such a community would be the natural custodian of Western civilization and would be so strong that no power on earth could prevail against it. One man more than any other arrested this development and turned the tide temporarily against it. That man was de Gaulle. No one else could have contributed so much to the moral renewal and material restoration of the French nation, but in a refined French way he also represented particularistic and nationalistic forces. These are the same forces that destroyed the Greeks in ancient times and they could again destroy Europe as they did in 1914 and 1939 if the infection were to spread from France back to Germany and to run its course unchecked. Now that de Gaulle is no longer on the scene there is more hope for Europe, but meanwhile isolationism and protectionism are reappearing in the United States.

The second dream which is not coming true as I hoped it would has to do with the place of Negroes in American society. I had hoped that after the passage of necessary legislation there would be an orderly evolution of Negro development in every sphere until they could participate fully and freely in the American way of life. But time has overtaken us. The migration of millions of people from the rural South to the northern cities occurred before they had acquired the education or the skills which would make it possible for them to compete successfully in the labor market. Further, a considerable percentage of these Negroes had been born and grown up without homes, and a home is the essential unit of civilized society. It followed that in every large city there were thousands of unemployed youths who had no roots in anything—no traditions, no families, no jobs, no community. But rootless youths with nothing to do could look at TV commercials by the hour and see what the white man was supposed to buy or to have. Consequently, on a stifling summer night when a riot started, they were psychologically prepared to break store windows and take whatever they could lay their hands on. The frustrations and hatreds that gave rise to the cry, "burn, baby, burn," are now developing into a theory of violence as an end in itself. "If America will not accommodate itself to our wishes, we will destroy America." This fantasy no doubt has considerable appeal to persons incapable of foreseeing the consequences of such a doctrine—incapable of appreciating that violence will necessarily be answered by force, and that the force at the disposal of the United States government is unlimited and could be ruthless.

The tragic fact seems to be that an increasing number of young Negroes, instead of being reconciled to American society, are being alienated from it. That is an appalling prospect. There is no ready "solution" for the mess we are in. But there are urgent things that have to be done—and at once. The federal government knows what these things are. The most urgent need is, of course, to create employment and to provide training in the skills required for employment. Further talk is worse than useless. Action is required on a massive scale—action of such magnitude that its cost would be equivalent to the cost of the Vietnam War. Otherwise we shall find ourselves shortly living in a police state. That is the nightmare that threatens to take the place of my dream.

There is, however, some ground for believing that through the work of Christian and Jewish religious bodies an atmosphere of sufficient good will may be created and maintained to avoid the worst—and that also as a result of this work, the conscience of white America may be appealed to as it has never been appealed to before.

My secular hope for the world lies with the freedom-loving English-speaking peoples associated with those Western European nations that share our political faith. My spiritual and ethical hope for the world lies with the reality of the Kingdom of God which Jesus announced and with those churches that witness to its reality and strive to make the will of its Ruler done on earth. Human life is not meaningless. Its meaning is best expressed through the affirmation of our citizenship in that City which has foundations whose Ruler and Maker is God.

Once when I was young, I do not recall where or when, I felt that I was in a great cathedral. In my mind's eye I saw my Master standing in front of the High Altar with a sword in his hand. I knelt before Him and as he touched me on both shoulders with the sword, he said: "You are my man." I am not a mystic and this was not a vision. It was a fact, and I knew that what He said was true. Over the years, I have tried to the best of my ability to serve Him as a true and faithful knight, and no man could ask for a better service.

Further, my own life has acquired far more meaning than it would otherwise have had because of Helen. Her encyclopedic interests have broadened my horizons, her brilliant intellect has stimulated my mind, her unlimited reservoir of energy has often set the pace for action, her social conscience, which is sharper than mine, has quickened my concern for the public weal, and her whole life has inspired me to try harder and live better. Besides her career in journalism and as an executive during the years 1930–46 when I was away two-thirds of the time, she ran the farm, maintained an ideal home, and brought up our two boys who between them carry on my major interests—one serving the church and the other the state. Helen has, indeed, been the good companion of my pilgrimage.

Occasionally, as evening draws near, moments of fulfillment occur which help to illumine and give meaning to one's life. I have known two such recently.

On February 23, 1969, we stood in the crowded sanctuary of the church of our younger son, Robert Day, the minister, in St. Petersburg, Florida. It was a desegregated church and the associate minister was a Negro, the Reverend Irving Elligan. We were there for the baptism of our grandson and my namesake, Francis Pickens, and since the father was the minister, it was right and proper for the associate minister to conduct the service. The sight of a black hand coming down on that little white head in the name of the Father, and of the Son, and of the Holy Ghost, and of tiny white fingers encircling a black finger for security, symbolized the beginning of fulfillment of some of my hopes for the South.

There was another moment of fulfillment on January 17, 1970, when we attended the inauguration of a new administration in Virginia. A Republican was becoming governor and Democrats were becoming lieutenant governor and attorney general. Democratic ex-governors were on one side of the rostrum and relatives of those about to be inducted on the other. We were there to see our elder son, Andrew Pickens, take the oath as attorney general of the Commonwealth. I could not believe my ears when I heard Linwood Holton, the Republican governor, in the presence of United States Attorney General Mitchell, quote John Gardner at length on the open society and by so doing detach Virginia from the national administration's so-called "southern strategy."

After the ceremony was over, Bill Tuck, the former governor who had told Brooks Hays some years before that "Pickens was poison in Virginia," came over and said, "Pickens, I also told Brooks that I loved you." On that pleasant note I end.

Too self-congratulatory, but forgiveable, considering how many defeats he suffered in good causes.

✐ Index